Psychoanalysis a Contemporary American Men

Debate over gender and especially the lives of men is currently at a fever pitch, particularly in the United States. New perspectives that capture the complexity of men and a rapidly changing gender landscape are therefore critical today. *Psychoanalysis and Contemporary American Men* challenges narrow stereotyped views of men by arguing that men are as complex and layered as women.

In the light of the recent #MeToo movement, stereotypes of men are being recycled. While aligned with the spirit of this movement, the authors worry that negative stereotypes of men are being perpetrated at the very time that men are renegotiating their gender experience. The authors present a critical non-heteronormative perspective addressing current gender transformations. Although the lives of men are changing, the stories that dominate the public sphere often represent them as narrowly phallic—controlling, detached, sexist, and homophobic. Seidman and Frank offer a counter point: men are also "guardians" driven to be useful and to do good, to live valued and purposeful lives. They argue that men are not only driven by a will to power but by an ethically-minded, relationally-oriented sense of responsibility to care for others, whether partners, children, or fellow citizens.

Drawing on historical, sociological, and psychoanalytic work, this book provides a nuanced, multidimensional construct of American men today. *Psychoanalysis and Contemporary American Men* will be of interest to psychoanalysts and psychotherapists as well as scholars and students of gender and queer studies.

Steven Seidman has written widely in the areas of gender, sexuality, queer studies, and American culture. His books include *Romantic Longings: Love in America 1830–1980, Embattled Eros: Sexual Politics and Ethics in Contemporary America*, and *Beyond the Closet: The Transformation of Gay and Lesbian Life*. He is currently a psychoanalyst in private practice in New York City, USA.

Alan Frank co-edited *Intimacies: A New World of Relational Life* (Routledge, 2013). He is a psychoanalyst in private practice in New York City, USA.

Relational Perspectives Book Series
Lewis Aron, Adrienne Harris, Steven Kuchuck & Eyal Rozmarin
Series Editors

The Relational Perspectives Book Series (RPBS) publishes books that grow out of or contribute to the relational tradition in contemporary psychoanalysis. The term *relational psychoanalysis* was first used by Greenberg and Mitchell[1] to bridge the traditions of interpersonal relations, as developed within interpersonal psychoanalysis and object relations, as developed within contemporary British theory. But, under the seminal work of the late Stephen A. Mitchell, the term *relational psychoanalysis* grew and began to accrue to itself many other influences and developments. Various tributaries—interpersonal psychoanalysis, object relations theory, self psychology, empirical infancy research, and elements of contemporary Freudian and Kleinian thought—flow into this tradition, which understands relational configurations between self and others, both real and fantasied, as the primary subject of psychoanalytic investigation.

We refer to the relational tradition, rather than to a relational school, to highlight that we are identifying a trend, a tendency within contemporary psychoanalysis, not a more formally organized or coherent school or system of beliefs. Our use of the term relational signifies a dimension of theory and practice that has become salient across the wide spectrum of contemporary psychoanalysis. Now under the editorial supervision of Lewis Aron, Adrienne Harris, Steven Kuchuck and Eyal Rozmarin, the Relational Perspectives Book Series originated in 1990 under the editorial eye of the late Stephen A. Mitchell. Mitchell was the most prolific and influential of the originators of the relational tradition. Committed to dialogue among psychoanalysts, he abhorred the authoritarianism that dictated adherence to a rigid set of beliefs or technical restrictions. He championed open discussion, comparative and integrative approaches, and promoted new voices across the generations.

Included in the Relational Perspectives Book Series are authors and works that come from within the relational tradition, extend and develop that tradition, as well as works that critique relational approaches or compare and contrast it with alternative points of view. The series includes our most distinguished senior psychoanalysts, along with younger contributors who bring fresh vision. A full list of titles in this series is available at www.routledge.com/mentalhealth/series/LEARPBS.

1   Greenberg, J. & Mitchell, S. (1983). *Object relations in psychoanalytic theory.* Cambridge, MA: Harvard University Press.

Psychoanalysis and Contemporary American Men

Gender Identity in a Time of Uncertainty

Steven Seidman and
Alan Frank

Routledge
Taylor & Francis Group

LONDON AND NEW YORK

First published 2019
by Routledge
2 Park Square, Milton Park, Abingdon, Oxon OX14 4RN

and by Routledge
711 Third Avenue, New York, NY 10017

Routledge is an imprint of the Taylor & Francis Group, an informa business

British Library Cataloguing in Publication Data
A catalogue record for this book is available from the British Library

Library of Congress Cataloging in Publication Data
A catalog record for this title has been requested

ISBN: 978-1-138-32850-1 (hbk)
ISBN: 978-1-138-32851-8 (pbk)
ISBN: 978-0-429-44863-8 (ebk)

Typeset in Times New Roman
by Florence Production Ltd, Stoodleigh, Devon, UK

To the men we've worked with. Our deepest gratitude for the opportunity to learn from them as we explored their and our lives.

Contents

Acknowledgments

We are grateful for the comments on various chapters by the following people: Jeffrey Alexander, Steven Botticelli, Michael Clifford, Patricia Clough, Raewyn Connell, William Cornell, James Dean, Michael Diamond, Martin Frommer, Dodi Goldman, Laura Impert, Michael Kimmel, Lynne Layton, Linda Nicholson, David Rappaport, Caryn, Jill Salberg, Sherman-Meyer, Arlene Stein, and Joseph Sullivan. We also thank our patients/clients who, in many cases, read and commented on parts of the manuscript.

Preface

It is admittedly odd to be relating a story of men renegotiating gender in more inclusive, flexible, sometimes radical ways at the very time that one of the most gender retrograde of men sits in the oval office. Yet, isn't this the way of change—uneven, concurrent threads filled with paradox and contradiction?

But, wait, there's not only Trump! Writing in the Winter 2017–2018, we're in the midst of an unprecedented wave of women exposing the underside, some might say—echoing some radical feminist arguments of the 80s—the hidden truth of manhood: a misogyny manifest in vile tales of predatory and violent behavior towards women. These are not, moreover, ordinary men; they are movers and shakers, the icons of manhood across long stretches of 20th century America.

Men at the edge of renegotiating gender? Really? Well, yes. As we see it, the "facts"—Trump and the #MeToo phenomenon—are not unambiguous or transparent in their significance. Two points are worth considering.

First, almost all of these men are of an older generation, the "mad men" generation. They came of age in a culture that took-for-granted men's dominance both institutionally and in the arenas of romance and the family. But, unlike previous generations of men, this one triggered second-wave feminism. And these men, Cosby, Weinstein, Ailes, Riley, Rose, Smiley, Conyers, were the fathers, husbands, colleagues, bosses, co-workers, lovers, and friends of the very women radicalized by these men's bad gender behaviors. Second-wave feminists laid bare modes of gender domination that most of us knew, but resisted thinking about and that few thought truly unjust.

Men's dominance, and some would say being a man itself, was about controlling and possessing women. Women were supposed to mirror men's fantasies and desires as inferior, emasculated subjects. Second-wavers made another crucial point: these men, unlike their fathers and grandfathers, had to contend with a different gender reality, namely sharing and competing with women in every aspect of public life. And, with the winding down of state enforced gender inequality, and with women moving en masse into public life, it was up to individual men to enforce their dominance through specific behaviors. This state of affairs often got ugly as men perpetuated a culture that subjugated women through a series of actions: by collapsing women into a caregiving stereotype, by sexualizing them in ways that deny their multifaceted humanness and autonomy, and by repeated acts of harassment, intimidation, and violence. In short, men sought to dominate women—and "lesser" men—rendering them subordinate and inferior.

Second, many of the women of the #MeToo movement are either baby boomers or post-baby boomers who are college educated and career-oriented peers of these men. They live lives very much like these men, including expecting others to respect their autonomy and dignity. These are not the women of their mothers' and grandmothers' generation, who lived in an era of legal patriarchy. Instead, born into a culture that in many respects took for granted the women's movement or at least the dismantling of state enforced patriarchy, these women came of age in the throes of personal and social struggles to claim their full entitlement to an expansive life, including an equal right to self-fulfillment at work and in their personal lives. We wonder: do the women speaking out against the behavior of these men assume that most of their women peers, and *most younger men*—the sons of the Weinsteins and Cosbys—share their outrage? In other words, does the potentially transformative power and resonance of their protests pivot on the understanding that these men represent a rapidly fading past and that the tide of gender change is on their side? This is not to minimize these women's outrage and courage, but to underscore a different point: underlying the story of individual men and women is a tale of social structural transformation. It is these younger men, those roughly below 40, that we would like to think there resides a potentially hopeful gender future.

One unintended and undesirable consequence of the current moment is the temptation to perpetuate narrow stereotypes of men—as predators and warriors, as misogynistic and homophobic, as testosterone-driven to subjugate women and other men. This would be unfortunate since, as we see it, such "phallic" representations are as one-sided as flattened, feminized constructs of women.

A principal theme of this book is that much of what is said about men is framed in narrow phallic terms. Such accounts reinforce a pervasive cultural misrecognition and inadvertently contribute to enforcing a cisgendered heteronormativity.

Conventional views of men, including in academic and psychoanalytic culture, have rarely strayed from a seamless language of phallicism. These representations highlight men's emotional containment, impenetrability, self-sufficiency, and their drive to dominate others. While this is important, such narrow phallic tropes cannot provide nuanced enough accounts of men's lives. It's as if dependency, longings for intimacy, and aspirations to be useful and good are not also vital aspects of men's lives. In particular, phallic perspectives neglect or minimize the ethical commitments that infuse men's lives with passion and purpose. Acts of caring for others —friends, lovers, kin, citizens—cannot be collapsed into instrumental or narcissistic behaviors. Men live and die for beliefs about personal integrity, a good life, social belonging, and indeed justice. We call this relational, ethical dimension of men's lives "guardianship."

We aim then to go "beyond representations of phallic men" in the specific sense of exploring the narrative tropes and arcs of personal life that speak to the multilayered (phallic and guardianship), multigendered, and tension-filled character of men's lives in contemporary America. The declining significance of patriarchy and compulsory heterosexuality has created expanded psychic and social space for men to negotiate more gender flexible modes of being and relating. Specifically, we argue that these broad social transformations have altered families and the very psychodynamics of gendering. Many boys are now growing up with post-traditional parent[s] who embrace their multigendered status. And, in contrast to their fathers and grandfathers, they are more likely to be comfortable with gay normalization and to approach gender and sexuality as arenas of personal choice and variation.

In this regard, we detect in America's changing gender landscape a new cultural dynamic: *the individualization of gender*. Many, especially younger Americans feel entitled to fashion their own gender experience, to determine for themselves what it means to be gendered. Is gender a ground of identity or an aesthetic of self-stylization? Is it stable and unitary or situational and shifting? Is gender a staging ground for dramas of personal authenticity or does its normalizing force create false selves? And, is it possible and desirable to aspire to live beyond gender, to step outside of gender scripts?

We're not suggesting a Whiggish tale of progress. After all, narrow understandings of masculinity and manliness remain compelling. Nor are we free from blowbacks and reversals. In the face of challenges to men's exclusive claims to masculinity by women and by a swelling chorus of post-phallic men, along with queer and trans* people, some men have doubled down on their investment in a hard-edged masculinity. We don't anticipate an end to the iconography of the phallic man. Rather, we're suggesting that long-term structural shifts are creating social and psychic environments making it possible for American men to renegotiate what it means to be a man. Many American men are today imagining lives beyond a narrow phallicism and beyond the regulatory order of cisgendering and heteronormativity.

Nowhere can the tensions between phallic and guardian gender threads, between gender as identity and aesthetics, between the construction and deconstruction of gender, be more fully and subtly explored than in the consultation room. We argue that psychoanalysis is ideally suited to expand and deepen the conversation about men's changing experiences. Psychoanalysts have sustained access to individuals' inner lives. Moreover, they have elaborated concepts of the psyche and dynamic languages of self and other that can capture something of the heterogeneous, contradictory, and shifting character of our subjective and interpersonal gendered experience.

The phallic man has always been a stereotype—reductive and one-side. It perpetuates the illusion of mutually exclusively and seamlessly feminine and masculine figures—women and men. In particular, it erases feminine-coded aspects of men's lives such as being vulnerable, nurturing, receptive, and relationally oriented. And this is a problem. What is unique in contemporary America, we think, is that more psychological and sociocultural space is available for men—and others— to renegotiate the terms of gender as part of their projects of self-and-world-making.

Drawing on our clinical experiences, we offer accounts of men who are negotiating the psychic and social contradictions of living in a time of gender uncertainty. We intend to spotlight the ways men struggle with phallic imagery as they craft gender textured and layered lives that often exceed cisgendered-and-hetero-normativity, while often refusing to acknowledge these post-phallic renegotiations.

As a sociologist and psychoanalyst (Steven), and as a psychotherapist and psychoanalyst in practice for 20 years (Alan), we aim to explore the intersection of the social and psychological or the way macro-social context impacts on the family and the psychodynamics of gender self-formation. Each chapter considers the ways phallic and guardian themes thread through men's lives from their very formation as men to struggles for authenticity and for vital erotic and intimate lives. In each chapter, we locate the psyche in a sociohistorical setting; there's no story of the psyche that is not also a story of the social (e.g. Rozmarin 2009, 2010, 2017) We concretize these broad themes regarding the interpenetration of the social and the psyche and the phallic and the guardian threads, and the individualization of gender, offering a provisional and exploratory series of inquiries into men and gender in early 21st century America.

Chapter I

Gender uncertainty in 21st century America

Psychoanalysis widens the conversation

"What's so bad about a boy who wants to wear a dress?"

This provocative question, the title of a 2012 *New York Times Magazine* essay, says a lot about gender uncertainty in the early decades of the 21st century. The author, Ruth Padawer (2012), narrates a series of stunning stories about boys who now and again dress like girls, but do not want to be girls. There's Alex, a 4 year old, who "pronounced himself 'a boy and a girl'. . . . Some days he wears dresses, paints his finger nails and plays with dolls at home; other days, he roughhouses, rams his toys together or pretends to be Spider-Man . . ." The author reports that between 2 and 7 percent of boys under 12 "regularly display cross-gender behaviors, though very few wish to actually be a girl." Rather than being an anomaly or abnormality, these boys' gender fluidity is said to align with shifts occurring among contemporary American men. "Boys and men do have more latitude these days to dress and act in less conventionally masculine ways. Among straight men . . . necklaces and pairs of earrings are almost normative, at least in some communities. Plenty of men wax their eyebrows, get manicures, and wear pink. These shifts have provided an opening for boys who buck some gender norms."

What we find especially telling in this essay is that it is boys that are gender unruly, and in the face of considerable social disapproval. And, their parents generally support their son's gender play while holding schools and mainstream medical authorities to account for not questioning their endorsement of rigidly cisgender (the rigid alignment of sex and gender) and heteronormative norms. This turn of events would have been unimaginable just 20 years ago.

Something new and strange is happening in post-World War II America. From at least the 1960s on, women have pioneered gender change. They have moved en masse into the workplace and public life, competing with men in most social fields and in the vanguard in forging new intimate relationships, including choosing single parenthood. As women mix and blend stereotypically masculine and feminine traits in their personal and public lives, they are shaping a culture that makes possible highly individualized gendered lives.

By contrast, men have often been resistant to gender change: they've balked at equal participation in housework and childcare; they've chafed at women bosses and often resented the challenge women pose as rivals in the workplace, the classroom and in politics. For some men, gender change has come to mean one thing: surrendering social privilege and a long-held sense of entitlement. For these men, going forward feels like going backward. Some resist by resorting to intimidation, harassment, or violence not only towards women but, at least for white men, towards minorities and immigrants. These men seem to be pining for a time when social respect and authority was conferred just for being a white man. But, curiously, even those men, who the sociologist Michael Kimmel calls "Angry White Men," may wish "to protect and preserve the dominance of American white men, [but] . . . in real life, are actually accommodating themselves to greater and greater equality—and, actually, liking it very much" (Kimmel 2015: 38, cf. Deutsch 1999: 184).

Unlike many observers of the gender scene, especially in the aftermath of the Trump election, we do not think it's credible to narrate American men's gender experience chiefly in the register of resistance and backlash or loss and resentment. However reluctantly, men are changing, indeed must change. [1] For some, perhaps many, change is trumpeted as a marker of personal enlightenment and social progress, and a welcome opportunity to renegotiate what it means to be a man. Interestingly though, *many men don't recognize, and refuse to articulate, just how different their lives are from their parents and grandparents.* Many are clinging to stereotypical tropes of American manhood, which have historically empowered men and have been repeatedly invoked as a common legacy defining the core of being a man.

Cultural misrecognition is pervasive. In the mass media and popular culture, men are often represented as a singular type; they are denied a complexity that has been claimed by women and, through their struggle, has grudgingly been recognized. Yet, if we listen carefully, and if we attend to men's actually lived lives, we can detect layered lives that often exceed heteronormative expectations. Without discounting or minimizing a muscular investment on the part of many men in a testosterone-driven uber-manliness, something undeniable in this Trumpian moment, we wish to underscore the way men enact cisgendered norms but also mix and re-assemble gender in ways that challenge heteronormativity (Anderson 2007, 2016, Bridges and Poscoe 2014, Corbett 2009a, Davis 2008; Harris 2009a, Heasley 2004, Reis and Grossmarck 2009, Schiller 2010a, Schrock and Schwalbe 2009, Ward 2008).

The politics of cultural misrecognition

Men's lives may be changing but public representations continue to endorse restrictive gender constructs. Popular culture and the mass media are shot through with cisgender and heteronormative norms. Men are rigidly and reductively contrasted to women. It's as if being a man is unthinkable without the presumption that manhood pivots on the repudiation of any and all dispositions, behaviors, and roles associated with women and gay men (Dietz 1998, Ezzell 2008, Kearney et al. 2015, Pecora 1992, Sheldon 2004, Vavrus 2002).

Read any newspaper and magazine, tune in to any TV news broadcast, and you find headlines and stories exposing men's sexual scandals, their ruthlessness in business and politics, their recourse to violence towards women and others, and their warrior bravado. Or worse: men are presented as sexual predators, rapists, corporate raiders, ruthless financiers, and corrupt, power-hungry politicians. The iconography of a seamless masculinity that pivots around power and wealth, aggressivity and dominance, and embattlement and heroic triumph, is the cultural lingua franca of men's lives. It's not that such symbolism bears no truth; rather, the ceaseless repetition of a narrow cluster of presumably innate dispositions, character traits, behaviors, and roles crowd out other imaginable realities. Stereotyping generates a seamless sameness. It becomes unthinkable to know men in any other way. Reality ends up repeatedly confirming stereotypical images, which in turn invests reality with a seemingly transparent self-evident quality. This cultural circularity lacks any awareness of its historicity and politics. This is far too often the logic of a heteronormatively-structured media.

For example, reflecting on the recent history of mass killings by young men, from Columbine to the Boston marathon killings in 2013, a *New*

York magazine columnist unambiguously announces: "evil may not have a single face, but it can be reliably found within one kind of body: that of an angry man in his late teens or twenties." While correctly noting that the shooters were men, this statement misleadingly claims that men's rage is biologically based: "men have testosterone, an aggression drug, coursing through their veins. . . ." Citing the neuroscientist and philosopher Sam Harris, the author insists, without any appeal to evidence: "the male proclivity to assert power through violence has been true for males, and not for females, for millions of years . . ." (Miller 2013).

In a similar vein, in a well-intentioned Op-ed in the NY Times, "Stop Violence, Start at Home," Pamela Shifman and Salamishah Tillet (2015), repeatedly and without qualification posit a fixed, set-in-stone link between male perpetrated domestic and social violence. "Men who commit violence rehearse and perfect it against their families first. Women and children are target practice, and the home is the training ground for these men's later actions." Their specific point surely merits serious consideration. However, by not qualifying which men are violent, whether there are significant variations among men depending on class, ethnicity, or sexual identity, and which forms of domestic violence are predictive of what kinds of social violence, the authors unwittingly reinforce the view that violence is simply part of men's very nature.

Media and pop cultural representations tell us what it means to be a man. They establish the parameters of cultural intelligibility, determining the legibility and legitimacy of any claim to being a "real man." The media concretizes gender norms by providing detailed accounts and images of what men should look like and how they should dress, talk, walk, and relate to others. Concrete "realities" are then invoked to authenticate stereotypic representations.

Stereotypes crowd out alternative or more complex notions of being a man. Images that fall outside a cisgendered heteronormative lens, for example, the hippie, the boheme, or the aesthete, the emotionally expressive and nurturing man, the dedicated, generative father, the effeminate or the trans* or queer man, are mocked or pathologized as defective or dangerous or exoticized as a spectacle, while being exiled to the social margins. And men that are not part of a narrow class-based, racialized normativity, for example, working-class men, Latinos, Black or Asian men, are often represented in demeaning, if not menacing ways as failed, incomplete, and inferior versions of manhood (Butsch 2003, Dixon and Linz 2001, Entman and Rojecki 2000, Harper 1996; Jackson 2006). The result is that a narrow cluster of stereotypical traits and images frame what it means to be a man. Complexity is denied, but the act of denial is unacknowledged. Aspects of men's lives are then obscured, literally not seen—even by many men.

Our point is not that all mass mediated images represent all men in stereotypically negative ways. Rather, representations of a one-dimensional masculine man carry authority precisely because they flood the media and popular culture, because they are often championed as iconic examples of manhood, and because they are authorized by experts or by the very exemplars of a stereotypical manly ideal. Moreover, such representations sustain their credibility and authority to the extent that they are presented as part of an iconography extending deep into America's history. Indeed, as historians have documented, popular Victorian notions of real men often pivoted around tropes of self-making and world mastery (Barker-Benfield 1976, Kimmel 1994, Rotundo 1993). Such constructions of manhood often found expression in heroic narratives: faced with grave dangers, men, despite great risk, rise to the challenge with acts of heroism, if not always triumph. In such tales, men's dramatic resort to violence proves redemptory, delivering themselves and others (families, religious communities, or the nation) into safety and freedom.

Meta-narratives of men: phallicism and guardianship

As a shorthand way to theorize such representations of men, we offer the admittedly provocative term: "phallicism." As we use this concept, it refers to a network of narrative themes and arcs, dispositional and behavioral traits, and normative expectations that function as a kind of metalanguage to make sense of men's lives or at least the lives of modern Euro-American men. Departing from conventional views of phallicism, we underscore the layered, contradictory, tension-filled dynamism of this construct as it frames accounts of men.

Phallicism is characterized, foremost, by the wish to be in control. Driven by a fantasy of self-sufficiency, control underscores an aspiration to impose restraint over impulses, emotions, and behavior. The unruliness of internal life is to be mastered in order to realize a thoroughly masculine self that projects a cool sense of self-possession. Phallic men are defined by sharp and hard-edged self-boundaries and a psychic containment and invulnerability that exhibit a striking emotional reticence, at times a wholehearted disavowal of sentimentality (Shamir and Travis 2002). As one psychoanalyst observed: "Phallicism has become a fortress of emotional self-sufficiency and impenetrability, wherein man has taken shelter, leaving him emotionally and psychically inaccessible" (Schiller 2010a: 135, cf. Elise 2001, Irigaray 2002). Emotional life may appear as the enemy, but, as we see it, phallicism is a specific cultural code of emotionality.[2]

Heightened psychic boundariedness is paralleled by a drive to control external forces. A will to control the other (animate or inanimate) manifests in a masculine culture featuring the objectification of the other, aggressivity and, ultimately, a social order structured by hierarchy.

But, complete control and self-sufficiency are impossible aspirations, as even phallic selves inevitably encounter the too-muchness and unruliness of their inner and outer lives, whether it is contradictory impulses and desires, many unconscious, or the mind-boggling excess and chaos of environmental forces. It's as if these forces have their own logic and power, resisting and mocking our most resolute efforts at control. Every effort to impose discipline and order is eventually frustrated and upended, exposing our ineffectiveness and impotence. Paradoxically, then, mastery risks, indeed invites, defeat, engendering states of helplessness and vulnerability. With this reversal of fortune, men find themselves, ironically, in a stereotypically feminine position of needing to be comforted and reassured in the face of their compromised masculinity.

Control, however, is not an end in itself; it is a condition of world-making and mastery. The animating spirit of phallic masculinity, its driving fantasy, is to forge a world that expresses men's unique personal vision, to impose on reality an order that bears their singular psychic imprint. Acquiring the requisite capacities, knowledge, and skills, phallic men project themselves into the world, aspiring and indeed expecting to inhabit it authoritatively. They aim to remake the world or, more modestly, impose their own singular imprint. In this regard, many men imagine themselves to be drivers of innovation and of self and collective reinvention.

Their grandiosity, however, comes with great risk. The phallic imperative to inhabit the world in expansive ways triggers anxieties about one's drive and capacity to translate desire into worldliness. How many men are immobilized by anxieties of inadequacy, anticipating failure, and humiliation? How many are stalled in imagined projects, utterly failing to launch, to make a worldly mark, even a light footprint? For these men, phallic expectations are crippling and mind-fucking; some crumble into states of powerlessness and defeat crossing over into an emasculating space of feminine submission and passivity; others are stalled in a mere pose of masculinity, terrified of being exposed and humiliated as fraudulent (see Chapter 5).

Despite the illusion of self-sufficiency, phallic men share a world with others, including their shared ambition of world-making. Each must countenance a reality principle: dependence on the other's recognition to redeem their claim to masculine authority. Recognition is contingent; it can be withheld or withdrawn at any time. And, in at least broadly liberal contexts, it's extended on condition of its reciprocity. Phallic men cannot then evade relationships of interdependency. Moreover, not all others are admirers; some are rivals—envious and wishing to surpass, even destroy, their competitors. Phallic men not only risk occupying the world but also holding their ground in the face of rivals. Despite a glossy, cool demeanor of self-assuredness, men inhabit a space of near-constant insecurity and anxiety, terrified by public dramas revealing their inadequacy and failure, rendering them potentially small and vulnerable.

Driven by a fantasy of self-sufficiency, phallic men are challenged by the experience of internal or external unruliness, excess, and chaos. To avoid defeat, and by implication, feminization, two responses seem paradigmatic in phallic tropes of manhood: flight or fight.

In the face of the too-muchness of psychic and collective life, a phallic self may take flight. This can take many forms, for example, a rejection of the emotional or a reaction formation that denigrates self-states of dependency and vulnerability; in short, a repudiation of affective and behavioral experiences culturally associated with the feminine. Flight is also evident in the well-worn masculine theme of escape from the quotidian through road trips, the rejection of domesticity, and the repudiation of sentimentality whether in the home, intimacy, or literature (Shamir and Travis 2002).

Alternatively, in the face of the unruly and the chaotic, phallic selves may resort to "fighting" or the exiling or eviscerating or submission of threatening and unruly forces. In this regard, masculine heroic narratives of resisting defeat, triumphing over menacing forces to secure order and freedom are iconic. In such dramas of restoration or liberation heroic acts of great fortitude, including the resort to violence, may be warranted as the threat escalates into a truly menacing evil; the danger must be crushed or expunged, by any means necessary. Such phallic symbolism has been foundational in accounts of American men's lives.

As a kind of metalanguage of iconic masculine men, phallicism has been a sustained target of critique. Male liberationists, for example, underscored the dark side of the masculine ethos of control: men haunted by a crushing isolation, loneliness, and sense of self and social estrangement (e.g. Farrell 1974, Goldberg 1976). Alternatively, second-wave feminists spotlighted phallic men's responsibility for women's sufferings. They pointed out that, despite the idealization of self-and-world-mastery, men still need women to provide the material and emotional labor sustaining their public lives. But such longings to be nurtured and comforted, to be receptive and penetrated, are said to trigger intense anxieties around emasculation. Phallic men sustain their masculine authority by repudiating such feminine longings at times by resorting to aggressive assaults on women and gay men (Barry 1984, Brownmiller 1975, Dworkin 1981).

Phallic men may present another kind of social danger: being unable to set boundaries in their quest for mastery. They threaten to render the environment, including living beings, into mere instrumentalities exploited for their own self-aggrandizement. Human and non-human animals are rendered inferior. In the face of resistance phallic men may leave a trail of bloodied bodies and wrecked communities. Again, in this phallic scenario, women—and all non-phallic selves—are expected to assume the complementary and subordinate role of domesticating and civilizing men's aggressive willfulness. Paradoxically, phallic men end up, once again, dependent on women or other feminized selves in order to sustain a stable social and moral infrastructure of domestic and public life.

It wasn't that long ago that phallic men were celebrated as decisive and heroic figures in American culture (think of the larger-then-life male stars of the Studio era from Gable and Cooper to Bogart and John Wayne). Such men were championed as adventurous and innovative, drivers of self and collective reinvention. Ambitious, sometimes ruthless, such men were admired as engines of social progress, builders of worlds of abundance, and agents transforming America into a world power. In the American imaginary, these men strode across history as paragons of virtue, even if flawed. Until recently, it was hard to imagine real men outside of this phallic iconography.

But times are changing. Today, there is a chorus of voices that speak of this iconic figure as slowly fading into the social background, as an anachronism, a failure, even a social threat (e.g. Scott 2014). For example, in response to women's forward movement, and a rapidly changing multicultural global work and social environment, this iconic masculine man is said to be tragically at odds with the current zeitgeist. Whether in the field of work, education, politics, or intimacy, phallic men depend on anachronistic and parochial thinking, outdated emotional and social skills, and rigidly competitive and aggressive behavior with little regard to the social consequences of their conduct. Stiff and insecure in their skin, defensive and often hostile towards women, non-whites, and non-Americans, such men are said to be ill prepared for a multicultural world that rewards personal flexibility, empathic communication, and respect for colleagues, clients, and consumers whose backgrounds and identities are diverse (Kimmel 2015, Rosin 2012, Searcey et al. 2015). Titles such as *The End of Men* (2012), *Angry White Men* (2017), and *Stiffed: The Betrayal of the American Man* (1999) voice a public anxiety that the very gender traits that had presumably served men and America so well are today barriers to personal well-being, social success, as well as national progress.

As we see it, this critique of contemporary American men is both on the mark and misleading. Spot on in that as men cling to a go-it-alone mentality and to a preoccupation with control and dominance, they will continue to lose ground in almost every sphere of personal and social life. Such men risk becoming caricatures of the heroic masculine men they still idealize. They are threatened with social marginalization and spiraling into a degraded social existence as many float in a world of substance abuse, drift in and out of dead-end jobs, or resort to a retrograde politics of resentment in a desperate effort to reclaim their lost status.

But such stories, which are today being told time and again (e.g. Brooks 2015), are far from the whole story. There is, as Lacan might say, a conflation of the signifier (phallicism) with the Real. But, as we see it, phallic imagery and tropes are one-sided and misleading as a foundational lens for comprehending men's lives. It's as if dependency and vulnerability, attachments, and longings for solidarity and community, belong exclusively to the province of women and "the feminine." Phallic representations neglect the ethical commitments that infuse men's lives with passion and purpose (Chapter 4). Men live and die for beliefs about integrity, goodness, justice, and social belonging.

With its preoccupation with autonomous world-making-and-mastery, a phallic metalanguage fails to grasp the *ethical cornerstone of American manhood: guardianship*. Aspirationally, to speak broadly, American men pursue self-and-world-making as a pathway to being socially useful by rendering themselves instruments of social beneficence and responsible stewards over worldly matters. To be sure, world-making serves as a marker of personal success, legitimating their claims to social authority. But, in our view, there is typically a higher purpose animating many American men: to form social worlds that benefit others—families, friends, citizens, and humankind. This ethical impulse is not comprehended in the metalanguage of phallic masculinity.

Arguably, at the apex of social usefulness is a willingness to take on the considerable responsibilities of guardianship. Bearing the trust of the public, men are expected to accept a moral duty to facilitate and care for the well-being of others, to be good stewards of the human and natural environment. Guardianship entails assuming responsibilities to provide for one's family and to be a good father and husband as well as friend and citizen; guardianship may culminate in sharing the ultimate responsibility of public governance as a commitment to promote the good of all citizens, whether this public spiritedness is expressed in joining a political party, social movement, philanthropic organization, or holding public office. In the final analysis, American men measure their worth in no small measure against the yardstick of social utility and effective guardianship.

Men must then be understood as ethical selves. They are animated by notions of rightness and fairness and by ideals of a life of integrity and moral purpose that extend beyond self-interest. Men use themselves for social benefit, for example, as generative fathers, as producers of goods and services, as entrepreneurs generating jobs and wealth, as protectors of the nation, or as cultural creators or entertainers. In their ethical life, men blend, to invoke stereotypical cultural codes, the masculine will to world-making-and-mastery with the feminine wish to be good custodians of life. Men not only allow themselves to be used by and for another, but measure their self-worth by their social usefulness and effective stewardship.

From this ethical vantage point, men must be seen as relational selves, as impacting on others, as experiencing themselves as part of others' lives, as living in part through and for others, and therefore as being in some meaningful way responsible for the other. Some of the key cultural tropes of femininity such as notions of a relational self, nurturance and social bonding, and an ethic of care in which self-interest is intertwined with interest of the other, are also at the center of at least a multidimensional construct of being a man.

Of course, guardianship is an ideal type. And, it is not without its own potential dangers. For example, the desire to be an instrument of social purposefulness may get derailed and inverted: the ethos of penetrating and using environmental and human resources for the public good can succumb to the narcissism of achievement and grandiosity. Or, guardianship can slide into an authoritarianism whether in the form of patriarchy (father knows best) paternalism (men know best), patrimonial (the male elite know best) or authoritarian populism (the leader as the true voice of the people). These negative potentials are not inherent in the ethos of a utilitarian and a public-spirited guardianship, but regressions, as it were, into narrow forms of phallic masculinity.

Recently, a trope that runs through both popular and academic narratives relates a tale of an historic shift from a more expansive culture of manhood to a narrow phallicism.

In *Angry White Men*, Michael Kimmel (2015) argues that in the era of industrialization, men fulfilled their roles as good husbands and fathers by being the primary breadwinners and family decision-makers. Men were also part of a fraternal brotherhood (unions, the military, bar culture, fraternities, men's associations, sports) and served as patriarchal protectors of the nation. However, as manufacturing jobs migrated beyond the nation's borders, and as more and more women participated in the paid labor market and virtually every sector of public life, some men, especially lower-income white men, have resorted to a rage-driven personal politics of misogyny and homophobia and, at times, racism, to reclaim masculine pride, if not actual power.

Similarly, in *Stiffed* (1999), Susan Faludi maintains that until recently men balanced a self-reliant, power-driven will to dominance with a commitment to being useful, in particular, to promoting the social good. "Even as the ethic of solo ambition gained ground [during industrialization], social utility remained a competing index of American manhood" (p. 12). Men were valued both for their accomplishments and leadership and for being good husbands and fathers, loyal employers, and employees, and good citizens willing to defend and die for their nation. "Men were not only to take care of their families but also their society without complaint; that was, in fact, what made them men" (p. 36) This America is disappearing. There's been a dramatic cultural shift to an "ornamental culture." Instead of a meritocracy, America's ornamental culture valorizes self-display and fashioning a sexy and stylized surface paralleling the triumph of a culture of celebrity. "Masculinity is [today] something to drape over the body. . . . It is personal, not societal. . . . Manhood is displayed not demonstrated" (p. 35). And it is violent. "As utilitarian qualities were dethroned . . . an ornamental culture encouraged young men to see surliness, hostility, and violence as expressions of glamour, as a way to showcase themselves without being feminized. . . . Celebrity masculinity enshrined the pose of the 'bad boy'" (p. 37). Not only do most men lack the economic wherewithal to realize iconic masculine ideals, this iconography has been downgraded as markers of yesterday's man. As Faludi sees it, many men have either surrendered to a growing sense of loss and rage or accommodated to a symbolic masculinity in which self-worth is no longer based on real accomplishments or social virtues.

We take issue with the main plotline of such narratives. Despite the current Trumpian moment, we hold that the long-term trend in the U.S. is more nuanced and contradictory. In particular, the opening of psychic and social space makes it possible for many Americans to renegotiate gender, at times beyond a cisgendered heteronormativity. The successive chapters of this book will make this case chiefly in psychoanalytic terms. Initially, though, we wish to present social science research in order to make a provisional case for our viewpoint.

Challenging orthodoxy: manhood without homophobia or misogyny

Men have always been more than seamlessly masculine. But today, the multigendered status of men is becoming more evident, even if not always recognized by men or represented in public accounts. Resistance to re-imagining men's lives has many sources: investments in "traditional" manhood by many men—and women; the defense of heteronormativity by straight Americans; a political investment by some feminists in a narrow phallic construct of men (Hooks 2004); and, not least, cisgendered heteronormative cultures that flourish in the worlds of business, the media, sports, the military, and the government that champion a competitive, sometimes ruthlessly ambitious and swaggering masculinity while also promoting a fraternal brotherhood of male privilege.[3]

There is another big reason for this cultural misrecognition: the view that men are defined chiefly by not being women—and not being homosexual. Straight manhood is said to be a defense—against femininity, whether in women, gay men, effeminate men, or men perceived as small, weak, needy, disabled, or unsuccessful. "While different groups of men may disagree about other traits and their significance in gender definitions, the antifemininity component of masculinity is perhaps the single dominant and universal characteristic" (Kimmel 2005: 97). In the American imaginary, real men are not women and are not gay—and not feminine, ever. In this scenario, misogyny and homophobia have been and continue to be the cornerstone of being a man.

But, what if this is not the case? It's time to seriously reconsider men's lives outside of narrow phallic symbolism that reproduce a rigid heteronormativity. Consider the following lines of psychological and social research.

Psychological research

A researcher observes: "Changes in societal roles now allow, and perhaps even require, men and women to possess traits once thought only appropriate to the opposite sex" (McDermott 2016: 4–5). Political Science professor Monika McDermott articulates a view that is now widely accepted among psychological researchers: regardless of the gender expectations attached to one's birth-assigned sexed status, our actual psychic and social lives mix culturally coded masculine and feminine traits.

In *Masculinity, Femininity, and American Political Behavior* (2016), McDermott cites a rich history of survey data and psychological research (cf. Auster and Collins 2000, Bolzendahl and Myers 2004, Fast 1984, Twenge 1997) that underscores a dramatic shift in the gendering of American's psyches: we no longer live in a bipolar but in a multipolar gender world. Specifically, while notions of ideal masculinity (achievement, dominance, and leadership) and femininity (warmth, nurturance, tenderness, and being loving) have changed little over the decades, traditional expectations that males should exhibit only masculinity and females only femininity are increasingly at odds with empirical reality (pp. 12–13). Researchers have documented that "it has become increasingly likely for individuals to take on (or admit to) non-traditional gendered personality traits. . . ." (p. 14). In particular,

> the level of masculine personality traits has risen significantly among women. . . . *At the same time, men's possession of both masculine and feminine personality traits has increased. Both sexes are now, on average, more likely than in the past to possess the personality traits of the sex role opposite the one once dictated to them by tradition.*
>
> (our emphasis, p. 15, 16)

In a 2011 national survey ("Gendered Personalities and Politics"), McDermott classified respondents into four ideal typical gendered personalities: "Traditionals" scored high in gender traits that correspond to expectations attached to their "biological" sex e.g. males registered high on masculine traits and low on feminine traits; "Cross-typed" personalities scored high on opposite sex personality dimensions and low on their own e.g. men scored high on feminine, low on masculine traits; "Androgynous" personalities measured above the median on both masculine and feminine traits and "Undifferentiated" personalities scored well below the median on both gender measures (pp. 16–17, 120). Her chief finding: "Few American adults . . . conform to a traditional gender/sex personality profile. . . . 67 percent each of men and women . . . possess . . . the traits traditionally expected from the opposite sex. . . . Roughly half of each sex possesses high levels of the traits once expected exclusively from the opposite sex. . . . *These results depict a society in which masculine and feminine personality traits are not the sole domains of men and women, respectively*" (pp. 17, 120). In particular, contrary to conventional stereotypes, "*men have gotten more feminine over at least the past five decades.* . . . It does at least seem [that] . . . men have changed with the times (our emphasis, p. 55).

The implications of this body of psychological research are considerable. In a traditional or cisgendered scenario, sexed status (m/f) aligns with masculine and feminine traits that dictate sex roles (breadwinner/caregiver) and gender identity. For example, males are expected to exhibit paradigmatic masculine traits ideally suited to leadership roles. But, this normative ordering is being upended. Sexed status no longer seamlessly aligns with the empirical distribution of gender traits and roles. To be sure, more women are caregivers, while more men are still breadwinners. However, most researchers have concluded that this alignment of sexed status and social roles is not dictated by biology but is largely explained sociologically. In short, the tight, causal link between biological sex, gender identity, and social roles has given way in psychological studies to constructs of a more plastic and multipolar gender order (p. 134). Accordingly, given their multigendered subjectivity, men's identity cannot be so easily described as a defense against femininity.

Sociological research

A unique gender-sexual order coalesced in post-World War II America. Central was state driven compulsory heterosexuality and the exiling from civil life of the polluted figure of the homosexual. Echoing this cultural moment, Kimmel wrote: "homophobia, men's fear of other men, is the animating condition of the dominant definition of masculinity in America [and] the reigning definition of masculinity is a defensive effort to prevent being emasculated" (2005: 39). The other side to a culture of pervasive homophobia was the idealization of a straight, seamlessly masculine man (Anderson and Robinson 2016: 252).

Why did a virulent homophobia become so central to establishing manhood at this time? The historic emergence of homosexuals into public life in the 50s and 60s is surely part of the story. But, this development stirred a deeper anxiety: men feared feminization and this anxiety was linked to a larger threat—the weakening of the nation under the spectre of communism (Corber 1993, D'Emilio 1983). After the heroic phallicism of the war years, men returned home only to find work in quasi-feminized jobs in an increasingly post-industrial service economy. And, despite postwar pressure for women to return to a domestic-centered life, they were inexorably claiming public lives alongside men as classmates, co-workers, friends, rivals, and bosses. These postwar social shifts triggered heightened gender anxiety among some men, but it did not lead to a thoroughgoing pollution of women. Straight men depended on women, and specifically their femininity in order to be effective intimate partners, mothers to their children, caregivers to their families, and colleagues to be trusted. Men could though divide them into good (ideal femininity) and bad (masculinized) women. And, they could express their anxieties in acts of sexual objectification and in fashioning a misogynist public culture.

Such ambivalence did not attach to the male homosexual. This personage could stand-in for a polluted male femininity. He represented a failed manhood in his stereotypical male femininity and non-heterosexuality. His fate was sealed as this figure came to symbolize a threat to family and nation. Homophobia could then serve as a site to enact a straight masculine ideal; and, only then could heterosexuality become the über signifier of a normative sexuality and gender. But, in its normalizing and disciplinary authority, this hetero-masculine culture imposed a costly burden on men: to always present a seamless masculine, straight self.

This hegemonic sexual-gender order has not disappeared. However, by the mid-90s another regulatory order emerged: heteronormative but not compulsory. The closet door is now ajar. As more and more gay men step out in private and public life, and as public expressions of homophobia are less tolerated, straight men have had to reconsider the proving grounds of their gender identity. Central has been the unthinkable: the renegotiation of their relationship to homosexuality and femininity.

Straight men today face a dilemma. As homophobia—and misogyny—are less available, how to establish a credible identity? In *Straights: Heterosexuality in a Post-Closeted Culture* (2014), James Dean offers one explanation: maintaining "soft" boundaries between a straight and gay world. In post-closeted social environments "in place of overt acts of homophobic prejudice, straight men . . . employ normative gender practices to indicate their heterosexuality [and their normative masculinity]." However, "gender-conventional gay men . . . undercut this strategy." Accordingly, straight men rely on "normative heterosexual boundary practices, which put social distance between oneself as straight and gay individuals, signifiers, and spaces" (p. 249).

Three ideal typical patterns of boundary regulation are sketched, each pivoting around either subtle homophobic distancing or antihomophobic boundary blurring. "Hegemonic straight masculine men" establish "aversive boundaries" by participating in seamlessly masculine practices, for example, exhibiting a hyper-heterosexuality or exaggerated aggressive and competitive behavior.[4] But even this aversive boundary pattern relies on "soft homophobic forms of informal exclusion, nonrecognition and disrespect" (p. 249). For example, straight men avoid befriending gays or styles of dress and comportment that are culturally marked as gay. Such social distancing, however, is increasingly difficult to manage as straights, especially younger men, encounter gays as kin, colleagues, bosses, co-workers, classmates, and in social environments where straights and gays mix. Boundaries are then selectively regulated, for example, straights may cooperate with their gay co-workers while avoiding socializing outside of work.

Interestingly, among the young men interviewed, the majority reported establishing a straight masculine identity while holding antihomophobic beliefs. They normalized gay men and endorsed either a weakening (type 2) or blurring (type 3) of the boundaries between straight and gay worlds. In the former case, a porous division was maintained, for example, entering gay spaces and supporting gay equality while disclosing their heterosexuality and enacting a conventional masculinity. Curiously, straight black men exhibited a particular ease in relaxing boundaries. Dean explains: "Black racial identity acts as a kind of inoculation against suspicion of being gay and instead it exaggerates his straight masculinity. . . ." (2014: 236, cf. Seidman 2004). However, racial privilege has seemingly made it easier for straight white men to blur the boundaries by embracing an uncompromising antihomophobia. They challenged the gay/straight and the masculine/feminine binaries. "We are witnessing," says Dean, "the development of antihomophobic heterosexual masculini- ties, which . . . aim to subvert the reproduction of normative heterosexuality and normative masculinity" (2014: 131, 260).

Although sociologists such as Dean (cf. Bridges 2014; Heasley 2004, 2005) document cracks in the wall separating straight and gay men, such border crossing has had clear, seemingly absolute limits: prohibitions against erotic contact between men and behaviors and roles culturally marked as feminine.

Recently, this sociological orthodoxy has been challenged. "Declining homophobia . . . permits otherwise heterosexual men to engage in same- sex [erotic] interactions in absence of sexual desires for men. . . . [Such] heterosexual men are no longer assumed homosexual for engaging in such behaviors" (Anderson and Robinson 2016: 250, cf. Savin-Williams 2017, Ward 2008). Researching gender shifts, the sociologist Eric Anderson (2007, 2009, 2016, Anderson and McCormack 2015) documents a culture of sexual flexibility among university students. Identified as straight, these men are open to homoerotic contact. "Throughout America's universities . . . there is a rapid and increasing frequency by which straight-identifying men are kissing their friends on the cheeks and lips, all without the fear of homosexual persecution" (2016: 254). Hugging, spooning, and bed-sharing are surprisingly commonplace. "All of these men said that they had shared a bed with another man not out of homosexual attraction, but heterosexual affection. . . . Of the 40 athletes interviewed, 37 had spent the night in bed with a heterosexual male friend and cuddled with him" (2016: 255–256). Stunningly, "40% of the 40 men . . . had engaged in a male-male-female threesome where some physical contact occurred between men." As one student remarked, "my friend was fucking her and I was making out with him. . . ." (2016: 256). As homophobia is stigmatized, "men are given a much greater range of gendered and sexual behaviors that they can partake in, while remaining socially heterosexual" (2016: 257).

Anderson's research challenges another long-standing sociological orthodoxy: men's resistance to participating in "feminine" terrains and, in particular, integrating feminine coded practices. Researching collegiate cheerleading, a sport that "has largely maintained its cultural script of femininity" (2005: 342), Anderson divided cheerleader's gender practice into "orthodox" and "inclusive" masculinity. In the former, men participate only in masculine typed tasks and present a hyper-heterosexuality that includes homophobic and sexist behavior. By contrast, inclusively masculine men "embrace the feminized underpinnings of their sport and largely value their gay teammates" (2005: 338). Despite the fact that most of these cheerleaders are former high school football players, Anderson found that they "were not only less concerned with mitigating homosexual suspicion . . . but they were also less concerned about associating with femininity . . . [and] far less concerned with the expression of femininity among other men" (p. 347). Indeed, "men in the inclusive group also participated in tasks traditionally defined as feminine. . . . This included allowing themselves to be tossed into the air (flying), standing atop the shoulders of others [including women], wearing clothing defined as feminine [sleeveless shirts zipped in the back], and dancing in the same erotic fashion as their female teammates" (p. 351). Anderson concluded, "with the performance of these tasks these men challenge the utility of binary thinking" (p. 347).

The cornerstone of phallic manliness has been the presumption that masculinity is exclusively associated with men and men with a seamless hetero-masculinity; research suggests that both premises are today questionable. More and more men, especially young men, seem to be establishing a straight masculine identity while embracing an antihomophobic standpoint and incorporating, however selectively, feminine coded ways of being and relating. At the same time, more and more women today are integrating stereotypical forms of masculinity in their comportment, behavior, and social roles. In the not too distant past, it was mostly blue-collar women, non-white and immigrant women, or mannish women and butch dykes, who exhibited masculinities, but were often stigmatized. Today, mainstream straight middle class women, not to mention queer or transwomen, display, unapologetically, their "female masculinity" (Halberstam 1998a). In a parallel, if decidedly more ambivalent way, as men's work life migrates from manual labor to white-collar office and service work, and as their personal lives increasingly pivot around relationships and domesticity, especially parenting, men's lives are converging in key ways with women. As they absorb culturally coded feminine psychosocial dispositions and practices, it makes less and less sense to conflate men with a seamless masculinity. As a normative cultural code, heteronormativity is more and more at odds with men's multigendered lives.

Individualization of gender

One point seems indisputable: what it means to be a man today is a matter of contention—and confusion! Even more dizzying, the very notion of whether gender identity is still coherent and credible is being publicly debated. Has gender become an ideological abstraction, an identity performance, or a normative mapping that speaks less and less to lived experience?

Without discounting the public pronouncements of gender certainty, indeed a virulence by some who insist on the naturalness and normality of a muscular phallic manliness, we believe this is a time of unprecedented gender questioning. We're witnessing the surfacing of new languages of gender complexity and transivity. Some speak of the multiplication of genders, others of the refusal of the very idea of a gender identity; such voices are challenging a dichotomous, complementary model of gender. Newspaper and magazine articles, with titles such as "Oregon Court Allows a Person to Choose Neither Sex," "What's So Bad About a Boy Who Wants to Wear a Dress?," "Beyond He or She" (*Time* cover March 2017), "More Fathers Who Stay at Home by Choice," "When Women Become Men at Wellesley," "Easing the Law for New Yorkers Shifting

Gender," and "A University Recognizes a Third Gender: Neutral," trumpet a time of radical gender uncertainty. Consider: in 2014, "Facebook decided . . . to offer fifty-six 'custom' gender options" (Brubaker 2016: 44–45). New binary-avoidant notions of gender such as the metrosexual, queer, genderqueer, queer straight, ungendered, agender, gendermut, polygendered, trans*, third gender, transgendered, pangendered, and gender non-conforming signal a re-imagining of gender beyond a cisgendered heteronormativity (Ahlm 2015, Brubaker 2016, Ehrensaft 2011, Halberstam 1998b, 2018, Hale 1997, 1998, Hansbury 2005, Rupp and Taylor 2013, Ryan 2015).

If pressed to succinctly describe what's going on, we would underscore a tension between the shaky but still socially effective edifice of heteronormativity and a culture of the "individualization of the self" that upends gender binarism.

By a culture of individualization we mean the notion that each individual feels a right or sense of entitlement, perhaps also a normalizing demand, to design a unique self (Ehrensaft 2011: 532, Goldner 2011: 166, Halberstam 1998a: 306). In such a cultural environment, there is an ambivalent relationship to identity categories, whether gender or age or race or sexuality. Such categories may be approached as a ground of individualization but may also feel constraining and impeding the fashioning of one's singular individuality. Speaking only of gender identity, some individuals may wish to craft their own unique expression of gender; for others, individualization entails rejecting a binary gender model; still others refuse any gendering, as this is said to signify an act of inauthenticity and unfreedom. Furthermore, as gender is experienced as more plastic than hardwired, and as a site of personal choice, individuals can re-imagine gender less as an identity than as an aesthetic or as part of the stylizing or designing of the self (Brubaker 2016: 132). That is, selves may look to gender less to present "who they are" than as a site of play or situational self-expression or erotic exploration (Hale, 1997, Harris 2009a). It's hardly surprising then that new theoretical languages of gender have been invented to capture the dynamics of individualization, e.g. performativity, assemblage, situational gender, fluidity, inclusiveness, trans*, or transsituated (Brubaker 2016, Cromwell et al. 1999, Halberstam 1998a, 2018).

The age of gender binarism has hardly come to an end. It is the tensions between its continued normativity and representations of gender plasticity, and between its grounding of identity and belonging and its critique as a form of imposition and domination, that perhaps defines the field of gender in contemporary America. At the root of this conflict-ridden, changing gender environment are broad social transformations in the relationship between the state, social institutions, civic culture, and personal life.

Cracks in the edifice of heteronormativity

The social world that rendered the figure of the phallic man coherent and compelling is in the midst of upheaval. Two broad shifts in the American gender landscape spell trouble for this iconic figure: the decline of the Victorian idea of separate spheres and the retreat of the state from enforcing compulsory heterosexuality.

The notion of a fixed social order marked by separate gender spheres (men/public, women/private), and clearly defined gender roles, had considerable popular appeal and normative force through much of the 19th and 20th centuries (Canaday 2009, Cott 1977, 2000, for a critique see Davidson 1998). Today, this Victorian ideal is buckling under the weight of new social realities.

Women from all social classes and communities are more or less fully engaged participants in public life. For example, women's share of the total labor force is close to 50 percent. They have established a considerable presence in many previously male-dominated occupations, from bus drivers, accountants, pharmacists, physicians, and surgeons to retail and corporate managers, lawyers, judges, professors, and police officers. Indicative of their changing economic status, about one-quarter of married women (and almost 30 percent among younger married couples) make more money than their husbands—compared to just 4 percent in 1960 (Wang 2013a). Nothing signals women's changing status more than the fact that motherhood is no longer an insurmountable cultural barrier to entering the paid labor force. One researcher estimates that "70 percent of women with children below eighteen are in the labor force. . . ." (Miller 2014: 2). Even more telling, roughly 60 percent of mothers with children under age three hold a paid job, compared to just 34 percent in 1975 (Miller 2014: 2).

To state our viewpoint in a stark way: the actual lives of women today, especially younger women, are in important ways "converging" with men. Notwithstanding ongoing disparities in income and wealth and continuing gender segregation in sectors of the workplace and elsewhere, many women today exercise institutional authority, are cultural creators and leaders in academia, the arts, and in the world of public opinion-making, pursue careers and financial independence, are forging their own personal and intimate lives, and, especially for those below thirty five, claim a right to erotic and personal self-fulfillment—with or without men (Rosin 2012). As the sociologist Kathleen Gerson argues in *The Unfinished Revolution: Coming of Age in a New Era of Gender* (2010), "underneath this general shift in work experiences lies a gender convergence. . . . Young people are closing the gap between male 'careers' and female 'jobs' [with] . . . more men and women . . . reject[ing] fixed gender divisions and separate spheres" (pp. 200, 203). The result is the "undermin[ing] of traditional forms of masculinity and femininity. . . ." (p. 206, cf. Parker and Wang 2013).

What about men? Status deflation, gender anxiety, and an anticipated drop in income go a long way towards explaining the well-documented reluctance of many men to pursue "women's work" (e.g. Blau and Brummund 2013, Cohen 2013). And yet, as manufacturing jobs and well-paying blue-collar work disappear, men are migrating to stereotypically women's work in sales, retail, clerical, and client-oriented jobs such as cashiers, bank tellers, food preparation, janitors, loan interviewers, and insurance and policy processing clerks. In particular, "men . . . with less than a bachelor's degree . . . have been moving away from traditional, blue-collar, middle-paying jobs—such as truck drivers, construction laborers, and factory workers—to lower-paying service jobs." For example, the percent of men working in food preparation, cooking, and cleaning or janitorial work has virtually doubled from "11 percent to 21 percent" between 1990 and 2013 (Kearney et al. 2015).

But, even for men working in stereotypically male jobs, a gender convergence in the workplace at a deeper psychosocial level is occurring. Consider the changing context of their work life.

Men routinely work alongside women, many of whom occupy so-called men's work roles and engage in culturally coded masculine gendered practices e.g. intellectual analysis, managerial decision-making or personnel hiring and firing. And, many men today work under the management and authority of women.

Importantly, the daily practice of work today, almost regardless of the occupational sector, requires a range of psychosocial capacities and relational skills that inevitably blend stereotypically masculine and feminine traits. This is obviously the case for men employed in retail, sub-managerial, and a variety of white-collar jobs. Their work requires stereotypically feminine marked dispositions and behaviors such as empathy and a capacity to do collaborative works that relies on emotional labor and intelligence. But, more to the point: more and more men, whether engaged in blue- or white-collar paid labor, are employed in multicultural and global work environments. Men are expected to understand and cooperate with co-workers and be attuned to clients of diverse genders, races, nationalities, and sexualities (Brooks 2015). In short, work life—and life outside of work—increasingly demands, and arguably is engendering, selves whose psyches and self-practices fall well outside the boundaries of both phallic masculinity and hyper-femininity. Rigid heteronormative gender identities and norms are increasingly in tension with what is expected and what is effective in the workplace and beyond.

Nevertheless, many men refuse to acknowledge the extent to which their lives have changed. They neither recognize nor narrate the ways their actual gender experience is at odds with tightly bounded notions of manhood (Cross and Bagilhole 2002, McDonald 2013, Pullen and Simpson 2009, Williams 1995). Such men seem caught in a cultural contradiction: claiming a public identity as seamlessly masculine even as their lives betray a multilayered, heterogeneous gendering.[4]

Men's changing lives have been widely noted in their reconsideration of the importance of parenting. Researchers agree that today, especially among younger men, being a good father (available, nurturing and engaged) is at the center of what it means to be a man (Coltrane 2002, Coltrane et al. 2004, Deutsch 1999, Diamond 2007, Doucet 2006, Eden and Nelson 2013, Gerson, 2010, Goldberg 2012, Kaufman 2013, Townsend 2002). This shift is not just aspirational. In a study of stay-at-home fathers, the demographers, Kramer and Kramer (2016), document that as "women are increasing their participation in the labor force and working hours … men [are] increasing their participation in household labor, especially in the realm of childcare." For example, "time spent by married mothers on household tasks has fallen from 35.7 weekly hours in 1965 to 18.3 weekly hours in 2010, while married fathers' increased time spent on

household chores for the same period from 4.7 hours to 9.5 hours ...
[And,] time spent on caregiving for children has increased dramatically
for fathers, from 2.5 weekly hours in 1965 ... to 7.8 weekly hours in 2008
(compared to 13.9 hours for women)" (cf. Bianchi et al. 2012, Livingston
2014, Pew Research Center 2013, Rehel 2014, for class aspects of this
shift, see Deutsch 1999 and Shows and Gerstel 2009). This change is
fueled not only by economic pressures confronting families, but by a
process, no matter how uneven and incomplete, of gender convergence
and equality. "There has been a growing acceptance of this reversal of
gendered roles in recent decades and a larger shift to a more egalitarian
division of paid and unpaid work in families. . . ." (Kramer and Kramer
2016). Indeed, many researchers describe a process of the de-gendering
of parenting. "Research on equally shared parenting demonstrates that
parenting need not be gendered" (Deutsch 1999, 2007; cf. Bilbarz and
Stacey 2010, Golombok 2015, Lorber 2005, Rehel 2014, Target and
Fonagy 2002).

As we see it, a neo-Victorian social ideal that pivots around a radical
division between a women-centered private domain featuring a specific
emotional economy and caregiving roles, and a male-dominated public
realm articulating a masculine emotional economy and authority claiming,
decision-making roles is in tension with an increasingly gender mixed and
messy social world (e.g. Halberstam 2018a: 133). Roles but also emotional
capacities and relational orientations are becoming less gender typed, or at
least there are wide stretches of our personal and public lives that fall
outside a rigidly cisgendered heteronormativity. Such spaces are less
gender regulated, at least less rigidly. In de-gendering social contexts, the
distribution and regulation of behaviors pivot on factors such as individual
capacity, interest, ambition, and merit. In particular, the de-gendering of
what has historically been rigidly culturally marked as feminine spheres,
roles, and modes of being and relating allows men to more freely circulate
across social spheres and roles and to expand the range of their emotional
and behavioral expression. Of course, we need to add: we're speaking
of a societal thread, arguably a trend, but one that exists alongside a
heteronormatively organized social order.

Paralleling a dynamic towards gender convergence, and more haltingly
equality, is an unmistakable trend towards the normalization and
mainstreaming of homosexuality. The once solid, seemingly unshakable
edifice of heteronormativity is cracking—and at a pace few ever imagined

(e.g. Anderson and McCormack 2015, Dean 2014, Eskridge 1999, Ghaziani 2011, 2014, Raeburn 2004, Seidman 2004, Stein 2012, Weeks 2007).

At the center of this transformation is a shift in the legal status of the homosexual from outsider to citizen. This development does not signal the end of a heteronormative culture but a retreat of the state from enforcing the compulsory status of heterosexuality. Consider the legal status of the homosexual in the era of the closet:

> The homosexual in 1961 was smothered by law. She or he risked arrest . . . for dancing with someone of the same sex, cross dressing, propositioning another adult homosexual, possessing a homophile publication, writing about homosexuality without disapproval, displaying pictures of two people of the same sex in intimate positions, operating a lesbian or gay bar, or actually having oral or anal sex with another adult homosexual. . . . Misdemeanor arrests for sex related vagrancy or disorderly conduct offences meant that the homosexual might have her or his name published in the local newspaper, would probably lose her or his job. . . . If the homosexual were not a citizen, she or he would likely be deported. If the homosexual were a professional . . . she or he would lose the certification needed to practice that profession. If the charged homosexual were a member of the armed forces, she or he might be court-martialed and would likely be dishonorably discharged and lose all veteran benefits.
>
> (Eskridge 1999: 98, cf. Ball 2011, Frank 2014)

The legal scholar, William Eskridge, concluded: "This new legal regime represented society's coercive effort to normalize human relationships around heterosexuality" (p. 18).

In the course of the 1980s and 1990s, Eskridge details a retreat of the state's "coercive effort" to enforce heteronormativity by embedding homosexuality in a web of criminalizing and disenfranchizing law and social policy:

> The gay rights movement had won many successes by 1981—judicial nullification or legislative repeal of laws criminalizing consensual sodomy in most jurisdictions, of almost all state criminal laws targeting same-sex intimacy, and municipal cross-dressing ordinances, of the immigrant and citizenship exclusions, of all censorship laws

targeting same-sex eroticism, of almost all laws or regulations prohibiting bars from becoming congregating places for gay people, and of exclusions of gay people from public employment in most jurisdictions. . . . Since 1981, an increasing number of states and citizens have adopted laws affirmatively protecting gay people against private discrimination and violence, recognizing gay families as domestic partnerships, and allowing second-parent adoptions by a party of a same-sex partner.

(Eskridge 1999: 139)

Despite a summary that does not include the striking down of sodomy laws nationwide (2003), the repeal of the "Don't Ask Don't Tell" policy permitting gays to serve openly in the military (2011), the legalization of same-sex marriage (2015) and the legalization of adoption by same-sex married couples (2015), Eskridge believed the U.S. was witnessing the emergence of "a post-closeted regime where openly gay people could participate in the public culture" (p. 124).

Equally remarkable is gay's heightened cultural visibility. In virtually every cultural sector, from newspapers to television, film, and music videos, there is today a pervasive gay presence (Gamson 2002, Walters 2001). A researcher's comments about television could be extended to many other cultural venues. "Throughout its first four decades, television virtually denied the existence of homosexuality. The families, workplaces, and communities depicted in most network programming were exclusively heterosexual. . . . [By 2000] gay-themed episodes and references to homosexuality were everywhere. . . . American television seemed obsessed with gayness" (Becker 2006: 3). Today, it is less the presence of gay, lesbian, queer—and now trans*—characters on the screen that disturbs Americans then their absence! Moreover, in contrast to the pathologizing and menacing stereotypes of the past (Gamson 2002, Russo 1987, Seidman 2004), these cultural figures, to the dismay of queer critics, are presented in the vernacular of heterosexual normalization e.g. gender conventional and marriage, family, and career oriented, and patriotic. And, even when presented as queer, they are no longer automatically polluted or pathologized (witness "Roseanne" or "Transparent"). To be sure, visibility doesn't mean equality nor does it necessarily entail recognition of gay/queer diversity (Becker 2006, Gamson 2002, Walters 2001). Still, it does signal a renegotiation of the foundations of a heteronormative order.

Heteronormativity is undergoing a process of de-institutionalization. The Federal and many state governments, along with institutional sectors such as multinational corporations and the professions, the healthcare system, and virtually all secular colleges and universities, have (1) retreated from systemic policies aimed at enforcing heterosexuality as the sole legitimate way of organizing personal and social life and (2) recognize the civil and intimate rights and the normalized status of lesbian and gay citizens.

While the legal and institutional scaffolding of heteronormativity is being chipped away, many state or county governments still lack antidiscriminatory statutes; churches and evangelical colleges across the nation continue to withhold rights and recognition; and, local shops, professional firms, church and sports organizations remain unfriendly, even hostile, to the LGBTQ population. In particular, the delegitimation of public homophobia has not meant its disappearance. Homophobia is embedded in the informal cultures of institutions from Wall Street to the military and the media; it is perpetuated by cultural codes that mark gender in binary terms, by social conventions that recognize gay identities and relationships but are silent, compulsively so, about homosexual desire, and by a culture that idealizes heterogendered intimacy, love and romance (e.g. Best 2000, Ingraham 2008). In short, homophobia continues to thrive in personal, interpersonal, and institutional practices of everyday exclusion and non-recognition that uphold the hierarchical boundaries between straight/gay.

Still, we are a long way from an era when state enforced compulsory heterosexuality was a nationwide condition. As the government and the courts have struck down the legal basis of the closet, and as the state and core civic and cultural institutions have retreated from officially enforcing heteronormativity, however incompletely, gay men and lesbians' evolving claims to citizenship status mark a giant step towards the Americanization of homosexuality.

Normalizing homosexuality suggests the de-gaying of social roles and modes of self and cultural expression stereotypically marked as gay. Alongside dynamics of de-gendering, this development alludes to an historic possibility: straight men being able to claim a wider latitude to feel, express, and behave in ways that exceed phallic masculine codes. They face considerably less risk of suffering the stigma of homosexualization and feminization and suffering the terrifying anxiety of self-mortification. This is perhaps the cultural significance of the so-called "metrosexual" or the "hybrid man"—men comfortable with embracing a range of cultural signifiers of male gayness and female femininities (Anderson 2009, Arxer 2011, Barber 2008, Dean 2014). Hybridization expands personal and interpersonal freedom, but hardly signals the end of heteronormativity; it coexists, often uneasily, with a cisgendered heteronormativity (Arxer 2011, Bridges 2014, Bridges and Pascoe 2014, Dean 2014, Messner 2007).

We're in the midst, then, of a significant social shift: not the end of heteronormativity and surely not the end of gender binarism, but its declining social authority. From this vantage point, the iconography of phallic masculinity is looking more and more like a caricature of men's actual lives. Virulent celebrations of this figure appear increasingly like backlash efforts to hang onto a past that is receding into history.[5] If we are correct, the historically wide gender and sexual divide between men and women, straight and gay, and the masculine and feminine, is narrowing. Psychic and social space has opened up for many Americans to experiment with their gender and sexuality, eschewing models that demand a one-sided, more or less fixed unitary identity.

Enter psychoanalysis: expanding and deepening the conversation

The current public discussion about American men has largely been carried out in a sociological and political register. While such perspectives are indispensable for understanding the changing sociopolitical environment that drives the formation and deconstruction of gender, a psychoanalytic viewpoint is equally essential. Only a psychodynamic approach can access the finely textured layers of men's lives as they navigate the confusing and conflict-ridden terrain of gender today.

Psychoanalysis challenges conventional perspectives by conceptualizing subjectivities as composed of multiple, contradictory, and shifting gender experiences. This messiness doesn't disappear when we grow up; it doesn't get resolved in a neat and clean way as we become adults. And, no matter how much we present ourselves as seamlessly gendered, our internal life remains complex and often unruly.

Psychoanalysts have underscored a core tension between our subjective gender experience—heterogeneous, transgressive, and contradictory—

and a cisgendered binary culture and have reminded us, much to our dismay at times, that the singular unitary gender performances of public life belie unsettled and tension-ridden subjective lives (Benjamin 1995, Corbett 2009a, Dimen 1991, Fogel 2009, Goldner 1991, Harris 1991, Layton 1998).

Psychoanalytic discourse offers a uniquely nuanced language to grasp men's internal struggle with their gender messiness, often in the face of a cultural—and psychic—compulsion to deny this unruliness. A psychoanalytic perspective makes it possible to know something of how men actually negotiate their personal and interpersonal lives, and what it feels like, even as many do not wish to acknowledge their internal unease. Psychoanalytical theory can help us make sense of our difficulties in managing a chaotic subjectivity as we present coherent gendered selves. It speaks to the psychic and sometimes social costs of "succeeding" in performing a normative gender, and the costs of failing, for example, status deflation and humiliation—and worse. From this perspective, psychoanalysts challenge us to tell stories about men that dramatize the tensions and contradictions of being compelled to navigate between our subjective gender heterogeneity and the heteronormative compulsion to publicly enact a seamlessly masculine self (e.g. Benjamin 1988, 1991, Corbett 2009a, 2009b, Layton 1998).

Psychoanalysts assumes that we live in two parallel, intersecting worlds. There is the objective, external world of people and things with which we transact the business of living. There is also an internal world made up of drives, feelings, wants, needs, and fantasies, but also emotionally invested representations of others or "internal objects."

From childhood onwards, we internalize important people in our lives; we make them a part of our subjective world. Better yet, we introject different aspects of others depending on how we experience them. These internal objects may only partially coincide with reality. Yet, they form a core part of our sense of self. They inform how we think and feel about ourselves and how we relate to ourselves and others. The formative force of these internal representations is based on powerful emotional attachments to significant others. Such figures serve as ideals, as good and bad objects, and as templates of how to relate to others.

What are the implications of such a psychoanalytic notion of subjectivity for gender identity? In the ordinary course of growing up, the child identifies with its parent(s). Despite a heteronormative gender binary culture stipulating that boys must identify exclusively with their father's presumed seamless masculinity, and repudiate the assumed seamless femininity of the mother, *psychoanalytic thinking suggests that this is an impossibility* (e.g. Aron 1995, Benjamin 1996, Corbett 2009a, Dimen 1991, Fast 1984, 1990, Freud 1925, Goldner 1991).

In fact, assuming a heterosexual, two parent family, each parent embodies and enacts a multiplicity of culturally marked gender traits.

Consider mothers. No matter how feminine a mother looks and acts, and no matter how much she identifies as a conventionally feminine woman, her internal life presents a state of gender heterogeneity and inclusiveness. Here we can only hint at this gender complexity (see Chapter 2). To begin, mothers embody multiple femininities—for example, the femininities of their mothers and of other women, perhaps a close friend, sister, aunt, or teacher. Their sons then engage, mostly unconsciously, with the multiple threads of femininity as they identify with their mothers, but also with the diverse femininities of perhaps their older sister or a teacher or an idealized pop star or public figure. And, these multiple feminine threads may be in tension or contradictory—pulling the young boy in different directions but also making possible a certain capacity to be gender flexible.

But also, a mother's inner life is composed of varied threads of masculinities. There is the masculinity of the "father-in-the-mother" (Corbett 2009a, Ogden 1989a). As a child, a mother identifies with aspects of her father's masculinity—not to mention the masculinities of other significant men—and women—in her life. Then too, as many women today live fully engaged public lives, with careers, higher education degrees, and perhaps as cultural producers, political office holders or social activists, they have formed selves whose dispositions, emotional economies, and conduct are, in the language of American cultural codes, recognizably masculine. Which masculine mothers do boys actually identify with and how do they weave these varied gender threads together?

A father too presents a multiplicity of masculinities, reflecting an identification with his own father's masculinities but also identifications with other important men in his life and with cultural tropes of masculinity that circulated during his formative years (Diamond 2007, 2009, 2015). But, in addition, sons internalize the masculine threads of their uncles, teachers, older brothers, or cousins, not to mention cultural icons and charismatic and fantasy male figures. As Corbett (2009b) says, "this internalization that is distilled as paternal is a combined voice including father's, mother's, sibling's, teacher's, coach's, minister's, and so on" (p. 364).

But also, cross-gender identification occurs not only between the son and the mother but also between the son and the father. The latter's internal world is composed of multiple femininities. His father's mother lives inside him—"the mother-in-the father"—but also the father identifies with other significant woman (aunts, cousins, older sisters) and, for that matter, with men whose femininity has been resonant. And, again, paralleling the status of many contemporary women, the configuration and texture of their lives today means that men cultivate dispositions, emotional capacities, and relational and expressive orientations that in American normative culture would be marked as feminine.

From this perspective, sons are formed in a parental environment that may be conventionally cisgendered and heteronormative but their subjective gender experience would have to be described as heterogeneous and messy. So, yes, boys internalize masculine parts of their fathers, but which masculinities—the rough playing dad or the hugging, tender dad? And they identify with dad's femininity, but again which gender threads— the father who's receptive and accommodating, even submissive to his partner, or the one that enjoys stylizing surfaces? And, which masculine parts of the mother does the child identify with—the disciplining decision- making mother or the accomplished career woman or perhaps the athletic mom? And, which of mom's femininities resonate with the son—her decorative, glamorous self or the holding, emotionally attuned mom? Boys then, have interiors filled with multiple gendered identifications and feeling-and-bodily self-states.

If, as many psychoanalysts now argue, we all live with such complex, layered gendered interiors, this can help shed light on our capacity to be situationally flexible in our gender negotiations. However, in compulsory heteronormative environments, such gender plasticity is something that has historically been denied, made illegible or scandalized and pathol- ogized. But if our internal life contains multiple gender identifications and dispositions, different parts of ourselves may be drawn on in varied situations. Many of us have a capacity to be gender flexible and to step outside of a gender script if the environment is at all hospitable (Harris 1991, 2009a). "In the individual's mind, gendered self-representations coexist with [a] genderless or even opposite gendered self-representations.

Thus, a person could alternatively experience herself as "I, a woman; I, a genderless subject; I, like a man" (Benjamin 1998: 113). Psychoanalysis then underscores a potentially gender mobile self, even if heteronormative social structures still make it difficult for us to recognize that capacity and to be aware of the ways we already engage in gender negotiation in varied social contexts.

Things get more complicated. We've argued that gender play is today tolerated, even celebrated, in some quarters. From this vantage point, there is more psychological, interpersonal, and cultural space for individuals to acknowledge and explore a wide range of their gendered experience. Yet, heteronormativity still rules, especially in core social institutions—the family, workplace, schools, the military, and churches, and in authoritative social roles or statuses. How do individuals negotiate their internal gender heterogeneity in the face of cisgendered norms that mandate the alignment of sex and gender and in a heteronormative culture that normalizes mutually exclusive, complementary gender identities? In particular, how is the tension between gender singularity and multiplicity, between homogeneity and heterogeneity managed in private, intimate, and public life? What psychological adjustments make such accommodations possible, and with what costs to the individual? As we detail in the chapters that follow, psychoanalysis offers a vocabulary of dissociation, projection, idealization, repression, and splitting to help make sense of the subjective dynamics involved in managing the contradictions of living in a heteronormative culture whose foundation may be shaky but remains intact.

To date, the conversation about men, especially in the media and popular culture, often relies on observations about men's public or institutional behavior. This yields a skewed view because, as we see it, bodies and behaviors in public are still thickly regulated by cisgendered heteronormative rules. There is considerable pressure in public life to present exclusively masculine or feminine selves that are seamlessly aligned with male and female bodies. This is true even as roles are less rigidly gendered, and even as there is more cultural tolerance for gender flexibility. As we see it, it is in private life that we can more clearly witness how men live both inside and outside of heteronormativity, and how they struggle to negotiate their own unique ways of individualizing gender.

In a similar manner, social science literature typically relies on men's self-reporting based on 1–2 hour interviews. We believe that such accounts are heavily heteronormatively scripted. Many men, as we've suggested, are either not aware of their gender complexity or resist narrating it because they remain fiercely invested in a cisgendered hetero-normativity with its presumption of male privilege. Accordingly, such interviews may convey a view that leans considerably on phallic symbolism.

In the safe, intimate space of the treatment room, week after week, month after month, often year after year, psychoanalysts (and other psychotherapists) have access to people's innermost anxieties, aspirations, affective states, and fantasies. Psychoanalysis provides a uniquely privileged window to inquire into the ways men are actually making sense of their gender, experiencing it psychically and socially, and living it, consciously and unconsciously, in everyday life. As analysts, we can relate stories of men that are otherwise unspoken and unheard. In short, psychoanalysis can widen and deepen the public conversation about American men today.

Analysts underscore the multiplicity and messiness of gender. And while many psychoanalysts are aware of the ongoing power of hetero-normativity, some underemphasize the extent and depth of its regulatory force across varied situations and institutional environments. Sociology can serve as a reminder of the ongoing macro-social power of heteronor-mativity. So, yes, gender can be, for many of us, more deliberate and situationally varied and playful, but the macrosocial context remains heteronormative and infused with a pervasive, even if understated, cis-gendering normativity. This tension is particularly heightened as we move from the private to institutional public spaces. But, it is no less present in our personal lives as is dramatically played out in our psyches and intimate lives. Many of us today are struggling to negotiate a series of tensions: between rigid normativity and flexibility, between gender as identity and gender as an aesthetic of self-stylization, and between gender as scripting of experience and a wish to claim a subjectivity free of gendering.

Notes

1 Men present an endless variety of experiences depending on factors such as class, race, sexuality, ability, disability, ethnicity, age and so on. In the context of a wide-ranging American popular and scholarly discussion about men, we think it's helpful to initially engage the debate at a general level. As we examine such issues as authenticity, sexuality, and intimacy in subsequent chapters, we attend to a range of differences among men. There is another

metatheoretical issue that we've struggled with. The very categories of male/female and man/woman are unstable and in their stipulated coherence a fiction; yet, they still speak to empirically-based patterns of social difference and hierarchy. Hence, like many researchers and theorists of gender, we employ these categories while recognizing that this implicates us in the politics of heteronormativity. As Butler remarked:

> Men and women . . . tend to be referred to in very stable and unanxious ways, as if we know what they are, as if the process of a successful normalization has already occurred, and grammar is the index of that stability. The theoretical apparatus threatens to normalize precisely what the theoretical argument seeks to call into question.
> (Butler 1998: 375, cf. Benjamin 1997: 391)

2   Does masculine "guardianship" differ from a so-called feminine ethic of care? Arguably, the latter might be modeled on the traditional mother-daughter bond, with its resonances of thick emotional ties, porous boundaries, and the blurring of self and other. In this scenario, "nurturing solidarity" becomes the chief trope of a feminine ethic. By contrast, caregiving for traditional men perhaps pivots more on the father/son guardian relationship, which underscores sharp self-boundaries and emphasizes responsibility and governance. Guardianship perhaps suggests a caregiving, but less sentimental and more felt and expressed in an ethical language of rights, brotherhood, privacy, and justice. This isn't to deny that men also incorporate a feminized ethic of care (e.g. Campbell and Carroll 2007, Kaftal 2009).

3   It may sound counterintuitive, but many women also remain fiercely attached to the coupling of men and phallicism. For some women their very sense of identity and self-worth pivots on men presenting themselves as the antithesis of femininity—the *not*-woman. Phallic masculinities that evacuate all traces of femininity may allow women to claim this terrain as exclusively theirs, and ground a distinct identity. And, in an American economy and society that continues to disadvantage women across racial, ethnic and class boundaries, some women may embrace this complementary gender model with the hope that men will live up to their ideal as providers and protectors.

Of course, feminists have taken issue with this über-feminine representation and the presumption that women desire men's protection. They have rethought the politics of womanhood, reminding us of women's agency and worldly ambitions—and indeed of a reality of women living publicly engaged autonomous lives. And, while most feminists today would likely embrace a nuanced, complicated account of contemporary men, there continues to be a reluctance among some feminists to let go of the iconic phallic ideal. Just as some women evoke phallic masculinity to secure their feminine status, feminists have historically, and some still today, appeal to this hyper-masculine figure to explain the discontents of women—misogyny, homophobia, sexual objectification, domestic violence, and gender inequality. After all, phallic men—unemotional, power driven, objectifying and self-aggrandizing—provide a readymade explanation for women's oppression. This cultural figure has, at times, proved an effective tool for political mobilization, and a convenient rhetorical pivot from which to celebrate the solidarity of sisterhood.

4   One strategy men deploy to maintain a conventional masculine identity at work is to re-label feminine work roles and practices as masculine. These strategies may allow men to effectively manage the cultural tensions in their work experience by, in effect, denying or minimizing the dissonant aspects of their gendered experience. However, such strategies also threaten to render the masculine/feminine binary incoherent. If what was culturally coded as feminine is repeatedly reassigned a masculine status, doesn't the category of the feminine lose coherence? And, if the very meaning of masculine is repeatedly being reassessed by incorporating the feminine, wouldn't this category lose its stability and coherence? How does masculinity establish its singularity without a stable feminine other? In more and more workplaces, there is no escaping the cultural contradictions of gender. Ultimately, men may resist acknowledging this conundrum by refusing to recognize and symbolize the ways their actual gender experience is at odds with an austere, bounded notion of manhood.

Some men, though, are beginning to re-narrate their sense of gender in light of their multilayered gender work experience. Recent research on gender and the workplace, often organized around the theme of "undoing gender" (Butler 2004, Lorber 2005, Risman 2009), speaks to a shift, however halting and uneven, towards the symbolization of gender fluidity (e.g. Campbell and Carroll 2007, Deutsch 1999, 2007, Kelan 2009, McDonald 2013, Powell et al. 2008, Shows and Gerstel 2009, Simpson 2004). To cite just one study, in researching student nurses, McDonald (2013) shows how male students not only engage in feminine coded practices but recognize and embrace their experience of gender dissonance. Consider Bill, a student who shared his view of what it means to be a good nurse. "You are going to have to have kindness, compassion, empathy, and sympathy. You know, after three days with some of my patients, I love them." The author comments: "because most of these characteristics . . . are culturally coded as feminine, Bill implies that being a good nurse requires 'doing femininity.' Doing femininity in this way . . . entails undoing masculine gender norms. . . . Bill undoes gender to the extent that in order to be a good nurse, he emphasizes commonalities with women, and resists dominant masculine norms" (pp. 570, 576). McDonald believes that:

> in a field that is female-dominated, women along with men enact masculinity and femininity, which attests to the fluid and shifting character of gender performances. . . . Performing gender successfully entails performances of femininity and masculinity for both women and men, requiring all nurses to do and undo dominant gender norms.
>
> (p. 576)

5   Given the waning of a patriarchal, heteronormative industrial order, old-styled patriarchal phallicism has not just disappeared; rather it is giving way to "symbolic phallicism." Lacking actual power, and indeed gradually ceding social authority to women in more and more areas of social life, and, in fact, living lives that are—subjectively and socially—more and more gender convergent, many men today are opting for symbolic expressions of phallic masculinity. Of course, the semiotics of symbolic phallicism varies among different populations of men. Generally speaking, though, the body seems to

have become a chief site to enact threads of a phallic masculinity. Its surface is fashioned and marked through bulk, muscularity, and hardness, accentuated by comportment and dress, by tattoos and piercings, and by a street-wise rawness and bad boy posing. Symbolic phallicism creates the illusion of male gender power and privilege, even when the reality often tells another story. If we are correct, symbolic phallicism is more informally and performatively grounded today than based on state and institutionally enforced social roles and statuses. Symbolic phallicism is the other side, the fading defiant echo of the gender unruliness and uncertainty of the lives of many men.

Chapter 2

Straight families making straight boys

Phallic and relational threads in boys' early lives

Heteronormativity is a structuring force in personal and social life in America. And, it is through a heteronormative lens that many social institutions, and too often the psychoanalytic community, have construed and regulated individuals, gender identity, and social roles (Corbett 2009b).

In exclusively sanctioning heterosexuality, heteronormativity denigrates and at times outlaws non-heterosexualities. It engenders a culture of homophobia. This fateful linkage creates a class of polluted desires and persons who are rendered inferior, at times disenfranchised and criminalized.

A heteronormative logic also assumes gender binarism, or the notion that there are two, and only two, contrasting but presumed complementary gendered selves: males and females who are expected to become hetero-men and women. This cisgender logic naturalizes gender dualism, and historically has been aligned with men's dominance, which in turn normalizes heteronormativity. Without gender binarism, the edifice of heteronormativity crumbles.

We believe that there are cracks in the foundation of heteronormativity. Movements for gender and sexual justice expose this organizing principle as a social construct, neither solid nor inevitable. And, feminists, queers, and trans* critics, among others, have advocated for forms of personal and social life that embrace variation and inventiveness against social conventions that freeze hierarchies and enforce static dualisms.

Along with long-term cultural and economic developments such as the rise of a service and knowledge-based economy and the pluralization of intimate and family life, these movements have contributed to broad shifts in the American gender landscape.

Women's changing social status has been at the center of these far-reaching changes. For many generations, the Victorian-inspired "doctrine of separate spheres" claimed that nature dictates women's proper place in the domestic sphere and men's authoritative role in the public realm. In the past half-century, as women have stepped into public life as fully participating citizens, there has been a considerable weakening of the gender marking of social roles. Today, many roles are less monopolized by one gender and less gender stereotyped. Individuals circulate across social roles and institutions with fewer gender restrictions. As more and more men and women occupy similar social roles, engage in parallel personal and social practices, and acquire analogous psychic capacities, interpersonal orientations and cultural values, there is a blurring of gender difference. Patterns of gender hybridization and a growing awareness of gender plasticity are now a routine part of America. For example, women who assume decision-making roles and manage people and things acquire modes of relating to self and others that have historically been associated with men and masculinity. The reverse is also true, even if in a decidedly more qualified manner. Many men find themselves in work and domestic roles that place a premium on communication skills, emotional intelligence, and being socially accommodating and cooperative. These sensibilities and ways of relating have historically been linked to women and culturally marked as feminine.

The public world is becoming gender messy. We are by no means witnessing the end of gender or gender binarism, but the loosening of the gender marking of many social roles and statuses. It is no longer credible to conceive of social roles or whole occupations (lawyers, engineers, professors, public administrators or airline stewards or nurses), or entire social sectors (politics, policing, healthcare, sports, and caregiving) as if they neatly divide between masculine and feminine and between men and women. Emotional states and social behaviors and roles that just a few generations ago might have easily sorted out between masculine/ men and feminine/women, at least at a cultural level, circulate today among individuals with less imprint from their socially assigned sexed status. There is less gender polarization and more mixing and mind-boggling variation—though still a gender order of marked inequality and threads, sometimes thick, sometimes violent, of misogyny. These contradictory and shifting developments form the cultural matrix of gender that many Americans face today.

This gender transformation has affected a sea change in the life of families and in the psychodynamics of gender formation. Mothers and fathers are less recognizable as representing a mutually exclusive seamless femininity and masculinity—a view taken for granted until recently by most Americans, social scientists, and psychoanalysts. Instead, adults—and children—present as multigendered selves. Arguably, this was always the case; but today, there is a *growing awareness of our multigendered status and expanded social and psychic space to embrace this gender complexity*. Indeed, for some this means stepping outside the very language of gender binarism and exploring a trans-or-post-gendered status. Today's parents may look like their grand-and-great grandparents; they may even speak a "traditional" (i.e. cisgendered) gender language, but their actual lives, as subjectively and socially experienced, are a world apart. For example, as fixtures in the workplace, middle class mothers bear a closer kinship with blue-collar working women of past generations than to the 1950s popular TV ideal of the all-too-happy housewife and mom. And, in contrast to earlier generations, many women today, especially younger women, are choosing economic self-reliance and claim an entitlement to a full personal and public life—something that not too long ago was the exclusive privilege of (white, straight, able bodied) men.

The complex gender make-up of many parents today, and the increasing normalization of their multigenderedness, has transformative implications for boys' development. In particular, "post-traditional" mothers will recognize themselves in their son's aspiring masculinity, with its worldly ambition and its claim to being an autonomous subject. And, in turn, many young boys will identify with their mothers as agents or, in Benjamin's phrase, as "subjects of desire" who project onto their sons their own aspirations for a purposefully chosen vital personal and public life. If boys' masculinity is not threatening to their mothers, indeed if they identify with it, boys will be more likely to stay attached to and identified with their mothers even as they gravitate—under the normalizing authority of heteronormativity and male privilege—to a more emphatic paternal identification. And, if boys' maternal ties are validated by their fathers, in part, because they are no longer perceived as a threat to their son's masculinity, and in part because their lives "converge" in many respects, fathers will encourage their son's ongoing attachment to their mothers. Indeed, as the work and intimate lives of post-traditional fathers incorporate culturally marked feminine self–and-relational styles, and not least a commitment to being a nurturing parent and loving companion to their son's mother, such fathers will represent figures of gender complexity to their sons. Far from rigid defensive constructs of a seamless phallic masculinity, a son's paternal identification, at least optimally, incorporates phallic and guardian or relationally caring modes of being and relating (Abelin 1980, Diamond 2017, Fast 1999, Herzog 2005a, Kaftal 2009). In such a family environment, a boy's paternal identification would likely reinforce his identification and attachment to his mother.[1]

If we've identified a cultural and psychodynamic current in contemporary America, this suggests a potentially hopeful development in *post-traditional families*.[2] Many boys will experience psychic and social spaces tolerant of gender complexity and variation; and while this gives to boys an expanded capacity to approach gender as a site of choice and individualization, it will also engender subjective dis-ease as gender identifications and dispositions may be internally contradictory or an overinclusive gendering might be in tension with a rigid cisgendered heteronormativity or the very regime of compulsory gendering may upend boys disposed toward an agendered or transgendered position. Still, one hopeful possibility stands out: homophobia and misogyny may be less firmly lodged in boys' psyches, as arguably they are less firmly sociologically rooted. As we see it, then, many boys and men today dwell in a contradictory, confusing, and shifting gender space. Negotiating manhood in contemporary America entails navigating a series of tensions: between a subjective and interpersonal opening towards gender heterogeneity and an ongoing cisgendered heteronormative imperative; between aligning phallicism with a guardian ethical relationalism; and, between a cultural order that thickly genders everything and a phenomenological heterogeneity that opens to a degendering of experience. Exploring aspects of these tensions is a chief aim of this chapter.

Mothers and sons: negotiating the psychic economies of identification and disidentification

Psychoanalytic accounts of self-development have often assumed a historically specific gender arrangement: a social world organized around separate, gender-specific spheres and roles. Women were expected to center their lives in the private sphere, focusing on their roles as wife and mother; men were to occupy the public realm, providing the link between the family and the broader social world (e.g. Cott 1977, Degler 1981, D'Emilio and Freedman 2012, Kerber 1988, Smith-Rosenberg 1986, Welter 1968).

In this broadly speaking male dominated and compulsory heterosexual arrangement, "good" mothers were expected to forge a thick bond with their dependent child. For some psychoanalysts, this dyadic unit has a worrisome aspect: a prolonged state of an infant-mother symbiosis threatens to trap the boy in a narcissistic and potentially homosexual and effeminate self-state (Corbett 2009b: 357–8, Green 1987, Stoller 1968, 1972, 1985). Boys are thought to face a daunting challenge: to shift their primary emotional attachment and gender identification from their mothers to their fathers in order to claim masculinity and eventually the privileges of a public life organized around an authoritative projection of manhood (Greenson 1968, Chodorow 1978, Johns 2002, Stoller 1968). But given the overdetermined identification and near-unboundaried intimacy with their mothers, establishing a masculine identity is understood as an inevitably discontinuous and traumatic process.

The key moment in this transformational process is said to occur during the Oedipal drama. The young boy shifts from a dyadic to triadic familial space that makes it possible for him to imagine a life beyond the mother-son dyad. The father is expected to play the key role: providing the son with a pivot away from maternal to paternal identification—and, accordingly, from primary femininity to masculinity and from domesticity to a public life. In his paternal function, the father serves as a "third," opening a space for the son to participate in a world of other subjects—one that cultivates symbolizing and reflexive capacities and anticipates the boy's eventual assumption of authority.

Central to the Oedipal drama is that the boy attaches to and identifies with his father. However, given a heteronormative imperative, the boy must contain or sublimate his libidinal attachment, transmuting it into an identification with the father as a moral authority. In this scenario, Oedipus presents a twofold challenge. First, to pivot away from a mother-centered world through the mechanism of disidentification; in effect, boys project their femininity onto a world of women and lesser men. Second, under the threat of emasculation and exclusion from the world of men, he must become a rival hetero-masculine subject. At that moment, to use Ogden's (1989a) formulation, the mother's place in the psychic life of the boy shifts "from an exclusively internal object to also an external object" as she becomes the object of the boy's sexual desire—the passive counterpart to an emerging phallic penetrating masculine self (p. 112). And, in a parallel but reverse manner, the father shifts in the boy's psychic life from a libidinally-charged identificatory love object to an identification with a feared and admired male figure. In this tension-filled triad, each parent, maintaining their designated gender role in a patriarchal and compulsory heterosexual order, contributes to the desired resolution: a solidly masculinized post-Oedipal proto-man standing alongside the father as a member of the tribe of adult heterosexual men.

In the narrative of disidentification, a successful Oedipal process inevitably involves loss and ongoing psychic conflict. Specifically, the boy, at least unconsciously, surrenders his deeply felt, emotionally rich attachment and identification to his mother—abandoning his fantasy of wanting to be like her or to be her. Disavowing what Stoller called his "protofemininity" was thought to be a condition of gaining an authoritative status as a phallocentric straight man; the loss compensated by the privileges granted to men in a patriarchal order.

Boys though are said to face an additional challenge: in contrast to girls, whose core-gendered identity is said to develop from an unbroken emotionally thick attachment and identification with their mothers, boys presumably lack an analogous relationship with their fathers (Chodorow 1978). To the extent that men's lives are centered in a ruthlessly competitive public world that devalues sentimentality and intimacy, they are emotionally and socially unavailable—at best minimally responsive to their son's psychic needs. Boys are compelled to rely on idealizations of fathers or draw from culturally iconic male figures to cobble together a legible and compelling construct of manhood. But such identifications are shaky, as they are not emotionally grounded in a father-son relationship built up in a continuous way over years. Accordingly, boys' masculine sense of self is thought to be fragile and unsteady; ultimately, behaviorally sustained by a hyper-hetero-sexualization, which blends a virulent homophobia and threads of misogyny with a one-sided ethos of self-mastery and dominance over others.

At the heart of the disidentification argument is a view of masculinity as essentially a defensive structure. The defining moment in a boy's early development is said to be the radical break from his mother and a realignment with the father. However, the latter tie remains weak due to the homophobic prohibition against same-gendered erotic attachment. Boys then forge a masculine identity by a twofold act of repudiation: of their feminine identification with their mothers and a melancholic foreclosure of their homoerotic attachment to their fathers (Butler 1995, Hansell 1998, Jay 2007). If, according to this account, boys manage to enact a more or less normative phallic hetero-masculinity, they can expect to join the tribe of straight men competing in a public world for success, prestige, and power. But this Oedipal triumph anticipates the burdens of phallic manhood: unrelenting competition, the imperative to contain and dominate the other and, therewith, equally relentless anxieties of not being big enough, hard enough, tough enough, expansive enough, and independent enough; in this scenario, phallic men ward off such haunting anxieties through an "obsessive-compulsive" defense pivoting around hetero-sexualization, and hyper-masculinization (Jay 2007).

Differentiation, not disidentification: a revisionist perspective

Disidentification is arguably an inevitable aspect of gender identity formation. Indeed, disidentification theorists offer complex psycho-dynamical explanations of how boys become hetero-phallic men and how hierarchies between men and women and among men are reproduced, as illustrated by Chodorow's (1978) elegant account of the reproduction of mothering and gender inequality. At issue is whether disidentification is the pivot for boy's gender formation—and by implication a psychological grounding of a heteronormative order.

Disidentification assumes that, given a symbiotic mother-son preoedipal bond, a boy's initial gender identification is primarily feminine. Hence, the chief drama: the traumatic Oedipal pivoting of his psychic center from the mother to the father. But, this viewpoint holds to a series of questionable assumptions: that individuation requires a sharp break from a mother to a father-centered attachment; that boys' identification with their mothers are exclusively feminine; that preoedipal boys lack a meaningful identification with—and attachment to—their fathers; and, finally, that boys Oedipal paternal identification is exclusively masculine and, given compulsory heterosexuality and patriarchy, that their masculine gender embrace is ultimately a defense.

Granted, the preoedipal infant's secure attachment to his mother forms the basis of a maternal identification; they want to be like their mothers or some fantasy of her. But do boys need to disidentify in order to establish a solidly grounded hetero-masculine identity?

The revisionist counterclaim strikes us as compelling: even as boys traverse the road from the preoedipal to the Oedipal, given good enough parenting they sustain a vital emotional bond with their mothers (Benjamin 1996, Diamond 2004: 361–365, 2009, Meissner 2005, Ogden 1989b). In this regard, Irene Fast (1984, 1990, 1999), drawing on attachment research, argues that individuation does not occur by severing and separating from a maternal attachment but through sustaining it. "If boys with a secure attachment to their mothers are more likely to achieve a solid sense of autonomy and individuation, might that be equally true of their achievement of a secure sense of themselves as masculine" (1999: 665–6)? In the process of individuating, boys forge a "core masculine gender identity" but remain attached to—and identified with—their mothers. From this point of view, separation via disidentification suggests an "insecure attachment" triggered by environmental breakdowns and anticipates defensive forms of masculinization, e.g. a rigid phallic narcissism, hyper-heterosexualization coupled with misogyny and homophobia, narcissistic rage or a schizoidal withdrawal (Fast 1999: 650; Diamond 2009, 2015). As Fast says, "dis-identification . . . signals failure in optimum development of masculinity, an organization too exclusively phallic, denying the *actual . . . nurturing possibilities* of a man" (Fast 1984: 72–73). Whereas a disidentification dynamic assumes a thinning out of internal life via a disavowing of femininity, an attachment-individuation perspective underscores the formation of an internally layered and differentiated psychic structure as boys incorporate paternal identifications alongside maternal one's (Diamond 2004, 2009).

One reason boys do not feel compelled to disidentify from their mothers is that in the course of *preoedipal* development they begin to acquire a secure sense as separate selves and as boys. In her psychodynamic rethinking of Freud's biologically-based notion of bisexuality, Fast (1984, 1990) proposes that in their first 18 months infants experience an "undifferentiated period" marked by gender "overinclusiveness." Children believe "that everyone has all sex and gender possibilities. Father can give birth although masculine [and] . . . a woman can have a male appendage and also be pregnant. . . ." (1990: 109, 1984: Ch. 1, 3; cf. Bassin 1996, Benjamin

1995, 1996). Gender identity consolidation occurs roughly between 18–36 months; overinclusiveness begins to give way to an awareness of sex differences. Children experience gender identity formation as a form of boundary marking and containment, and, as such, it is an experience of loss (Fast 1990: 109). As much as individuation grounds gender identify formation, the latter anchors the making of a separate, reflexive sense of self. "From the time of sex ascription at birth, members of the boy's entire social surround . . . will treat him . . . [as] a boy. By about 18 months, then, the boy will have established significant constellations of 'boy' interaction patterns by which he understands his world and acts in it. . . ." (Fast 1999: 634). By the age of 3, children have "a sense of belonging to [a particular] sex" with specific "gendered ways of perceiving, thinking, feeling, and acting" that operate in a binary logic (Fast 1999: 645; cf. Bassin 1996: 174). Instead of undergoing an abrupt and wrenching process of maternal disidentification and separation, revisionists suggest that preoedipal infants become boys as part of a process of individuation while remaining attached to and identified with their mothers.

Furthermore, disidentification arguments mistakenly assume that the primacy of the mother-infant bond means the absence or backgrounding of the psychic presence of the father, except as disrupting the mother-son fusional dyad in order to facilitate individuation. But, the father is an ever-present and deeply felt formative force in a boy's life. As Diamond (2017) says, "the father's *actual, preoedipal involvement* helps establish a loving trusted dyadic bond, an isogender relationship between father and son. . . ." (p. 307, cf. Fast 1990: 107). Indeed, the preoedipal boy uses his father "to consolidate his gender identity" (Fast 1999: 303, cf. Freud 1921: 105).

This critique underscores a major fault line among disidentification theorists: mirroring a heterogender binary logic, they have not theoretically integrated the notion of multigendered selves. Commenting on Stoller and Chodorow, Sweetnam (1996) observes: "Neither theorist has been able to consider the idea that gender may be made up of identifications with *both* parents and that boys . . . may *include* their identifications with mother in their gender identity rather than *necessarily* need to repudiate feminine identifications in favor of masculine ones" (p. 443).

Assuming good enough parenting, in the ordinary course of development boys do not disidentify from their mothers. By roughly 2–3 years of age they already experience themselves as separate selves; still deeply attached to their mothers, they are also rivals for the love of their fathers. Furthermore, as we've argued, becoming a subject is inseparable from becoming a gendered self. In a thickly cisgendered familial matrix, infants assigned a status as males establish an internal sense of themselves as male and boys between 18–36 months (Fast 1990: 113). From this perspective, the mother-son bond does not threaten gender emasculation. Moreover, boys' maternal identification cannot be collapsed into a seamless femininity; instead, a boy's introjection of the mother is layered and richly textured, irreducible to rigid mutually exclusive gender binary codes. How to describe the phenomenology of a mother who penetrates her son with her breast and fingers, authoritatively handles or maneuvers him as she cleans or bathes him or changes his clothes or lays him down to sleep—hardly experiences that fit neatly into the cultural markings of femininity. And, in patriarchal heteronormative environments, mothers are invested in their boy's masculinity as a sign of normalization and successful parenting. A boy's early Oedipal challenge is not to substitute paternal for maternal identifications; rather, it is to expand his interior life to accommodate varied, ambivalent and contradictory identifications and to occupy a differentiated intersubjective psychic space while negotiating a heteronormative imperative.

Ultimately, the disidentification thesis stands or falls on its logic of identification. But here its credibility seriously falters. This viewpoint fails to incorporate both the idea that boys identify with their mothers and their fathers *and* that each parent is multigendered. "We must dispose of ... the assumption that every identification with a woman is a feminine identification and that every identification with a man is a masculine one. ..." (Fast 1999: 680). Even in a compulsory hetero-gendered order, mothers have their own history of masculine identifications based on attachments to their fathers and other significant men in their lives (Diamond 2009: 38, Fast 1984, 1990). Likewise, they incorporate the masculine threads of their mothers, akin to what Ogden (1989a, 1994: 199–201) refers to as "masculinity-in-femininity" or what recent theorists refer to as the paternal imago in the mind of the mother (e.g. Green 2009; Target and Fonagy 2002). Mothers are a chief source of masculine identification. As Corbett says, "masculinity is just as likely to be transferred from mother to son as it is from father to son" (2009a: 103). Boys then internalize and metabolize these masculine threads as part of their maternal identification. And, if a boy's attachment to his mother is facilitated by an identification with his mother's masculinity, many mothers in turn embrace their sons as extensions of their fathers and are experienced, as well, through the lens of their identification with their own fathers (Ogden 1992).

Considered solely from a standpoint of maternal identification, the Oedipal shift to a more salient paternal identification in a heternormative gender world is not necessarily discontinuous or traumatic. The Oedipal challenge is less about managing a sharp pivot from the mother to the father than renegotiating the dual status of the mother. In the heat of the preoedipal bond, roughly around age 3, the mother functions as both an environmental or holding presence and a sexual object (Winnicott 1965b, 1992). But, in the context of the Oedipal transition, boys struggle to sustain their thick emotional connectedness and dependency on mothers while also orienting to an Oedipal mother as an object of desire (Ogden 1989a: 143, 146). To the extent that the "father-in-the-mother" functions as a third, mothers unwittingly provide the psychic space for boys to identify with this hetero-masculine other; this facilitates an Oedipal transition while sustaining their attachment to the preoedipal mother (Ogden 1989a, Diamond 2015, 2017). Boys face an additional Oedipal challenge: assuming a compulsory heterosexual order, they inevitably feel considerable pressure to present a narrow, often rigidly hetero-masculine phallic self and to disavow their overinclusive gendered interiority. It is here, in the crucible of the Oedipal hetero-masculine mandate, in the tense juxtaposition of heterogeneity and a rigid binarism, that the dynamic of disidentification is enlisted on behalf of normativity. Overinclusiveness is pressed to bend to exclusivity, to the psychic economy of complementarity mirroring its sociological counterpart—compulsory heterosexuality (Benjamin 1996, 1997, also Dimen 1991, Goldner 1991).

To press this revision further, the theory of masculine formation as enacting a logic of gender disidentification presupposes a traditional gender order: a fixed and rigid division between men and women with each gender exclusively associated with a seamless masculinity or femininity. And the two genders, and in this account there are only two, are framed as mutually exclusive and complementary, forming a phantastical unity.

By contrast, we again wish to underscore a key point that is still sometimes ignored in psychoanalytic accounts: mothers today are not the "Moms" of yesteryear. As more and more women are integrated into public life as wage laborers, professionals, public officials, leaders of organizations, and as cultural creators, their gendered experience is decidedly more layered than the construct of a one-dimensional, seamless femininity. As they occupy varied social roles and participate in a public world demanding stereotypically masculine capacities to negotiate complex environments, women experience self-states that increasingly fall outside a heteronormative gender binary code. This psychic complexity informs their parenting.

In post-traditional families, we would expect mothers to forge a narcissistic identification with a masculine son, validating his emerging boyhoodness. No doubt, traditional mothers contribute, consciously and unconsciously, to constructing versions of hetero-masculine boyhoods; but, post-traditional mothers identify with and validate their sons' hetero-masculinity while also presenting a public figure of a multigendered phallic self. These mothers, moreover, would be more likely to provide psychic and social space for their sons to explore gender as a zone of individualization.

Furthermore, as boys undergo an Oedipal drift to the father under the force of heternormativity, post-traditional mothers would be less likely to encounter their sons' blanket rejection or abrupt detachment. In post-traditional families, we would expect sons to remain attached to their mother's, to sustain an identification with their mother's nurturing but also phallic presence. As we said, given heteronormativity, one challenge for boys is to hold the tension between the environmental and the sexual mother. A boy's Oedipal turn to the father is in part driven by an identification with the latter's sexual claim on his mother as a sign of manhood, that is, straight manhood. Nor will post-traditional mothers likely disengage or punish their sons as they claim a straight boy-ness by identifying with their fathers and fantasies of phallic masculinity. And, boys' attachments to their fathers will not necessarily be threatening to mothers, especially post-traditional one's, since they too are worldly subjects. As we see it, mothers may experience a temporary thinning of their ties to their sons as their paternal identification thickens during the Oedipal juncture; still, mothers will likely be supportive of the father-son bond as they recognize something of themselves in a son's trajectory into a wider world—and identify with the father's struggle to manage public life while being a generative parent. Even assuming an ongoing heteronormative social environment, the language of disidentification and parental rupture becomes less resonant than one of progressive internal differentiation as boys navigate the Oedipal transition and the eventual challenge to effect a potentially integrative post-Oedipal position (Bassin 1996, Benjamin 1995, 1996, Davies 2015, Diamond 1998, 2009, Fast 1990, Seligman 2017).

As mothers' psyches and interpersonal lives represent, in the language of American culture, a multiplicity of masculinities and femininities, indeed as their private and public experiences seem less and less congruent with a rigid binary gender code, boys internalize complex and often conflicting gender representations—with some questioning the legibility of gender coding itself. This perspective strikes us as especially compelling today as many women are economically and socially independent and comfortable with the desiring, ambitious self-and-world-making phallic parts of themselves. Accordingly, through a boy's attachment to his mother, he incorporates a chaotic mix of culturally coded feminine and masculine gendered ways of being; and, through experiencing their mother's multigendered self, some boys forge an awareness of gender as a site of self-fashioning, including the possibility of a genderqueer or trans* self. We are alluding then to a potentially expansive gender environment: many boys today experience themselves and others as less rigidly gendered, and will, perhaps, be less compelled, especially as heterosexuality and cisgendering is less compulsory, to disavow or denigrate feminine marked modes of being and relating and non-hegemonic expressions of masculinity (Corbett 2009a, Reis 2009: 62–63).

The logic of disidentification as an account of boys and men is arguably comprehensible in the context of patriarchal and compulsory heterosexual organizing patterns, as such viewpoints initially took shape in the decades following World War II. The state, civic institutions, and a public cultural matrix enforced highly restrictive gender and sexual norms. Personal variations were marked not only as psychic abnormalities and forms of social deviance but, against the horizon of the Cold War, as threats to family and nation. In this context, boys' too-intense attachment to their mothers or, for that matter, to their fathers, generated heightened anxieties—fears of effeminacy and homosexuality. Disidentification theorists, to speak somewhat loosely, universalized a specific socio-historical organization of heteronormativity, family, and psychic formation (e.g. Corbett 2009a: 5, Freeman 2008, Person 1995).

With the declining social significance of a rigidly state-enforced hetero-gender social order, the disidentification argument loses considerable credibility. Revisionist theorizing might be read in part as a response to this changing sociopolitical configuration. But, if the former theorists took compulsory heterosexuality as the unexamined historical context rendering their ideas legible, we wonder whether in highlighting an overinclusive and fluid gender logic, some revisionists might underestimate the ongoing power of heteronormativity and men's continued privileged social status. For example, Fast describes the innumerable ways a parenting environ-ment, saturated by gender binary norms, forms the cultural matrix for the gendering of children from birth onward. However, without situating this gender logic in a male-dominated, compulsory heterosexual context, "sex differentiation" can be read as if the making of boys and girls is an innate, internally driven "maturation" process. Moreover, the ways in which such normativities (i.e. phallic masculinity and heterosexuality) engender tensions and instabilities pivoting around the anxious haunting of forbidden homoerotic and feminine longings, repeatedly evoked and disavowed—this, too, is part of the gendering of selves but is largely absent in the differentiation model.

Fathers: recovering the relational dad

The disidentification perspective offers a psychodynamic account of the making of boys-to-men exclusively in a phallocentric language. From this perspective, infants become boys by repudiating their mothers whose femininity threatens emasculation. Through their authoritative imposition of boundaries, fathers penetrate and break up the mother-son dyad, making it possible for sons to acquire a seamlessly masculine self. Unfortunately, fathers are all too often absent or shadowy figures. If too removed, too idealized, or too feared, boys, once again, are threatened with phallic collapse. Compelled to cobble together masculine selves in ad hoc, emotionally thin ways, boys are often left insecure and unsteady, facing a world threatening emasculation by women and powerful men. Boys and men bolster a shaky gendered self by embracing a defensive phallic masculinity that leans heavily on an ethos of uber-masculinization and hyper-heterosexualization. According to this gender logic, everything coded as feminine—emotionality, relationality, receptivity, intimacy—is squeezed into the province of women or "failed" men. In this way, disidentification theorists explain—but also unwittingly reproduce—a rigid phallocentric heteronormativity that leaves no place for the ethically-oriented, relational or guardian aspects of manhood.

Some time ago, Emmanuel Kaftal (2009) noted that this viewpoint fails to make sense of something he encountered in his practice: the way men create social bonds of caring, moral purpose, and commitment. Blinded by phallocentric constructs, and arguably culturally resonant associations of femininity and intimacy, Kaftal didn't initially grasp that men have their own ways of establishing emotionally rich, ethically infused social ties. Many expressed their intimate connectedness through imagistic rather than narrative vocabularies; they described solidarities based on repeated episodes of being together and experiencing one another; as one of his clients said, "if people want to know me, they must experience me" (p. 308); and, some described forming bonds of fraternal belonging by virtue of being and doing this or that together; one client insisted that "our mutual attention creates a subtle but powerful emotional bond" (p. 307).

Kaftal wondered about the preoedipal roots of these intimacies, in particular, the role of the nurturing father. He cited Greenspan's (1982) view that fathers' "availability may enhance ... the depth and range of affect in the early attachment patterns. . . . [He] will ... provide ... a beneficial set of experiences through which the infant comes to know himself, others and *a world of loving relationships*" (our emphasis, p. 323). Reflecting on Kaftal's prescient essay, Fast (1999) underscores his multidimensional construct of manhood. "Kaftal's contribution brings men's relational and affective development to the fore. He suggests that in the preoedipal period a boy optimally establishes a relationship with his father that is affectionate, supportive, non-competitive, and facilitating. . . . This relationship permits him to find a model for affective attunement and relatedness in boy-father relationships and to include it in his identity as masculine" (pp. 229–330). In other words, Kaftal's essay reminds analysts of a truth often forgotten: men negotiate interpersonal life, including fathering, with multiple templates for relating that reach back to vital attachments to their mothers but also to their fathers. In this section, we begin where Kaftal left off: the preoedipal roots of men's intimacy-seeking in the father-son relationship.

With few exceptions (e.g. Abelin 1980, Blos 1984, Greenspan 1982, Ross 1979), standard psychoanalytic views, until recently, depicted fathers as narrowly phallic, barely registering as emotionally engaged parents but all-too-present as haunting figures of moral and social authority; idealized perhaps, but in their remoteness fathers have been viewed as unreal, almost phantasmatic figures—to be feared and either submitted to or destroyed. Ultimately, their heroic triumphs in the world of work and governance were said to mask a tragic failure as parents and as intimate confidants.

Indicative of this phallic conflation, fathers have been understood in terms of fulfilling a "paternal function." If nature and socialization destine women to assume a "maternal function" centered on an almost obsessional mothering, nature and social expectations assign men to a paternal function: facilitating individuation by penetrating and interrupting the mother-son fusional dyad. If mothers prepare the emotional ground for autonomy, fathers are said to actualize this potential by bringing the child into a cultural order of symbolization and other subjects (Diamond 2007, 2017, Freud 1939, Herzog 2001, 2005, Harris 2009, Kalinich and Taylor 2009, Liebman and Abell 2000, Perelberg 2015, Target and Fonagy 2002, Trowell and Etchegoyen 2002).

Perspectives that collapse fathering into the role of providing sons with a path from maternal dependency to a post-domestic public world, and with a blueprint for a normative hetero-masculinity, presume a narrow phallocentrism. By contrast, assuming a multidimensional gender grammar, we aim to bring the father back into the heart of the family—to its preoedipal beginning and to his layered presence as a nurturing, loving figure alongside his phallic, paternal role.

Mother-father–infant: the triadic structure of preoedipal life

In traditional families, with their dichotomization of social roles, women typically assume the "maternal function." They are expected to be the primary parent from the initial postnatal period—Winnnicott's "primary maternal preoccupation"—up until the Oedipal drama, at which point the focus of development is said to shift to the father. But, recent revisionist views hold that the father has a central, formative presence from birth through preoedipal development and beyond (Diamond 1998, 2017, Herzog 2001, 2005a, Green 2009, Kalinich and Taylor 2009, Liebman and Abell 2000, Target and Fonagy 2002, Trowell and Etchegoyen 2002).

There may be, as Winnicott (1965b, 1965c) said, no baby without the mother, but there is no mother-baby unit without the father.

Psychoanalysts have long argued that a good enough (traditional) father holds the familial environment during an extended maturation process. As a subject formed and destined to claim a life as a public figure, the father sustains the mother-infant unit but, in doing so, signals to the child a world beyond the family, one they're fated to join. In Diamond's apt phrase, the father "watches over" the family (Diamond 1998: 257, cf. Green 2009). He makes it possible for his wife to forge a symbiotic bond, which, at least for many traditional parents was the marker of good enough mothering. Moreover, throughout a child's development she was expected to sustain her primary maternal function, only gradually reclaiming her status as a full participant in domestic and civic life.

In this regard, the traditional father has an additional role: he lays claim to the mother as his sexual partner, thereby creating a space between her and the infant. By repeatedly calling her back to their exclusive sexual-romantic coupledom (Herzog 2005a, 2005b, 2009), he contributes to sustaining her separateness and status as a cultural subject. This is a vital paternal role: the father helps a mother to contain her adhesive or fusional impulses, but also her periodic return to the spousal unit contributes to modulating her anxieties of anticipated separation and loss. Simultaneously, in establishing a space between the mother and the child, the parental sexual coupling facilitates the child's emergence as a separate self (Diamond 2017: 305, 1998: 251). Moreover, in claiming the mother for himself and in establishing the father-mother couple as a unit apart from the child, a son has an important, formative experience of the father: he "provides his son [with] an object of identification able to locate *maleness within the matrix of intimate relationship[s]*" (our emphasis, Diamond 2007: 1118). In other words, the father is experienced as a relational and loving subject parallel to, but different from, the son's intimate experience of his mother. Optimally, then, an alliance is forged between the mother and father that is the unseen and unthought ground of a good enough mother–father–infant environment (Abelin 1980, Diamond 2007, 2017, Herzog 2001, 2005a).

But, even if the traditional father is not present in an everyday, fully engaged way, he remains a formative symbolic presence. The father is present in the mind of the mother as a paternal imago; this masculine imago is an amalgamation of the mother's identification with a lineage of fathers, including the father of her child and perhaps other iconic male figures (Diamond 2017, Green 2009, Kalinich and Taylor 2009, Perelberg 2015, Target and Fonagy 2002). The paternal imago is unconsciously communicated to a son and is integral to the way he forms a maternal identification and attachment. This perspective underscores a father's role beyond "watching over." The symbolic father serves as a third and invites the child into a world apart from the mother-son dyad. Triangulation is then intricately woven into the preoedipal dynamic, regardless of the actual presence of the father. The formative environment for boys—and any gendered child—is a triadic one consisting of independent relationships with the mother, the father, and the mother/father dyad (Abelin 1980, Davids 2002, Diamond 1998, Green 2009, Herzog 2001, 2005a, Marks 2002).

There is an additional point to be made: the paternal imago underscores an unconscious gendering dynamic. A mother communicates the paternal imago through the various ways she relates to her son and his father. Although. we should not collapse this imago into a seamless masculinity, boys will experience their mothers—including their mother's experience of themselves as unconsciously projecting onto them a particular type of self-in-the-making—a boy.

Assuming a heteronormative family environment, mothers will recognize and respond to their child with a penis as male, as a protoboy. From being assigned a sexed status at birth to the naming of the infant, and in virtually every aspect of relating to the infant, the child with a penis is being imagined and made legible by the mother as a male and as a boy-in-the-making; to be precise, as a hetero-masculine boy since gender is only legible in a compulsory heteronormative context in rigidly cisgendered terms.

Mothers' mirror their love and admiration of their sons consistently and in an overdetermined way as, and only as, straight and masculine. The traditional mother responds to the infant as already gendered, thereby presupposing and authorizing cisgendered norms. And the infant, imitatively and through unconscious identifications with such mirroring constructs, no doubt internalizes a sense of itself as not just human, as not just a living, loved self, but as a gendered self along with incorporating a heteronormative matrix. Maternal identification underscores a child identifying with, indeed, wanting to be the gendered construct that is the mother's unwavering representation of him. The child with a penis wishes to be identified by others and by himself as a boy and, roughly between 3–5, as a straight boy.

The unconscious life of the father-son bond

Paternal holding is at one level a series of transactional actions: reproducing the material life of the family, containing affect and establishing boundaries, and enforcing rules and facilitating individuation. But holding is more than that, and fathers are more than phallic or authoritative, legislating men. Fathers participate in creating and caring for a new life— and the new life of the family. Such parenting cannot be reduced to a series of discrete, sharply boundaried, instrumental actions to be followed by paternal withdrawal and serving as a symbol of a post-familial cultural order. Instead, from birth onward, good enough fathers assume expanded responsibilities as they are expected to sustain the material and affectional-moral life of the family.

In traditional arrangements, they are expected to assume a public life of work and governance, which makes possible an emotionally saturated, integrative domestic sphere pivoting around mothers' devotion to their child. In this scenario, the good enough father assumes a largely background role. Yet, fathers are no less devoted to the child and family, no less immersed in its solidary-creating dynamics, even if their expected paternal function often leaves them on the outside, seemingly detached from the day to day life of the family.

Immersed in the making and maintaining of family life, fathers' devotion is at one level expressed in the considerable sacrifice they must bear. To wit: even as they sustain the family psychically as well as materially they must also manage their own ambivalent feelings about being marginalized and having to defer, if not surrender, longings to be a more fully nurturing and constant presence in the precious but quickly moving moments of the child's early life (Herzog 2001, 2009, Green 2009, Richards 2009, Target and Fonagy 2002).

Optimally, paternal sacrifice and containment is made possible and purposeful by an abiding ethically committed loving attachment to the idea of the family. Specifically: love for his wife who is also the mother of his child; love of the mother-infant bond; love of the child who is his, and is both him and not him; and love of the family as a unit, as a kind of living force of which he is a part and, traditionally, a condition of its possibility. In this immersive, devotional love, the mundane—the endless sacrifices, responsibilities, and deferrals—is infused with a higher moral significance. In each of these aspects of familial identification, the father, at least traditionally, is in the background, often unacknowledged and culturally marked as secondary. However, as an ongoing series of acts of attachment and immersion, as the quotidian behavior of watching over is infused with ethical significance as a joint creator and participant in this sphere of love and familial solidarity, the paternal function cannot be reduced to a series of transactional and legislative roles and actions.

Holding is, moreover, the staging ground for forging a loving bond between father and son (Diamond 1998: 307). Optimally, a real, embodied father is present from pregnancy through birth onward. Fatherhood is potentially generative not only in making a new life but in the re-making of his own life. The father-child bond is potentially transformative: he not only experiences himself as the co-creator of a life that he is now and in principle will always be a part of, as it will be a part of him, but, through parenting, especially a son, he re-experiences and renegotiates aspects of his own psychic life.

Inevitably, the father is thrown back to the way his father parented him and to the child he was with his father and, to some extent, to the boy and man he became in no small measure because of the way he was fathered, because of the particular father he had, because of the man his father was. Indeed, he may experience himself as the man he is and the father he is because of his father; he is a man made in the image of his father, perhaps as his father's ego ideal or sadly as the failed or "bad" man his father was or felt himself to be.

In the experience of return, a new father may feel that he bears the utmost responsibility for his son. Unconsciously, he carries the weight of his son's fate, of the kind of boy and man he will become; it's as if the boy and man his son will become reflects in no small measure his fathering; and, who he is will more or less dictate how he will father. Phantasmatically, his son will be the kind of son he "makes" by virtue of who he is. This may be the narcissism of the über-masculine "Western" subject; but, such an unconscious immersive and projective fusion deeply binds the father to the son and the son to the father who, we assume, experiences himself in part through his father's experience of him and through his identification with his father's projections of him.

We're alluding to a layered transgenerational dynamic: the father's experience of his son is in no small part mediated through an identification with his father, rather than as an independent object. The son, then, experiences himself through the ways his father experiences him, which pivots on his father's experience of his own father, and so it goes in an infinite regress. The child at once bears the character of the man the father is, of the child the father was, of the man the father's father was, and the child the father's father was, and so on (Marks 2002).

To add another layer: the child experiences the father as the boy the father would have liked to have been had he been fathered otherwise. Fatherhood is in some sense a corrective or redemptive practice. In re-enacting his own father-son dynamic, a father is in some sense the father he wished he had; and, in a parallel manner, the son might become the boy and man he wished he was or might have become. The child is inevitably a site of phantastical enactments: the boundaries between the child, his father, his father's father, and so on blur and interrelate in mindboggling unknowable ways; and, as a new life, the infant with a penis, bears the gendered fantasies of present and past fathers, bearing the illusory promise of a son, of a boy, and eventually a man, who can be both the same and other than who his father is and who his father's father and their fathers before him were.

From this psychodynamic perspective, the father would seem to unavoidably enact a psychic drama with his preoedipal son. It may be a redemptive drama: he redeems himself, and perhaps his father, by becoming the father he wished he had and by imagining his son as the son he wished he were. But a tragedy is also possible: his own early trauma gets reenacted through reproducing his father's failed parenting. In a Fairbairnian (1952) scenario, a splitting may drive not good enough fathering. Perhaps feeling he failed his good father or was undeserving of a good father, this traumatic scene is transferred to the present father-son dynamic. The son may be unconsciously positioned as a persecutory object to be punished by the father, confirming his own badness and his father's failed parenting. In the grip of a lineage of not good enough fathers, he enacts a tragic drama of failed parenting with his son, reproducing his—and his father's—traumatized childhood in his son. There is no escaping the transgenerational making of selves.

Parenting is impossible to conceive without deep unconscious iden-tifications and attachments. In particular, there is an inevitable narcissistic identification underpinning the father-son bond. As we've argued, the father experiences something of his own boyhood in his son; he imagines his son as he was, as if the son wants, feels, desires, and needs what the father as a child needed and desired. But also, he imagines this new life as a life he wished he had with a father he wished he had, who he may now feel he is. He fantasizes a son occupying self-states he wished or wishes for himself. Arguably, the child can never be entirely other than the child imagined by the father, including the child he may have wished he could have been. The circulation of projective and introjective identifications between father and son propel the sort of deeply felt, loving but also ambivalent attachment that good enough parenting entails. For the traditional father, it makes possible a lifetime of sacrifices, endless obligations and deferrals. It's not hard to understand how such identifications and attachment dynamics can have undesirable outcomes—especially if unmetabolized bad objects attach to the father's own childhood and haunt his parenting. In such cases, a father's absence, his hostility, rejection, shaming or his jealousies and envies, will wreak havoc on the son—and the family.

The dynamics of identification are inextricably gendered. Fathers' idealize their designated male children in a specific way: their own ego ideal is projected onto the child. This is a gendered ideal; it cites the kind of man he would like to be or became. A very specific gendered idealization is projected onto the child: from birth onward, the infant with a penis is imagined as already gendered as a male, as fated to be a boy, a straight boy. Paralleling the experience with his mother, a child is experienced through the lens of a gendered normativity; in traditional families, he is imagined as embodying, as if the very telos of his being, a seamlessly hetero-masculine boyhood. He is expected to inhabit this ideal, indeed to do so in perhaps fuller ways than his father. The child with a penis, the male, the boy, is experienced through this idealization as an extension of the father's gendered fantasy of him; but, ironically, it is this narcissistic identification that in part attaches the father to his son and is drawn on to build a vital bond. Diamond aptly calls this "narcissism, in the service of connection" (1998: 257–8).

A child then knows himself through gendered paternal and maternal projections and mirroring idealizations. Moreover, a son's identification with the father, an actual embodied father, intensely present and then absent but in ways that, at least in traditional families, symbolize authority, has the force of likeness. Between 2–3, the child with a penis knows he's not the mother, not a girl, but a boy. He finds sameness in the father—an idealized figure. The boy luxuriates in this likeness, in the collapsed identification; he radiates this idealized sameness back to the father, this sense of being like his father who, in good enough parenting, recognizes aspects of himself in the boy and validates his son's growing sense of being a hetero-masculine boy. In such moments, "the father ... is then able to become 'engrossed' in, and protective of, his newborn with whom he feels a *'loving union,'* while concurrently experiencing the infant's 'otherness'" (Diamond 1998: 257–8). A powerful father-son bond is potentially forged in a matrix of largely unconscious identifications, projections, idealizations and attachments.

Benjamin's formulation of identificatory love speaks to this formative unconscious grounding of the preoedipal father-son bond (Benjamin 1988: 106, 1995: 122, Freud 1923, Klein 1957: 242) "The father," she says "is ... not just the non-mother, the third symbolizing a space of separation ... but for *the growing boy a figure of deep attachment, identification, and love*" (Benjamin 1991, 1996: 31). The son wants to be like his father, indeed to be him. Moreover, "identification is not merely a matter of incorporating the ideal, *but of having a relationship with the person who embodies it*" (our emphasis, Benjamin 1996: 30). The father-son bond is experienced as an actual love affair. "The identificatory homoerotic bond is the prototype of ideal love—a love in which the son seeks to find in the other an ideal image of himself" (Benjamin 1988: 107, 1991: 284, 1996: 31). Given a son's identificatory love toward the father, and the father's narcissistic identification with his son, an intense affectional-erotic intertwinement occurs, a fusional dynamic in which the space of difference is, at least in moments, collapsed into mutual idealization and likeness that provides the unconscious cement to the father-son bond.

This homoerotic father-son love is inextricably gendered. The father recognizes and validates "the child's sense of being a subject of desire" (Benjamin 1988: 31, 1995: 124). Benjamin seems to suggest the making of a particular kind of masculine self: desiring, entitled, world-making-and-mastering, in a word, phallic. But we wonder whether the kind of bonding she describes, the fusional at times collapsed space of mutual identification and idealization, which is facilitated by an actual relationship of attunement and caring, doesn't also speak to fathers as relational, loving men. As Herzog (2005a) says, the father-son bond pivots around both "harmonious" (soothing, comforting) and "disruptive" (competitive, tension generating) attunement. "A father optimally, is already cavorting with his infant in his particular mode (disruptive attunement) as well as trying to interact in a more maternal mode" (Herzog 2001: 57). Sons' then experience fathers as phallic but also relational, intimate subjects, at once generating playful forms of conflict yet "maternal" in facilitating a quiet comforting psychic and interpersonal equilibrium. What the good enough father experiences in parenting, a son also experiences—namely, an integration of the maternal side of himself, a foregrounding of relational intimate-seeking that is part of the deep satisfaction of fathering and, optimally, of men's adult lives. Through fathering men can recover "the disavowed . . . early maternal and paternal attachments [that] serve to further the linkage between this fatherly provision and the adult's formation and strengthening of a maturing sense of maleness" (Diamond 1997: 459)

Individuation and gender imposition: the psychodynamics of subjectification

The question of maternal identification is at the center of psychoanalytic accounts of individuation. For infants assigned a male status, there is said to be a singular challenge: to claim the appropriate gender identity they must shift the ground of their being from the mother to the father, a potentially traumatic development given the fusion-like mother-son dyad and the more episodic and mediated father-son bond associated in traditional families. Analysts relate a story of separation in which, optimally, a protoboy effectively claims psychological independence vis-à-vis his mother. Disidentification perspectives hold that maternal repudiation and the disavowal of a primary feminine identification are a condition of securing a normalized status as a boy. Revisionists agree that boys must shift their psychic allegiance to the father in order to claim a legible gender status. They hold however that this is a process of internal differentiation, one in which boys, under conditions of good enough parenting, sustain their maternal attachment and identification.

Despite feminist interventions, many analysts are still prone to describe this process as a quasi-natural "maturation" dynamic, as if humans are innately propelled to claim psychic independence. Perhaps, but, there are sociological conditions that underpin and drive the specificity of this psychodynamic process. For example, a mother-son symbiotic bond, as elaborated by Winnicott or Mahler or Stoller presupposes a traditional family in which women's primary status is as a wife and mother; her chief role is to parent. This family arrangement, moreover, assumes the normativity of the notion of separate spheres (men/public, women/ domestic) and a condition of compulsory heterosexuality with a tilt toward patriarchy. If a heightened anxiety attaches to the mother-son bond, this speaks in part to its pivotal role in social reproduction, i.e. in being responsible for the making of straight masculine, public-oriented men complemented by straight, appropriately feminine, domestic-oriented women. The anxiety is quite specific: the fear that a mother's adhesive attachment will emasculate a male child, and, as such, endanger heteronormativity and patriarchy. The anxiety surrounding traditional mothering, moreover, presupposes culturally specific norms of manhood that pivot around autonomy and self-sufficiency as well as aggressivity and a will to power.

The question of boys individuation, as its been addressed in much psychoanalytic thinking, is legible only if we take for granted a social context in which women are the primary parent, in which families are expected to produce cisgendered heterosexual masculine subjects, in which a father's function is to facilitate the movement of the male child into a cultural order; in short, individuation as its been posed since Freud, has often assumed social conditions organized around compulsory heterosexuality and a patriarchical-leaning doctrine of separate spheres and gender roles. In such a context, the question of boys' development has been linked to unstated, often unthought, anxieties about societal reproduction. We do not wish to collapse the psychic into the social or deny a singularly psychodynamical process in explaining boy's psychic independence. Yet, in a context of cisgendered heteronormativity, individuation is inevitably a gendered sociopolitical dynamic.

With this contextualizing frame in mind, we want to return to the question of gender identification and to its originary moment: the mother-son bond and maternal identification. For disidentification theorists, maternal identification is collapsed into femininity; by contrast, revisionists stipulate a mix of stereotypically feminine and masculine identifications, thereby reworking Freud's notion of original bisexuality in a social constructionist manner. We wonder: is such a binary framing of gender identification still complicit with the normativity of gender binarism?

In this regard, we wish to ask: what is it about a son's experience of his mother that is identified with and introjected?

Despite the cultural marking of the mother as "feminine," and maternalness with an über-femininity, we wonder whether this has much resonance for a preoedipal child prior to functioning in a categorical gender mode (ages 3–5)? By the latter, we mean a capacity to identify themselves and others, and a wide range of feelings, desires, behavior, social roles, and cultural styles, in categorically dichotomous gender terms. We assume the gendering of the preoedipal child but, with psychoanalytic feminists, believe that their regulation is thin and irregular. Importantly, there is an absence of a reflexive gender self-monitoring. Hence: the overinclusive and fluid gender experience of the preoedipal child. But, the notion of overinclusiveness seems to assume that the range of a child's bodily and subjective states is describable in conventional gender terms. Again, we wonder: do such accounts collapse subjectivity and gender and thereby unintentionally authorize a logic of compulsory gendering? Early preoedipal children would seem to inhabit subjective states featuring an almost chaotic heterogeneity of sensations, excitations, movements, affectional states, and, to use Laplanche's term (1997), "enigmatic messages" that arguably are *not experienced as gendered and may be illegible in terms of cisgender codes*. If so, this raises a question: what is the relationship between gendering and subjectivity, in particular, gender identification and subjectivity?

Consider: mothers play, handle, carry, hold, clean, and gaze at their child in tender and gentle, but also in forceful, controlling ways; sometimes her talk is soft and sweet but other times projects a commanding, even scary voice and countenance. She placates and soothes her child but also coerces and can be uncompromising in setting boundaries. Even during infancy mothers come and go as they circulate between the child and his father, between the care of the child and other domestic and non-domestic matters. Mother's relate to their children in ways that mix presence and absence, penetration and reception, forcefulness and tenderness, decisiveness and surrender. In virtually all of their discrete task-oriented practices mothers weave together behaviors that, from afar might be describable in culturally stereotyped gender terms as feminine or masculine, but, up close, such descriptions seem thin and more like a cultural superstructure.

Consider cooking: mothers cut, chop, order, arrange, direct, and manage a complicated series of actions. We cannot assume that a preoedipal child experiences these coordinated and purposeful mix of heterogeneous behaviors in anything like clear gender binary terms, or indeed as gendered at all. And, if they do, would they identify with her forcefulness, her adept coordination of bodily acts, or her capacity to organize and arrange this complexity—and would this be experienced as feminine? Or, would they identify with her being in the kitchen as a "being for" her husband and children, what hegemonic cultural discourses might mark as feminine?

The child, it seems to us, experiences the mother as powerful and commanding alongside being tender and, at times is harmoniously attuned, at times not. The somewhat chaotic heterogeneous experience a child has of a mother, perhaps gendered in some ways but also not, forms part of their interior lives; presumably, it figures in a child's maternal identification and somehow in the dynamics of subjective formation and gender identification.

How then to think about the intersection of an emerging categorical gender identity and subjective states that exceed such identifications? We suggest the notion of gender imposition. It is as if formal gender identification is something that happens almost apart from, but also alongside of, but also constitutive of, but also in tension with, a child's heterogeneous subjective states.

To state the obvious: gendering begins at birth—in the marking of bodies as sexed, male or female. "Except in rare cases, the infant's genitals at birth result in unambiguous sex ascription to the infant as boy or girl. That identification is in fact binary and perhaps monolithic. . . . The infant is either . . . one or the other" (Fast 1999: 677, Thomson-Salo and Campbell 2017). Further: subjective states are being gender marked as a child incorporates a familial environment saturated with gendered names, voices, bodies, countenances, clothing, gestures, movements, activities, play, social roles, etc. However, in so far as the child has a limited capacity to engage in reflexive gender self-monitoring and is not yet fully implicated in thick and formulated family-based modes of gender regulation, preoedipal gendering is not fused with subjectivity. Over-inclusiveness is possible: boys/girls and moms/dads can mix gender traits. And, little anxiety is attached to a toddler's gender fluidity as long as they remain more or less normatively cisgendered. Overinclusiveness is also possible to the extent that the preoedipal child almost fully inhabits the insular, constricted environment of the family. Would we then be mistaken to conjecture that not only do the boundaries between the feminine and the masculine remain porous as gender is a site of play, but the boundaries between gendered and non-gendered subjective states are relaxed as the former is not yet a chief anchoring point of identity and self-regulation?

Still, as Fast says, by roughly the age of 2 a child is claiming an "I" that is gendered—as male/female and boy/girl and absorbing, imitatively and through identifications, how males "do" boyhood. But boy-ness is not just a status claimed solely by virtue of maleness, but redeemed performatively within the norms of gender legibility; and in doing so, the protoboy is unwittingly incorporating and authorizing a cisgendered and hetero-normative order. Shortly, all too soon, this boy-ness will become a primary identity he must claim and enact hourly and daily in order to warrant recognition of gender and psychic and social normality.

Oedipus marks the decisive, fateful developmental juncture: inclusive-ness gives way to mutually exclusive complementary gender and sexual identities; males are expected to become straight masculine boys (Benjamin 1988, 1995, Corbett 2009a: 10, 55). The story has varied little since Freud. In the face of castration anxieties triggered by their libidinal rivalry with the father, sons' abandon the mother as a sexual object and, ideally, reinstate her as the environmental mother. But boys learn something else: they can't have their father. There's a twofold foreclosure: no mother but women and no father but also no man, ever! In return for this disavowal, boys get to claim an identification with their father as a man, indeed a man who has his mom, a straight man. This psychodynamic account in which gender (same-gender identification) and sexuality (cross-gender desire) diverge has been tweaked since Freud. In particular, some analysts argue that a boy's identificatory love for his father is sustained along with his gender identification; homoeroticism is then still in play in the Oedipal drama even as it is formally proscribed (Benjamin 1996, Davies 2015). And, formal identifications, gender and sexual, are understood as contradictory and ambiguous, never settled once and for all or ironed out into a seamless coherent interiority (e.g. Benjamin 1995: 18, 77, 1996, Harris 1991). To wit: the gender of the identifying subject and the identified object are ambiguous, despite conventional identifications. For example, a male identifying with his father may subjectively experience himself as a girl identifying with a male father or a girl desiring the male father or a boy identifying with a female father or a boy eroticizing a male father. The point: we cannot unambiguously read an individual's gender and erotic life by only attending to manifest normalizing identifications. Nevertheless, few analysts disagree that the Oedipal moment marks a significant change in subjectification, e.g. expanded capacities for mentalization, symbolization, and intersubjectivity. From a gender point of view, we would say that Oedipal boys in traditional families experience something potentially traumatic: gender imposition.

In the throes of Oedipus, boys in traditional families are enjoined by the full authority of virtually every aspect of their environment to present, consistently and unambiguously, a normalized boy-ness or risk humiliation and exile from the tribe of men. Gender imposition entails a compulsory demand to performatively present as a conventional boy and that means a straight boy (Goldner 1991, Layton 1998). To effectively manage this performative expectation, a child is expected to be able to operate in a categorical gender mode. They must absorb gender as an organizing framework and experience gender as pervasive, stretching deep into one's interior and across all aspects of social existence.

Gender stipulates a dichotomous order: males and females, masculine and feminine, boys and girls, men and women. A cisgendered alignment is posited: males/masculinity/boys/men or females/femininity/girls/women. This alignment is complementary: bodies and temperaments, statuses and roles are imagined as naturally and normally meshing, uniting to form integral wholes. In this way, gender is inextricably understood as heteronormative. The Oedipal boy is expected to be an active participant in this gendered order, citing and enforcing its normative and normalizing authority in his daily practice.

In the dynamic of gender imposition, then, the child absorbs gender as the order of things, as the way he knows himself and others. The unruliness of bodily, subjective life is sorted out and given meaning and coherence through the lens of gender. It makes possible an ordering of interior and exterior life. It is a way to be and to reflexively organize and regulate oneself. It is a foundation upon which to formulate an identity and to give personal life form and purposefulness.

Gender imposition entails a dual dynamic: to render all subjectivity gender legible and to align internal and external life according to a cisgendering normativity. Subjective life is then unavoidably fraught; a chaotic and unruly matrix of sensations, excitations, desires, feelings, and fantasies threaten the normalizing compulsion that drives gender imposition. Inevitably, subjectivity is a site of considerable anxiety and psychic work as its unruliness must be contained and managed. Recognition of oneself as normal and good, as warranting love, respect and belonging, is at stake. From this perspective, gender performativity may be experienced as a traumatic imposition. Indeed, for some boys whose temperament disposes to sensual and affective fluidity and mobility, the compulsion to performatively enact a cisgendered self may feel distressingly at odds with a subjectivity resistant to gendering per se (e.g. trans* or agender identifications) or to a rigid cisgendering normativity that organizes many families.

But, admittedly, for many boys gendering is gradual, almost imperceptible, as if a natural part of maturation. Imposition may go unformulated since there may be no space in and outside of families to represent gendering as anything other than a natural process. There is, though, a marked experiential transition from preoedipal overinclusiveness to Oedipal exclusivity. Fast speaks of the child experiencing a restriction and loss, as if recognizing he cannot be all that he wishes. Although Fast describes this shift as if it's an inevitable individuating process, it is about enforcing a gender normalizing imperative—to be a masculine straight boy. This is a formative moment where, at least in traditional families, there is little or no space to imagine alternatives and where the child experiences a loss without the possibility of mourning. In the Oedipal drama, a vague sense of being a boy must give way to presenting, repeatedly and unendingly, an unambiguous identity as a straight masculine boy.

The unstated ground, indeed a driving force, of Oedipus is social. Between the ages of 4–5, the child begins to exist beyond the domestic sphere in a world of formal schooling and expanded socializing with kin, friends, teachers, administrators, and perhaps childcare workers. He is more fully in the social world as a subject but also as a representative of the family. He is expected to be more self-regulating and socially skilled, exhibiting the psychic and social traits recognizable as a good citizen (Alexander 2007). But also, he must present this good self in a normalizing gender vernacular, i.e. one associated with constructions of a cisgendered straight boyhood. In the absence of good enough parenting, some boys may navigate this psychic terrain embracing an exaggerated hetero-masculine manliness—with all the bad consequences we have witnessed inside and outside of the treatment room (Diamond 1998, 2009, 2015, 2017, Herzog 2001, 2009, Pollack 1998).

Afterword: a comment on post-traditional families and parents

In post-traditional families, both parents feel entitled to work and aspire to share parenting decisions and responsibilities. Importantly, post-traditional parents feel entitled to choose the kind of family they want, including whether or not—and how—to have children (Golombok 2015, Rosenfeld 2007). Following the logic of this chapter, we continue to assume two cisgendered straight parents living together. We focus on post-traditional parents born after 1980.

Coming of age in the late 1990s and after, these parents grew up in a very different social environment from their parents and grandparents. Unlike their parents, post-traditional parents likely had mothers that worked, many fulltime and career oriented, and many remaining in the paid work force during their child's early years. This change speaks, more generally, to a trend in the past few decades towards gender convergence and equality. In this regard, post-traditional men are likely to have women friends, classmates, and work colleagues sharing many of the same ambitions—foremost, economic independence and a self-fulfilling personal and intimate life. They may well have had fathers for whom the counterculture and the social justice movements of the 1960s and 1970s, along with multiculturalism, were formative. They likely inherited from their father's doubts about what previous generations took for granted, especially in regard to matters of gender and sexuality. One such matter is homosexuality. Young parents are part of a cultural shift towards gay normalization and mainstreaming; more than likely, they know lesbians and gay or queer folk as family or friends or as classmates, co-workers, cultural creators, and pop icons.

We're alluding to a significant change in parenting culture. Post-traditional family environments echo broader cultural shifts. For many Americans aged 40 and younger, personal and intimate life is less unequivocally and unthinkingly tied to rigid ideas of normal gender and sexuality. Compulsory norms of heterosexuality and cisgenderedness have been challenged; they no longer feel like "the order of things." In a parallel manner, while misogyny is still woven into American culture, as signaled by the events that prompted the #MeToo movement, the willingness of many women to go public, the firing of powerful men, and the seeming widespread public support for an anti-sexist culture, speaks to a broad, if highly uneven, cultural shift: a recognition of women's entitlement to be autonomous subjects. Post-traditional family cultures have absorbed broad currents of anti-homophobia and anti-sexism; rigid constructs of personal life are less normative.

Two additional points seem crucial. First, where an older generation of parents may have taken for granted "the family," post-traditionalists assume that family is chosen, e.g. one or two adults, children or not, same gendered or opposite gendered, and so on. In these new families, men are expected—and are motivated—to assume more of the day-to-day parenting. The data is pretty clear: Post-traditional fathers may not want to clean or cook, though more do, but they definitely want to parent— longing for a nurturing father-child bond. Fathering has become a key aspect of younger men's identity and aspirational selves (Chapter 1). Second, the boundaries between the family and public life have become undeniably porous and blurry. In particular, pop culture and digitalization are today part of the preoedipal family culture. As Corbett put it: "The family is less a fortress, more a clearinghouse, open to the currency of social forces. . . . The 'outside' society is indelibly 'inside' the family" (Corbett 2009b: 360, Altman 2011, Bonovitz 2009, Corpt 2013, Dimen 2011, Goldner 2011, 2014, Harris and Botticelli 2010, Hartman 2011, Layton 2002, 2006b). Less the insulated "haven in a heartless world," families echo the busyness and noisiness and at times the frenetic rhythms of public life.

Children in many post-traditional families encounter different kinds of parents then those of past generations (Ehrensaft 2007, 2011, Golombok 2015).[3] In particular, gender is approached less as a destiny making social status; it is increasingly recognized as a sphere of individualization. For many younger Americans, selves are understood as "designed" or self-authored and gender flexible. In a similar manner, many post-traditional parents have likely experienced periods of sexual-intimate experimentation, including homoeroticism, participation in a culture of hook ups, cohabitation, polyamory, and so on. Many millennials embrace a culture that is fiercely libertarian.

The culture of parenting is changing. With many mothers working, and many fathers prioritizing parenting, the notion of a divide between women's/maternal and men's/paternal functions is losing credibility. Many mothers, like fathers, come and go, are nurturing but also disciplining, represent domesticity but also a wider public life—in short, blend stereotypical feminine and masculine traits in their familial and public lives. Similarly, fathers, like mothers, engage in nurturing, caregiving practices as central to their domestic lives; they soothe and comfort as well as feed and play with their children; in Herzog's (2001, 2005a) terms, fathers are harmoniously and disruptively attuned to their children.

As the line between mothering and fathering blurs, we question theorizing parenting in terms of a maternal and paternal function. Post-traditional parenting may still be gendered, but, given converging parenting practices and a culture enjoining and legitimating parenting as a core value irrespective of gender, we doubt whether there is anything about being female and a woman or male and a man that mandates specific parenting roles. Overwhelming evidence underscores a trend toward the de-gendering of parenting practices (see Chapter 3, Davies and Eagle 2013, Deutsch 2007, Doucet 2006, Golombok 2015, Target and Fonagy 2002). By invoking a universalistic language of maternal and paternal functions, analysts perpetuate a misrecognition of actual parenting practices in many families, and are perhaps unwittingly complicit with a cisgendered normativity (Davies and Eagle 2013, Freeman 2008, Samuels 1996).

Children of post-traditional parents encounter historically unique family environments. They experience manifestly multigendered parents, mothers and fathers engaged in overlapping parenting practices, and grow up in family and public cultures increasingly respectful of gender and sexual variation. Such families, optimally, provide the social and psychic space for children to more freely explore matters of identity and personal life. Departures from a rigid cisgendered heteronormativity are tolerated, indeed increasingly discursively validated. Are we mistaken then to assume that many of these children approach gender and sexuality as sites of choice and variation? Will not many of them find in their family culture, and in the very lives of their parents, support for a personal life that values individualization and, accordingly, frames gender and sexuality as occasions to explore their own dramas of authenticity and self-fulfillment? As we see it, this is a hopeful moment in the midst of America's current retrograde identity politics.

Notes

1 We've assumed a two-parent, gender conventional, heterosexual family. We are admittedly uneasy about further normalizing this arrangement, but offer two rationales. First, psychoanalytic theory has assumed, and still does in no small measure, the two parent heterosexual family in its accounts of gender formation. Accordingly, we think it compelling to show that, even assuming this family type, boys' gender development is still in need of considerable rethinking. That said, in subsequent chapters we speak to family variations theoretically and through case studies. Second, although there is a rich archive of sociological research and scholarship on non-normative families, there is not yet a parallel body of psychoanalytic literature on gender formation in such families. To be sure, there are trenchant analyses of the clinical challenges of engaging social differences of race, class, sexuality, and so on (e.g. Adams 2009, Altman 2011, Bonovitz 2009, Corbett 2009a, Drescher 1998, Gump 2000, Layton 2006b, Miles 2012, Samuels 2006, Sherman 2005, Suchet 2004, 2007, 2010). There is also psychoanalytic research on, say, growing up gay or lesbian, but almost all of these accounts assume a straight family in which struggles around identity occur in the context of a compulsory heterosexual and cisgendered social environment (e.g. Blum and Pfetzing 1998, Blechner 1998, Corbett 2009a, Drescher 1998, Isay 1989, Lewes 1988, Magee and Miller 1998). There are very few psychoanalytic studies of children, specifically boys, raised in gay or queer or trans* families (see Chapter 3). Similarly, psychoanalysts are addressing the challenges race and class differences present in the treatment room, but there are still precious few accounts of self-formation in poor families, single parent or multigenerational households, or racially or class-based marginalized families.

2 The admittedly clumsy categories, traditional and post-traditional, are used to delineate changes in American families in the 20th and 21st centuries. These concepts are intended to serve as ideal types or crude markers of a complex social transformation. Each concept suggests patterns that arguably are dominant at specific historical periods; they do not of course capture historical realities in their complexity nor do we assume a simple linear progression. They have, at best, a provisional heuristic value. And yet, such general concepts are helpful as an initial mapping of changes and as a way to identify patterned empirical differences. For example, we are aware that in the high period of "traditional families" (say 1900–1950s), there were non-traditional families, especially among immigrants, poor Americans, African-Americans, non-heterosexuals, bohemians or radicals. We would argue though that today not only are post-traditional families more acceptable, but many Americans feel a right to decide what family means and what form of family they want; this sense of being entitled to choose, along with growing public recognition of the pluralization of families, is at the heart of what we mean by post-traditional (Gamson 2015, Golombok 2015, Rosenfeld 2007).

3 As the sociologist Phil Cohen writes: "At the end of the 1950s, if you chose 100 children under age 15 to represent all children, 65 would have been living in a family with married parents, with the father employed and the mother out of the labor force. Only 18 would have had married parents who were both

employed. As for other types of family arrangements, you would find only one child in every 350 living with a never-married mother! Today, among 100 representative children, just 22 live in a married male-breadwinner family, compared to 23 living with a single mother (only half of whom have ever been married). Seven out of every 100 live with a parent who cohabits with an unmarried partner (a category too rare for the Census Bureau to consider counting in 1960) and six with either a single father or with grandparents but no parents. The single largest group of children—34—live with dual-earner married parents, but that largest group is only a third of the total, so that it is really impossible to point to a "typical" family. With two-thirds of children being raised in male-breadwinner, married-couple families, it is understandable that people from the early 1960s considered such families to be the norm. Today, by contrast, there is no single family arrangement that encompasses the majority of children (2014b: 3).

Chapter 3

Gay boyhoods and fathers
The gay Oedipus and beyond

In the cultural and political effervescence of the 1960s and 1970s, the idea of compulsory heterosexuality [CH] became central to gay/lesbian politics (Birkby et al. 1973, Jay and Young 1972, Knoedt et al. 1973, Myron and Bunch 1975, Rich 1980, Wittman 1972). CH entails state enforcement of the normative status of heterosexuality through legislation, laws, and the assignment of rights. It both enfranchizes and idealizes heterosexuality and disenfranchizes and pollutes homosexuality. The "straight state" is reinforced by the core institutions of American civil society and its culture, from TV and religion to expert discourses spanning the social sciences and the medical and mental health fields. The institutionally enforced imperative of heterosexuality is woven into the fabric of daily life, for example, in the tolerance of pervasive homophobia, in the stigmatizing and violence toward gay people, and in the censoring of gay-affirmative speech.

A regulatory order based on CH creates what has come to be called the closet. The avoidance of exposure and the mere suspicion of homosexuality typically compel individuals to make life-shaping, destiny-making decisions, for example, about jobs, marriage, and friends. No less impactful, the closet compels the deliberate and systemic self-monitoring of every aspect of self-presentation in order to avoid any trace of signifiers of homosexuality. CH is not a regime of genocide or ethnic cleansing; the homosexual is tolerated but only as an abject personage invoked to justify heteronormativity (D'Emilio 1983, Eskridge 1999, Seidman 2004).

From roughly the 1980s and 1990s, the state began to retreat from the systematic enforcement of heteronormativity. More and more institutions, especially bureaucratized and global ones, have normalized and integrated gay men and lesbians, and the intolerance of public homophobia is now a marker of enlightenment and social progress for many Americans. Heteronormativity may still be hegemonic, but it does not carry the oppressive weight and scale of the state and big institutions.

Sadly, but unsurprisingly, through the 1980s and arguably well into the 1990s, psychoanalysis contributed to sustaining CH (Domenici and Lesser 1995). Memoirs and reports of the time, from patients and practitioners, relate a dismal tale of the pervasive homophobia of many practitioners and the virtually uncontested heterosexism of psychoanalytic institutes (Dominici and Lesser 1995, Drescher 1995, Duberman 1991, Sherman 2005). Leading psychoanalysts from the 1950s onward took heterosexuality as a central marker of normality and health, homosexuality functioning as an über symptom of pathology and mental illness (Bergler 1956, Bieber et al. 1962, Socarides 1968).

Heterosexism was built into the cornerstone of psychoanalytic theory: the Oedipal complex. To achieve a "normal" cisgendered heterosexuality, the child was expected to negotiate an opposite-gendered eroticism and a same-gendered identification. Specifically, in the face of castration fears, boys were expected to abandon their rivalry with their fathers for the mother; instead, they were to identify with their fathers, duly compensated by assuming male privilege, while substituting for the mother a suitable female object of desire. This Oedipal dynamic was facilitated by presumptively heterosexual parents and sanctioned by a compulsory heterosexual social order. In this heteronormative account, the homosexual represents the failure of Oedipal development (Drescher 1998). Terrified by castration fears, and confronted with an unavailable father and an adhesively attached mother, the homosexual boy is said to retreat from paternal identification into a preoedipal mother-son bond and a maternal-feminine and homosexual identification (Drescher 2002, Frommer 2000, Green 2003, Isay 1989).

The heteronormativity of this account went virtually unchallenged until well into the 1980s (exceptions include Friedman 1988 and Marmor 1980), despite the ambiguities and contradictions of Freud's own views. Two texts, each squarely within the psychoanalytic establishment, announced the beginnings of a major re-examination: Richard Isay's *Being Homosexual* (1989) and Kenneth Lewes *The Psychoanalytic Theory of Male Homosexuality* (1988).

From "why" to "how": Oedipus from a gay perspective

Lewes did not offer a critique of the ethics and politics of psychoanalytical accounts of homosexuality; nor did he propose an alternative theory of gay boyhoods. Instead, the brilliance of his breakthrough text was its deconstructive analysis of Freudian and post-Freudian psychodynamical accounts. As befitting someone trained in literary theory in the 1970s and '80s, Lewes exposed the semantic contradictions in orthodox psychoanalysis and its textual incoherence as concerns the question of homosexuality.

Lewes zeroed in at the foundation of psychoanalytic accounts of homosexuality: the Oedipal complex (1988: 77). A homosexual object choice presumably signaled the failure of Oedipal negotiation; the boy regresses to a preoedipal position, manifested in a narcissism and an overidentification with the mother.

Lewes makes the case that Oedipus is equally open to hetero-or-homosexual outcomes. He offered a series of compelling arguments. We sketch three of them.

First, as does Freud, Lewes assumes that the son actively pursues his mother as the primary sexual object; he also assumes the boy experiences a crippling castration anxiety in the face of his potentially emasculating father. Still, the boy remains fixated on her. If he indeed abandons his mother as an erotic object to preserve his phallus, as is expected in the normative Oedipal drama, he suffers a *"self castration. . . . This passive phallic phase may predispose a son to 'a certain type of homosexuality'* . . ." (p. 79). In effect, in defending against emasculation the boy may experience himself as impotent and passive—as a collapsed phallic self. Accordingly, he may embrace a feminine identification leading to an inverted Oedipal dynamic.

Second, drawing on the Freudian notion of a bisexual disposition, Lewes suggests how the very logic of Oedipus unfolds as easily towards a homosexual as a heterosexual outcome. In line with Freudianism, he posits that "even in the most normative masculine development, there are important feminine trends. . . . There is always at least a partial disposition to feminine identification. . . ." This is "quite important because the Oedipus complex uniformly impels the male child away from a masculine libidinal stance." A homosexual development is doubly possible. On the one hand, "if the child . . . unconsciously preserve[s] his tie to his mother by identifying with her and consequently choose[s] future objects on a homosexual narcissistic basis." On the other hand, "if he chooses the passive alternative, he may try to preserve his penis, but in so doing he may have to be subject to his father and adopt the 'inverted' Oedipus complex, thus becoming the father's passive sexual object" (pp. 79–80).

In a third formulation, Lewes underscores the dynamic aspects of gender and sexual identification. "The child is seen as bound to both parents by positive libidinal ties. Because of his preoedipal identification with his father, which corresponds to his identification with his mother, the child's relation to his father is not simply rivalry, but . . . ambivalence. And just as his primary bond with his father is libidinal and not simply aggressive, his relation with his mother is not simply affectionate and libidinal, but includes the same ambivalence and rivalry. . . . The child takes his mother as a libidinal object and regards his father a rival. But he also takes his father as an object, and hates and competes with his mother as a rival for the loved father" (p. 80). Contrary to the rigid normative logic of sexual complementarity, Lewes suggests that, like masculinity and femininity, heterosexuality and homosexuality remain psychodynamically at play during boys' Oedipal drama.

In the spirit of deconstructive critique, Lewes invokes Freud to challenge the normative Oedipal story. He does not however elaborate an alternative, non-heteronormative account of gay boyhoods. This was left to Richard Isay. Working within the mainstream of psychoanalytic thinking, including its putative empiricist grounding in a body of clinical observations, Isay made the case for a unique male homosexual Oedipal dynamic. Moreover, reflecting the normalizing politics in urban gay America at the time, Isay insisted that being gay is a natural and typical human variation, or, as Chodorow (1976) and Mitchell (1978, 1981) argued a "compromise formation" as ordinary as male heterosexual development.

Isay's thesis is at first take stunningly simple: "Individuals are born homosexually inclined or, stated otherwise, homosexuality is 'constitutional in origin'" (1989: 4, cf. Lewes 1988: 80). Between 4 and 6 years of age, protogay boys become aware that they are different from siblings or peers. Alluding to the Oedipal story to come, he observes that many of the adult men in treatment (most born before or proximate to Stonewall) were able to recall childhood homoerotic fantasies associated with male peers or superheroes. Isay interprets these fantasies as disguised desires for their fathers. Recalling one patient, he comments that "many of his [patient's] therapy hours dealt with his longing for his father. He remembered that it was his father who would read him Superman and Captain Marvel comic books and that he felt warmth and pleasure while sitting on his father's lap. It became clear . . . that his sexual interest and excitement over masculine comic book heroes at age four were displaced and disguised expressions of his repressed sexual feelings toward his father" (1989: 26).

In these gay adult men, Isay thought he discovered an Oedipal dynamic *"except [that] the primary sexual object of homosexual boys is their fathers"* (1989: 29). Given the heteronormative context of the time, such fantasies, no matter how exciting, were deeply troubling; most boys knew that they were different and that there was something forbidden and wrong about such desires. Despite its prohibitive and dangerous status, these boys were still drawn, erotically and affectionately, to their fathers.

Notice: Isay reverses the then standard account. Whereas that viewpoint held that it's the remoteness of the father that drives the boy into the embrace of the mother, ultimately enacting an inverted Oedipal drama, Isay maintains that the father's distance is a reaction to their son's erotic attachment or his gender non-conformity.

> Particular to the childhood of homosexual boys, however, is that their fathers often become detached or hostile . . . as a result of the child's homosexuality. Fathers usually perceive such a child as being "different" from other boys in the family, from themselves, or from their son's peers. These boys may be more sensitive, [display] more aesthetic interests, may not be involved in competitive activities, and may be more seclusive than heterosexually inclined boys. This may lead both to the father's withdrawal and to his favoring an older or younger male sibling who appears to be more sociable, more conventional, more "masculine". Some of the fathers of homosexual boys, whether consciously or unconsciously, recognize that their sons have both a special need for closeness and an erotic attachment to them. These fathers may withdraw because of anxiety occasioned by their own homoerotic desires, which are usually unknown to them.
>
> (1989: 34, 1987: 284)

Isay concludes: "Thus the 'distant' absent or 'hostile' father is often the *result* of his son's homosexuality and not the cause of it" (1987: 284).

In Isay's account, homosexual desire is not an expression of gender identification, for example, a boy's excessive attachment to his mother. Instead, homosexuality is understood as an innate dispositional state needing no further explanation. But what does need explaining is the curious fact that most of the gay men in his consultation room were, in the dominant cultural codes of the time, markedly feminine.

The standard explanation appealed to either temperament or to an adhesive, co-dependent mother/son bond driven by castration fears or the mother's narcissism. Isay offers a different account. Just as protoheterosexual boys identify with the masculine traits of the father to "seduce" the mother, protohomosexual boys identify with the femininity of the mother to gain their father's interest. After a series of vignettes, Isay surmizes that "each of these *men* illustrates another *normal developmental issue* in the early sexual life of some gay men: they assume opposite-sex characteristic in order to acquire and maintain the attraction and attention of the father. [Furthermore], there is no evidence that such identifications are associated with castration anxieties. . . . Although partial identifications with both parents are inevitable in all children, I am stressing here the attempt to acquire the father's love . . . as one important motivation for identification with the mother in some gay men" (1987: 286–288). In Isay's view, this heightened feminine identification might also help account for boys' passive sexual desires and fantasies, triggered by their "ubiquitous, repressed, erotic desires for the father" (1987: 286–288). But, again, Isay is quick to reiterate a principal thesis "*in my clinical experience, the same-sex object choice appears to occur before the homosexually inclined child makes such [gender] identifications*" (1987: 282).

But, in reaction to their father's remoteness, don't these boys end up embracing an overly dependent, adhesive attachment to their mothers? And, in the face of a father's unavailability to his wife, wouldn't the mother forge an emotionally dependent attachment to their "sensitive" sons? No doubt there are powerful mutual identifications and entanglements between mothers and sons. Yet, Isay insists that for many of these boys, and their mothers, they experienced each other as rivals, competing for the affection and erotic love of the father (1989: 30). The standard view fails to appreciate "that many gay men may . . . be envious and competitive with women, a feeling that they are often not aware of which originates in the rivalry with the mother for the father's attention. Perhaps the mothers' sense that and try to keep them from their fathers . . . or envy the son's closeness to the father" (1989: 48). To the extent that such boys are in a tense rivalry with their mother, they will be able to renegotiate gender as adults. "For many boys this feminine identification persists into adulthood, [but] for others it disappears. . . ." (1989: 30). Despite the marked femininity of many of the gay men he treated, Isay insists that he did not witness any "gender identity or gender role disturbance in my 40 homosexual patients" (1987: 288).

After the pioneering work of Lewes and Isay, there were surprisingly few efforts to elaborate a uniquely gay Oedipus. Instead, there was, as we will address shortly, a shift from developmental themes to a focus on the subjective experiences of protogay boys. While there were no major reassessments, there were efforts to fine-tune Isay's developmental account.

In particular, two issues invited comment. First, how was hetero-normativity communicated to the son? Second, given the son's heightened identification with the mother, and his father's rejection, how do such boys come by a sense of themselves as boys and men-in-the-making?

In Isay's account, heteronormativity was conveyed primarily through the father's unavailability and at times overt rejection of his son's erotic-affectional interest. Arguing that Isay downplayed the active role of both parents, Scott Goldsmith (1995) suggested that heterosexual parents take for granted the child's heterosexuality and expect the son, indeed actively press him, to display the appropriate cisgendered, heterosexual behaviors. In particular, he was expected to demonstrate his paternal identification through a consistently normative masculine performance while also displaying a normative sexual interest in his mother.

Nowhere are these hetero-gender normative expectations more powerfully at play than in the Oedipal drama. Parents encourage their sons to cultivate a competitive but admiring relationship with their fathers "as part of the rituals of same sex parental identification" while fostering a "childhood romance with their opposite-sex parent" (Goldsmith 1995: 133). Goldsmith argued that the Oedipal dynamic doesn't just happen, but is made to happen; it is aggressively enforced, often unconsciously, by the parents. The boy experiences heteronormativity as an imperative, as "the natural order of things." Unfortunately, and sadly, "for the homo-sexual boy . . . parental Oedipal expectations run contrary to [the erotic-affectionate-gender experience of the boy], and therefore confound this stage of development" (p. 133). The protogay boy confronts an unforgiving Oedipal challenge. "For a successful resolution of this stage of development, homosexual boys must learn to master not only loving and erotic feelings towards the father but also his anger and aggression towards the mother, and fear of reprisal from her. . . ." (p. 114). The spiraling expectations to negotiate the Oedipus by displaying sexual and gender behavior at odds with his "personal idiom" make Oedipus a time of trauma for the protogay boy. He becomes "a 'double agent,' harboring one set of feelings while being called upon to enact another" (pp. 116–117).

Homosexuality is not only experienced as the wrong desire but a sign of the wrong gender (Drescher 1998: 237). Despite a preoedipal awareness of gender identity, it is during Oedipus that the child is expected to be recognized as a boy. This doesn't just happen; instead, the family stages a drama in which the boy is to claim a straight normatively masculine status. How does this young child manage a protostraight boy status when he actually wants what his mother wants and when his father has made it clear that that he isn't the son he wants? Once again, he's forced to "becomes a double agent and . . . something of an 'imposter'" (p 117).

The protogay Oedipal boy is tied up in gender knots, caught in the vortex of gender and sexual expectations at odds with his disposition and desire. Repelled by his father, he is driven into the embrace of his mother—at once idealized and envied for possessing the love object he desires (pp. 122–123). But also, the boy's awareness of being a boy and yet wanting to be the mother or be like her prompts considerable gender anxiety and confusion.

Goldsmith holds that a protogay boy's gender negotiation may get played out in caricatured expressions of masculinity or femininity. Some recoil from their femininity as a source of self-hatred, embracing a hyper-phallic masculinity; others fold into a version of gay male femininity driven by a longing for the father's love that remains psychically gripping.

These pioneer theorists of the gay Oedipus were of their time; their gay standpoint made possible a revised Oedipal story that avoided pathologizing protogay boys while exposing the developmental impact of CH. However, their essentialist notions of identity and at times flattened view of the dynamics of identification didn't allow them to deconstruct a cisgendered heteronormativity and imagine a more layered and contradictory gender and sexual field.

The psychodynamics of gay suffering

To reiterate: between the late 1980s and the early years of the present century, a wave of analysts aimed to critique heteronormativity in psychoanalysis; to sketch a distinctive—but "normal"—Oedipal trajectory for protogay boys; to reconsider clinical approaches to a gay clientele; and, finally, to explore the way heteronormativity yielded forms of existential suffering.[1] It is to this last theme that we now turn.

In their phenomenology of protogay development, these analysts assumed two cisgendered straight parents in a more or less traditional family (male breadwinner/female mother). Furthermore, they focused on the experience of boys' homosexuality while avoiding conflating being protogay and a "girlyboy" (Corbett 1996); markedly effeminate boys may or may not be protogay. Their observations were based on adult men born roughly between 1940–1970.

In this historical setting, the protogay child likely experienced only one reality: a cisgendered heterosexuality. This would be felt as the more or less seamless "order of things" (Moss 2012: 75–76). Whether it's kin, peers or popular culture, the reality—communicated in virtually every manifestation of language, imagery, and behavior—was heteronormative. If gay and lesbian figures, actual or representational, were introduced, they would have been mocked and exiled to a space of abjection and utter disgust (Moss 2012: 75).

This hetero-cisgendered culture was baked into the life of the family—in the exclusive presence of gender conforming straight kin, in ordinary family talk and play, and in the *unending idealization of a cisgendered heterosexual order*, for example, in family origin or romance stories. A hetero-cisgendered social reality was the uninterrupted cultural context for the formation of the protogay boy's subjectivity.

In a heteronormatively saturated family culture, trauma is the almost unavoidable accompaniment of being gay. Under conditions of compulsory heterosexuality [CH], protogay boys grow up lacking a consistent validating mirroring or being recognized and lovingly embraced for who they are (Blum et al. 1997, Canarelli et al. 1998, Frommer 1994, Green 2003: 182–183, Molofsky 2013). Such boys struggle to metabolize their intensely-felt but hidden homoerotic longings. "For this child, there is no empathic other who can help him to modulate affect states, process information, and verbally encode . . . [their] . . . particular 'experiences.'

. . ." (Blum and Pfetzing 1998: 434). For example, finding himself repeatedly with other boys and men in varying degrees of undress and bodily contact, the protogay boy experiences, time and again, an erotic "over stimulation . . . [creating a] tantalizing inner world of longing. It is relentless cycles of attraction, hope, excitement and arousal alternating with states of disappointment, loss, despair and grief that give their inner world a unique form and content" (Phillips 2003: 1441). Phillips (2001, 2003) underscores the "too muchness" of a desire that is repeatedly evoked and disavowed. How do these young boys manage a haunting fear of exposure and a pervasive sense of shame and rage—none of which find direct expression or social recognition?

The child not only experiences misattunement, but, worse: he is exposed to parental disapproval and hostility, especially by the father in response to any trace of erotic-affectional longings for his love (Blum and Pfetzing 1998: 431, Corbett 1993: 353, Drescher 1998, Isay 1987). Canarelli et al. (1999) link negative mirroring to narcissistic trauma. "The child's strivings for closeness and acceptance evoke responses in parents. If these reactions . . . are colored by distancing, rejections, devaluation, contempt and anxiety, the child understands that his strivings are bad and that there is something about him that must remain hidden or be changed." In the face of parental misattunement and misrecognition, "growing up gay is a process characterized . . . by isolation, marginalization, and disenfranchizement, as well as perceived and actual threat of annihilation . . . internalizing hostility and loathing. . . ." (p. 55).

The agonies of a protogay boy are intensified by his collusion with his parents. As he senses that "there is something terribly bad and wrong with my desire, perhaps my very being," he must remain unknown to his parents. Indeed, he will not experience the other, any other, as experiencing him as fully known and as loved for all that he is. To protect the parent/child bond, however compromised, he does what he can to ensure that his parents will never know this truth about him. He learns to disguise and dissemble to make sure he will never, ever be fully known. Secretiveness is not, then, an episodic event; rather, it is a regiment of relentless self-vigilance. He must be acutely tuned to other's expectations and potential suspicions. Are certain toys off limits? Do I need to modulate the tonal resonance of my voice or avoid or learn certain gestures? Who can be touched and how? At what point does staring betray an erotic desire? The closet may begin with an initial awareness of varying too far from cisgendered heterosexuality, but unfolds into a compulsory straight masculine performativity.

The protogay boy strikes a pose of insincerity with the very people he loves, who love him, who he is dependent on, whose recognition and support he desperately longs for; these are the very people he wants to be! Knowing that if the most important people in his life fully know you they will withdraw their love and sever the parental bond, triggers a psyche-bending, dislocating experience. Imagine, the burden born by the protogay child—not only unrecognized and unsupported, but his truth and its denial is never to be spoken.

The absence of a validating-and-loving parental mirroring *throughout childhood* upends and disturbs the very "structuralization of the self" (Blum and Pfetzing 1998). Protogay boys cannot escape feelings of otherness, badness and wrongness. "The desires of the [gay] boy can acquire an aura of the forbidden, or of the immoral," Drescher writes (1998: 230). And, in the face of the overwhelming taken-for-grantedness of compulsory heterosexuality, he inevitably internalizes a homophobic and arguably a misogynistic self-denigration (Brady 2011, Isay 1989: 48, Moss 2012, Roughton 2001).

The experience of self-hatred is not easily, if at all, containable. Badness may saturate his entire being as homoerotic desires "include a broader array of affectional wishes, attachments, behaviors that [would] make numerous people in the young boys world uncomfortable" (Blum and Pfetzing 1998: 431). His most intimate desires and feelings may come to feel opaque, object-like, as if an unwanted, alien implant of some bad object (Grand 2016). Worse still, such boys may feel utterly alone as they blame themselves for their badness, as they feel only they can know of this, and, as they are alone in their abject otherness:

> Unlike being black or Jewish, the gay man as [a] child is both typically alone with his "differentness," as well as often unclear, confused, conflicted, horrified by "it." Unlike the black child whose parents are typically also black. . . . the proto-gay child, typically not only does not have gay parents, but doesn't even know what "gay" is except as a very nebulous and negative thing. . . . Even the black child adopted by white parents has the potential empathy and help from his

parents in identifying and valuing his "blackness"; the proto-gay child almost never has this. [His gayness] remains unobvious to the outside world and is then "managed" internally alone with varying degrees of consciousness and unconsciousness.

(Blum and Pfetzing 1998: 431, cf. Ehrensaft 2011)

How does a young boy with limited capacities to process his sexual-gender variance, and virtually no environmental recognition, defend against psychic unraveling and a crushing self hatred? In the face of daunting challenges, many of these boys resort to splitting and dissociation (e.g. Phillips 2003: 1440). "Unable to react emotionally and/or thoughtfully to the trauma," write Blum and Pfetzing (1998),

the individual is forced to keep its presence undigested and though a powerful influence, it's kept . . . out of consciousness. As a result of this inability to react to and truly experience the traumatic event[s], the "experience[s]" then become subject to a "splitting of con-sciousness" or "dissociation. . . ." These traumatic experiences are laid down as unconscious memory traces . . . powerfully influential, reactivated later in life.

(p. 432–433)

Homoerotic desire is split off from the boy's broader psychic economy. For example, intense homophobia may prompt a radical dissociation from his sexuality but at a great cost: self-hatred. Or, compelled to isolate homoerotic longings, his subjective and interpersonal life may be shot through with a series of binaries: the division between a hidden self, felt as core and real, and the visible, cisgendered, heterosexual inauthentic self or between desire and affect or between affective-bodily excitations and longings linked to the homoerotic parts of the self and those associated with non-polluted parts of the self; such splits may be overlaid by a moral divide: the good non-homoerotic self and the bad homoerotic self or the good boy associated with the desexualized, gender conforming self, and the sexual and gender-bent bad boy; these internal divisions may form a global division between a private/public self, the former being the true and real self but hidden, the latter being performative and defensive, pivoting on deception and a false transparency (Drescher 1998: 266, Gonzalez 2013).

Suffering narcissistic injury and haunted by feelings of wrongness and badness, is it any wonder that as adults these gay men encounter troubles in living? Hungry to be known and loved, but on guard against re-traumatization, many gay men are said to externalize and sexualize such longings. As Blum and Pfetzing (1998) see it, this dynamic explains gay men's putative preoccupation with bodily attractiveness. Some fantasize that the attention and admiration they expect to receive from sculpting beautiful, sexy bodies will satiate this hunger. "If the inside can't be changed the outside can. . . . Dwelling on the body surface is an attempt at self-cure and consolidation, as well as an effort to protect oneself from a truly dangerous event" (Canarelli et al. 1998: 55). Unfortunately, this preoccupation reproduces their loneliness and shame. It is one more deception, a sadly devastating one, as being desired for one's body can never fulfill the emotional hunger for self-acceptance and for another's sustaining love.

Sexualizing psychic longings for recognition and love is said to be another defensive strategy typical of many of these gay men. This dynamic has two dimensions. First, instead of engaging other gay men as psychically layered selves, they are viewed and valued through a narrow lens as sexual selves or as composites of eroticized bodies, sexual acts and pleasures, and cultural markers of one's own sexual desirability. Second, sex is reduced to a carnal experience dissociated from emotional vulnerabilities and intimate longings. Reflecting on sex in the Stonewall era, Francisco Gonzalez (2013) remarks: "Because sexuality had been split-off, relegated to an exile status as unaccepted and unacceptable, so-called sexualization had become the matrix of attempted repair." Sexualization inevitably frustrates as it disavows vulnerability, thins out intimacy, and "forecloses interiority" (Gonzalez, 2013).

Sadly, in the view of these analysts, gay men have elaborated a culture that is often impulse-ridden, hyper-sexualized, and threaded by a hypermasculine misogyny that reproduces childhood's saturated with shame and loneliness (Blum et al. 1997, Canarelli et al. 1998). Despite coming out and the illusion of liberation, such "compromise formations" ironically reproduce the closeted state of the protogay boy through psychic splits, dissociations, disavowals, and unexamined shame (Halperin and Traub 2009, Love 2007, Stein 2004).

Queering gay boyhoods in the epoch of the closet

"First-wave" gay standpoint psychoanalytic thinkers were in sync with second-wave gay justice movements. Their chief themes were identity affirmation and consolidation, coming out and community building, forging intimate relationships and social integration. These analysts were pioneering. From revising Oedipus to deconstructing heteronormativity in psychoanalysis, they generated novel standpoints on the ways social oppression informs psychodynamics. Curiously, though, whereas feminist psychoanalytical theories fairly quickly entered into the analytic mainstream, this has been less the case for gay perspectives. No doubt, the reasons for this marginalization are complex; one reason perhaps is that some of its key theoretical assumptions were time-bound and lost credibility as this field underwent fairly rapid change in the 1990s and after. We address three areas deserving further theoretical consideration.

First, the question of identification. Gender identification haunts this literature in a way that sexual object choice does not. The latter was of course highly fraught, as historically the question of "why" had assumed the abnormality of homosexuality. Gay standpoint theorists by-passed the origin debate by stipulating homosexuality as largely a matter of temperament or biology. We have no quarrel with that assumption. Gender identification however was decidedly fraught; in particular, how to make sense of the so-called effeminancy of gay men, at least those who made their way into treatment? Standard heteronormatively informed analytic accounts were variations of the theme of failed Oedipus and the regression to an enmeshed mother/son dyad. Despite critiquing such accounts, gay standpoint analysts continued to lean on maternal identification to explain gay male femininity.

After surveying the available clinical reports and research, Goldsmith (1995) conceded the undeniable association of femininity with gay boys and men (cf. Friedman 1988). Recoiling from their father's rejection, boys embrace, however ambivalently, their mothers and an emphatic feminine identification. But, and here we take issue with Goldsmith, wounded by the father's rejection of his erotic-affectional longings, are there not other parts of the father—and the father-son bond—that a boy may attach to and identify with? Goldsmith doesn't ask: "which father" is desired and which father is disidentified and identified with? Similarly, if a boy is drawn to his mother, which parts of his mother are identified with and which are disavowed? In both cases, as Goldsmith acknowledges, gay son's experience attachment and separation, desire and repudiation, and love and envy. Goldsmith operates with a thin, unidimensional notion of identification and disidentification.

Likewise, Isay (1989) assumes that, in the aftermath of a father's repeated rejections, protogay boys identify with their mothers. To be sure, this identification is ambivalent as she is also a rival for his father's love and therefore an object of jealousy and envy (1989: 29). But, again, which mother does he identify and disidentify with—the receptive and soothing mother or the mother desired and claimed by his father or the desirous and phallic mother? Identifications and disidentifications are not singular, unambiguous events, but multiple and contradictory.

A multidimensional dynamical view of identification would seem to be a condition of rendering sexuality intelligible. So, even assuming that homosexuality is largely dispositional, we still need to account for its specific configuration of desire, fantasy, and relational form. Only some notion of multiple identifications can help us to make sense of the gendered and erotic lives of gay men who, like all men, blend being receptive and penetrative, passive and active, as well as phallic and desirous of intimacy.

Despite challenging heteronormativity, many gay standpoint theorists continued to assume that identification and desire must be on different tracks. Normatively, boys identify with a same-gendered object while desiring an opposite gendered one; in a parallel manner, protogay boys are said to identify with an opposite gendered object while desiring a same gendered object. It's as if "normal" selves can't identify with and desire the same object.

Breaking from this heteronormative logic, Martin Frommer (2000) bridges gay standpoint theorizing with feminist, queer psychoanalytic work. In opposition to "psychoanalytic theories that stress the polarity and independence of identification and desire," Frommer "favor[s] . . . a more varied dynamic [with] anxious tension between [them] . . ." (p. 196). In particular, he takes issue with a viewpoint that collapses the dynamics of sexual object choice into a binary of difference and sameness. In this sexual logic, gay men are said to exhibit a desire driven by likeness or sameness. But this perspective, Frommer reasons, pivots on a reduction of sameness to the genitals of the gendered object (something even more problematic in an era of men without penises and women with penises). Thus, gay men are said to choose a narcissistic object (p. 195).

Against this reductive theorizing, Frommer points out that the sameness of genitals in gay male sexuality may conceal the real turn-on for some men, namely the eroticization of difference. Gay men may sexualize men precisely because of the ways they are different. For example, a slight, heady, smooth-bodied man may be attracted to another man's bigness, thickness, hairiness or mix of muscular bulk with vulnerability and receptiveness. Knowing the genital status of the sexual object tells us precious little of erotic life. In eroticizing his father is the boy sexualizing his father's bigness and invulnerability or is it his sameness as a gentle and tender man? And, in the throes of desire, does he experience himself as a large man like dad or a small boy admiring a big, powerful dad, or perhaps he becomes a seductive, submissive girl?

Frommer's point is straightforward: we know very little about erotic life if we only know the gender of the object (p. 195, Sedgwick 1990). He urges that "we ... conceive of erotic experience as hinging less on the hollow concept of sexual orientation [with its unidimensional axis of sexual identity] and more on a dynamic interplay of contradictory identifications and complementarities" (p. 205).

Second, the question of agency and subjectivity. With parallels to critical race theorizing that exposes systematic racism and its social correlate, the ghetto, and radical feminist theorizing revealing a misogynist, hierarchical gender binary order and its social correlate, a devalued women's sphere, gay liberationists introduced the notion of compulsory heterosexuality and its social correlate, the closet. It was however first-wave gay standpoint analysts who inaugurated an inquiry into the psychodynamics of the closet by posing the question: what is the impact of CH on the formation of the subjectivity of young gay boys? Their homoerotic variance in a heteronormative environment was the socio-psychological context for the formation of gay subjects.

As we've seen, protogay boys were said to suffer the trauma of repeated environmental failure rooted in homophobic-saturated families; as a signifier of gay oppression, agency collapsed into managing a bare psychic existence. Psychically convulsed, and with little capacity for self-consolidation, protogay boys became a shadowy reflection of a virulent homophobic culture; it was all they could do to survive by relying on a false self.

We wonder: in delineating the ways psychic closetedness crushes "the spontaneous gesture" (Winnicott 1965b) and inhibits the elaboration of a "personal idiom" (Bollas 1989), in effect, compelling a life-shaping compromise formation, do these analysts deny these boys capacity to resist and act as subjects? Do they unwittingly invoke a traumatized crumbly self to expose the ruthlessness of CH? Also: Don't protogay boys retain a capacity to withdraw or protect themselves from psychic assault, perhaps taking refuge in an inwardness that might allow some generativity? Don't good enough parents, despite the homophobic injuries they unwittingly inflict, also provide them with emotional and cognitive resources that make possible psychic consolidation and resistance? Don't protogay boys have capacities, including the formation of a developing ethical sensibility, which allow some decisional autonomy? After all, many protogay boys coming of age in the 1960s and 1970s did forge richly layered, often expansive and vital lives, whether gay-identified or not (Nardi et al. 1994, Reinhart 1986, Stein 2000). We need not minimize their suffering to also allow that they were still subjects, often resisting the crushing implications of CH and in the long run forging lives of integrity and purpose.

In this regard, we were taken by a comment of Francisco Gonzales (2013) to the effect that in their secret lives, in the relentless reflexivity that was the fate of so many protogay boys, some found a way of "*coming to be as a cultural subject.*" What was it about closetedness that allowed some to become "cultural subjects," and what kind of subject is that?

Our thesis can be stated simply: a defining condition of psychic closetedness is being an outsider in a compulsory heteronormative world. Inadvertently, this outsider positioning creates a potential space for boys to imagine themselves as unique subjects. Briefly, being inside but existing outside of the family (and normative society), however burdensome, however unbearable, also facilitated in *some boys* a "reflexive inwardness." Living a part of his life as an outsider made possible, perhaps even necessitated, a capacity to dwell inside himself, to consider what was it about his desire and longings that were so fraught and troublesome. This inwardness unfolded, in some boys, into a cultivated capacity towards "interiority" (Slochower 1999). That said, we are all too aware that some boys likely experienced a collapse of this transitional space, a paralysis of mentalization, as their thoughts and feelings were simply too much, too terrifying to hold.

Accompanying inwardness, many protogay boys cultivated a capacity for social reflexivity. Wishing, indeed mostly compelled, to manage their secret lives, such boys developed a keen "hermeneutic capacity;" they learned to read cultural codes that governed sexual and gender intelligibility in order to maintain their status as a good, loved son—and to avoid a shattering psychic experience of unwanted exposure.

Protogay boys didn't just survive; they became agents, however constrained, capable of resistance and of fashioning world affirming self states, even if at times only in their imagination; as such, they became protogay subjects—meaning-making, reflexive, intensely feeling and desiring selves (on children as agents, see Ehrensaft 2007: 280, 2011: 535–536; 2014).

But, what kind of *cultural subject* did they become? To be succinct: subjects who apprehended themselves and others through a "theatrical" lens. How could it be otherwise given lives at the very intersection of a series of dualities—inside/outside, continuity/discontinuity, sincerity/deception, realness/artifice, manifest/latent, and normalization/eccentricity. A theatrical sensibility gravitates toward intensely felt, exaggerated forms of expression, an eccentricity that at times extends into the grotesque, the melodramatic, and the carnivalesque (think drag, camp, balls), and a performativity (role playing, gender fluidity, social constructedness) that opens to reversals, historicity, and parody. In the closet, "I am not who I appear to be nor, likely, are others." A theatrical cultural sensibility doesn't so much dismiss the real or the true as claim that its embrace of performativity and extravagance make possible perspectivist, constructionist, and queer or deconstructive ways of thinking about realness, truth, and beauty. Thus, by embracing the eccentric or grotesque, the very subject position occupied by gay men in CH discourses, such transgression opens to ways of thinking and being that expose the social construction of reality and the contextual legibility of normativities. Is it any wonder that many gay men gravitated to parodic modes of relating to themselves and others?

It will not be lost on the reader that this stipulation of gay subjectivity—theatricality, performativity, emotional intensity, extravagance, parody—falls decidedly on the feminine pole of the gender spectrum. And, how could it not be, given their exile from hegemonic masculinity and an affinity with the "feminine position" as simultaneously a sexual subject and object, an idealized and denigrated figure, an insider and outsider.

Indeed, if we follow the writings of some cultural critics (e.g. Clum 2001, Halperin 2012, Koestenbaum 1993, Miller 1998), many gay boys and men have historically displayed a *cultural affinity* to what at the societal level is marked as "feminine," for example, the Broadway musical, opera and their divas, interior design, and the Hollywood Queens of the studio era such as Crawford, Davis, Dietrich, and Garbo rather than phallic icons like Gable, Bogart, Cagney, Cooper, and Wayne. In their stylistic and gender textured aspects (e.g. the abrupt shifts from speech to singing, the intense emotionality of its stars, especially the women, its over-the-top costumes and exaggerated gestural performances in movie and Broadway musicals and opera), these cultural expressions evidence precisely the kind of phenomenological sensibility that we've characterized as theatrical. The affinity of gay men with these cultural forms is not about wanting to be a woman or acting out a deep-seated identification with their mothers and all things feminine; instead, gay male femininities speak to their unique cultural struggle to find ways to express their own femininity that is neither a desire to be a woman nor a repudiation of being a man (Halperin 2012: 377–382).

Third, the question of the psyche/social divide. Isay (1989), Goldsmith (1995), and Green (1987), among others, underscored the gender variance of many adult gay men in treatment. Boys' marked femininity was considered a key tell anticipating their eventual gayness. As we've seen, gay male femininity was typically collapsed into a boy's maternal identification. However, these analysts did not consider the cultural meanings of gay male femininity, as if it's to be conflated with female femininity. But, as we suggested above, this is far from clear.

There was no serious effort to situate gay male femininities in its historical context. Social expressions of gay male femininity, from the making of a gay icon of Judy Garland to gravitating to feminine-typed jobs in interior design or the cosmetic, beauty, and fashion industries were presumed to be rooted in their deep-seated psychological femininity. Setting aside well-known epistemological objections to conflating psychic and social levels of analysis, gay male femininity was not only a homophobic stereotype that saturated public life in the 1950s and 60s, but it was a chosen identity marker in threads of the urban gay world. As a cultural expression, gay male feminine performativity was a way to be known, a signifier of community belonging, and perhaps a way to stake out a uniquely gay male gendered experience—neither being a woman nor a misogynistic man. Arguably, it was another instance of gay men claiming but queering an abject status (feminine men); as such, it was transformed into a defiant ironic statement of the plasticity of gender and their resistance to gender normativity.

There is a social/psychic conflation, as well, in their accounts of "sexualization." As we've seen, some of these analysts explain gay men's sexual "obsessiveness," their focus on the body, sexual performance, and the uncoupling of sex from emotion and intimacy, as a desperate but futile search for a love denied them growing up. Sexualization is then viewed as a defense, one that reproduces a terrible aloneness and otherness.

This perspective though fails to consider the context-based cultural meanings of sexualization. Many gay writers of the time defended, indeed celebrated, gay male erotic culture for opening spaces of sexual exploration and exuberance and as a unique way of building friendships, romantic intimacies, and forms of community and political resistance (Altman 1982, D'Emilio 1983, Lee 1979, Seidman 1991, Ch. 6, White and Silverman 1977, Wittman 1972).

Consider gay cruising sites such as tearooms (public bathrooms). Tearoom sex would seem to exemplify the point made by some analysts —body centered, act oriented, lacking emotion and intimacy, and, as such, degraded (e.g. Isay 1989: 53). However, culturally speaking, the significance of tearoom sex may not be so straightforward. By rendering these normatively desexualized public spaces into arenas of erotic desire, tearoom sex may have been experienced as acts of queering or resignification. These men arguably contested what heteronormative conventions stipulate as an appropriate sexual space (the bedroom, not a public bathroom); they also challenged the so called higher moral purposefulness of sex, that is, as a mode of family-making or an expression of romantic love and intimate solidarity. In a dramatic way, they were perhaps provocatively declaring that there is no natural or right sexual space, and neither nature nor god dictates what sexuality is and should be. In tearoom sex, gay sexual subjects seem to announce that sex bears many purposes; as individuals, we create our own meanings and spaces as sexual.

Even more outrageous, culturally speaking, they were perhaps claiming that these spaces, ostensibly intended for evacuation, can also be overflowing with desire and bursting with erotic fantasy. It's almost as if gay men as outsiders were going to make one of the "insides" of straight society into a queer space—resignifying the abject as a site to re-imagine "the sexual." By making these desexualized public spaces into fields of erotic play, gay men were making straights uncomfortable, upending their taken-for-granted reality. Their transgressive sex was messing with the private/public, sexual/non-sexual, evacuation/penetration binaries that organize straight life. The transgressive parallel in Stonewall culture is the resignifying of the evacuating parts of the body as sites of desire and pleasure, including penetrating the anus with cocks, tongues, dildos, fingers, and hands, thereby scandalizing straight culture. Our point: social or cultural logics have their own distinctive forms and meanings apart from psychological dynamics. They form an irreducible formative context for the making of gay male subjectivities.

Boys and fathers in the era of the declining significance of the closet

Two social changes have altered the context for understanding gay boyhoods and fathers in contemporary America.

First, a shift from compulsory heterosexuality to a heteronormative order that is sustained less by state and institutional law and policy than by a culture of cisgendered and heterosexual normativity and idealization. This change underpins the emergence of a parallel formation of post-closeted conditions. The latter makes possible new forms of gay publicness and civic integration. No matter how unevenly and incompletely, gays are today part of American society—protected by the state and big institutions. One consequence is the marginalization of the Stonewall narrative of coming out of the closet.

A second key change is the pluralization of families. The traditional two parent, male breadwinner/female mother family in a state-recognized marriage is now a distinct minority. There's been an explosion of "new families" and a growing awareness of this diversity.[2] We can no longer assume the normative nuclear hetero-cisgendered family unit as "the family." Today, it's just one of many, even if it's still promoted, often aggressively, ideologically. In this context, individuals claim a right to fashion their own vision of a family. They can legitimately decide to marry or not, live together or not, be monogamous or not, and have children or not—within or outside of marriage. There is then a growing sense that family and intimate life is a zone of purposefulness, rather than its form and function hardwired into our bodies or psyches or fixed by tradition, or god. Today, it's not only gays and lesbians who have families of choice, but, increasingly, all Americans (Weston 1991).

These two parallel developments are central for grasping shifts in gay boyhood and fathering (cf. Brady 2011, Cohler and Galatzer-Levy 2013). Growing up sexually or gender variant today is in many families a world apart from previous generations. Protogay boys not only have more latitude in defining and embracing this variance, but they can anticipate a more hospitable familial and social environment. In part, this is so because many younger straight parents have normalized being gay. And, more dramatically, gay men can today choose to be parents. Accordingly, in this changing social context, boys have psychic and social space to re-imagine personal life, including the fantasy of one day choosing to establish a gay or queer family. In this concluding section, we consider the impact of this broad social transformation on the psychodynamics of protogay/queer boyhoods and fatherhoods.

Let's be clear. Closetedness remains a position that few, if any, gay boys and men can fully escape. Yet, for a subset of these boys and men, the Stonewall narrative has been marginalized, indeed criticized for leaving in place a cisgendered heteronormativity, or for installing a new disciplinarity around homo-normativity (Duggan 2002).

Boys born roughly from the mid-90s on do not necessarily become aware of their sexual-gender variance earlier than previous generations. However, their experience of this variance is significantly different in several noteworthy ways.

First, they are not likely to feel that this difference marks them as an abject Other. There may be a time of isolation and self-questioning, but this will typically be telescoped compared to previous generations. Today's protogay boys have access to affirmative gay and queer representations through popular culture, the internet, and, in real-time where sexual and gender non-conforming folks are encountered as kin, friends, peers, neighbors, or as activists and public officials. Public life is shot through with normalizing but also defiantly transgressive expressions of gayness and queerness. The result: protogay boys grow up with wide access to a range of identity representations generated by mainstream and countercultural publics.

Second, a subset of protogay boys either do not relate a coming out story or speak of the absence of a protracted, anguished coming out.

Indeed, many declare that there was no closet to come out of; they just knew they were different and felt no need to declare themselves to family or peers. It was something that was just known and acted upon (Murphy 2016, Savin-Williams 2005, 2016). Although their initial awareness of sexual and/or gender difference may be distressing, it does not necessarily trigger trauma or psychic dislocation.

Third, many of these boys do not link their difference with an identity. Although some couple homoerotic desire to a gay identity, many do not; they resist, indeed rejecting such identities as a form of misrecognition and, as such, a source of constraint by stipulating a unitary and fixed status. In place of a rigid gay/straight binary, young boys enter a cultural space marked by the proliferation of identity categories—queer, pansexual, ambisexual, multisexual, polysexual, fluid, or just sexual or asexual. Such labels are understood as temporary markers of where they are at a specific moment, rather than core identities that reveal in some deep-seated, static way who they really are. The marginalizing of identity categories expresses their sense of the situated and shifting character of desire. They claim the freedom to be in the moment, to relate to themselves as an object about which they wish to experiment with varied expressive modes of being and relating (Cohler and Hammack 2007, Hammack et al. 2009, Murphy 2016, Savin-Williams 2005, 2017, Rupp and Taylor 2013).

Fourth, many of these young boys insist that their sexuality cannot be separated from their gender. The Stonewall generation of gay men typically uncoupled sexuality from gender. They centered identity on their sexuality while embracing an almost seamless, at times hyper-phallic masculinity. It was as if they were declaring "we may be gay but we're not fags!" In the post-Stonewall context, many gay or queer men insist on the inseparability of gender and sexuality, and on avowing their femininity (Hennen 2008, Sycamore 2012). Their preferred labels, if pressed, signal a sexual/gender blending and the renegotiating of femininity, e.g. genderqueer, trans*, transgender, polygendered, queerboi, or boidyke.

Post-Stonewall perspectives contest the Stonewall disavowal of gay male femininity. This speaks, in part, to the power of trans* discourses for generations coming of age in the last decade or two (Brubaker 2016, Erickson-Schroth 2014, Halberstam 2017, Kuklin 2014, Stryker 2008). Against the Stonewall sexualization of identity, which left hegemonic masculinity in place, the question of gender, especially male femininity, is now center stage. But also, the engagement with male femininity speaks to an altered parental environment. More men are engaged fathers, and display their own version of male femininity, while many mothers, as fulltime paid workers, present varied versions of female masculinity and femininity. Gender is experienced for many protogay/queer boys as, optimally, a site of choice and variation.

Coming of age today is less about the ordeal of negotiating a stigmatized sexual identity—the closeted position—then navigating sexual/gender variance understood as dynamic and contextually shifting—the post-closeted position. Protogay and queer boys are today struggling with incorporating versions of male femininity as part of a project of designing selves that move in and out of a gendered and sexual world of solid identities as men and women or gay and straight. For this reason, we might more appropriately speak of protoqueer boys or kids alongside protogay boys.

For the generation of protogay boys coming of age in the last decade or two, Stonewall narratives often feel outdated, as they struggle with many of the same issues as their straight peers, for example, negotiating identity and relationships, peer acceptance and social belonging, and anxieties about jobs and the future. Many of these boys blend into mainstream American life. But, some come of age as protoqueer or trans* kids. They relate neither to Stonewall nor assimilationist, post-gay narratives, both of which reproduce a cisgendered heteronormative order. Queer or trans* kids feel like outsiders to both heteronormative and homonormative regulatory orders since their very existence assumes the interpenetration of sexuality and gender and an anti-normalizing personal politics. Growing up protoqueer, boys may feel more of an affinity to trans* kids than to protogay or normatively straight boys.

A reality check: America is still heteronormatively structured. Protogay and protoqueer boys know this. A cisgendered normativity saturates American life. It's the background noise gays and queers hear wherever they find themselves; there is no escaping it, but today the volume is often low, static-like, only to be jolted by an act of violence, a menacing or mocking stare, a ridiculing remark, a thinly disguised homophobic joke. The haunting presence of the closet persists across generations despite the fantasy of living a post-gay life. And yet, it's not trivial that this saturatedness is today interrupted, even absent in large stretches of daily lives. Gays and queers circulate between positions, never fully inside or outside a social regime organized by a cisgendered heteronormativity.

Enter dad! Not the father who came of age against the backdrop of Stonewall, but the dad born in the 1980s and after. Who are these fathers? Granted, there are many different fathers, stamped by the considerations of class, race, religion, sexuality, gender, national origin, disability, and so on. But a few things can be said in order to highlight the changing gender context of fatherhood (cf. Ehrensaft 2007, 2011).

Straight or otherwise, cisgendered or otherwise, fathers today are more engaged as parents than their fathers and grandfathers. Being a good father has become central to men's emotional and ethical sense of identity and integrity. Across class, race, and sexual/gender variance, the research is clear: a good father spends time with his child, connects in playful, loving ways, shapes a child's moral compass, and aims to provide emotional and material familial support (e.g. Deutsch 1999, Doucet 2006, Kaufman 2013, Townsend 2002). That fathers fall short, often far short, should not blind us to their moral commitment and aspirations.

Into this altered matrix step new gay fathers. Born roughly in the late 1970s and 80s, they chose to be fathers outside of heterosexual marriage. Positioned between Stonewall and a third-wave of gay/queer life, these fathers can be roughly mapped in terms of three ideal typical positions: Stonewallers embracing being gay as a social identity; post-gay men who marginalize their gayness as they aspire to a fully normalized status; and queers situated against a cisgendered, hetero-homo-normative order. Notwithstanding these varied social identifications, most new gay dads, like their straight counterparts, at least among the working and middle classes, chose fatherhood after establishing steady jobs or careers, usually in their late twenties and thirties.

Gay men, however, face considerable obstacles—financial, institutional, cultural, and personal—to becoming fathers. From cultural bias to institutional discrimination by adoption and public agencies to costs that can edge into the six figures, and, not least, self-doubts instilled by a homophobic culture that stigmatized gay men as the antithesis of the good parent, their path to fatherhood is difficult and filled with myriad bruises. Such challenges underscore a crucial feature of becoming a gay father: parenthood is chosen by at least the primary parent as if it was fated. Some talk of parenthood as wired into their psyches, as "predestined" or as if born to be a parent, and of equal, if not more importance, than having a partner (Goldberg 2012, Stacey 2011). Only resolute and sufficiently resourced gay men can sustain the bumpy and costly road to becoming parents (Goldberg 2012).

Researchers suggest that there are unique socio-psychological dynamics of gay parenting. For example, gay dads are more process-oriented and egalitarian then their straight counterparts as they negotiate domestic and child-caring tasks. In stark contrast to traditional families, the division of parental practices is based on the earning potential of each parent, job flexibility, emotional capacity and motivation, and parental status as primary or that of a stepfather. In line with post-traditional straight fathers, gay fathers typically mix stereotypical masculine (e.g. rough play, sports, competitive games, disciplining by rewards and punishments) and feminine parenting styles (e.g. soothing, quieting behaviors, tenderness, feeding, cuddling). As one researcher put it: "Gay male and female parents alike nurture, discipline, socialize, subsidize, organize, challenge, confirm, delight, and inspire their children, as well as disappoint . . ." (Stacey 2011: 83). In the context, moreover, of documenting the overall effectiveness of gay parenting (e.g. Golombok 2015: 176–179, 199), researchers have found that children of gay parents will be somewhat more sexually and gender flexible and tolerant (Bilbarz and Stacey 2010, Stacey and Bilbarz 2001).

Two broad conclusions stem from this research. First, based on her own research and a wide ranging review of the literature, Golombok (2015), perhaps the leading researcher in this area, argues that the structure of the family, one or two parents or straight or gay, matters much less than its processual or dynamical aspects, for example, the well-being of the parents, their stress levels, whether or not parental conflicts are violent, histories of depression and substance abuse, the quality of the parent/child relationships, whether parents mix warmth with clear boundaries, or whether there is a good fit between a child's temperament and the parent (pp. 5–30, 202–204). She concludes, "family processes are better predictors of children's psychological adjustment than is family structure" (p. 204). Second, gay and lesbian families, like many post-traditional ones, underscore the telling point that the gendering of parental roles or functions is by and large a matter of social convention, not a genetic or biologically-based capacity. Summing up the research literature, the sociologist Judith Stacey observes that gay parenting suggests "that an individual parent's character, capacities, and foibles count for more than biology or gender conventions do in shaping parenting behaviors. . . . Gay parenting gives the lie to the popular, but misguided, naturalist belief that women and men are inherently different kinds of parents" (2011: 83, cf. Deutsch 1999, Doucet 2006, Target and Fonagy 2002, Golombok 2015).

The melancholy of gay fathers

Shifting to a phenomenological register, we want to press a point often neglected: the importance of gay men's unique history and social status in the making of fatherhood. Specifically, even if gay fathers have come of age in a post-Stonewall context, as young boys they undoubtedly grappled with the psychodynamics associated with the closet. Furthermore, as parents, even if living in a post-closeted urban center, they still encounter misrecognition and a myriad of heterosexist and homophobic micro-aggressions (e.g. Stein 2013: 207). How does their unique social status enter into gay fatherhood, in particular, as fathers of sons—straight, gay, or queer?

Parenting is generational. In becoming a parent, we experience repeated instances of temporal dislocation as we travel fluidly, often in mindboggling ways, through time, as the past, present and future intermingle confusedly. With the arrival of our son, we re-experience something of our own childhood; our own boyhood comes to life through a heightened identification with the child (Beebe and Lachmann 2014, Stern 1985, Winnicott 1965c). And, as we are drawn back in time to our own beginnings, we return to being the child of parents who may or may not still be among us. Of course, we are continuously, often abruptly and with a jolt, thrown back into the present through the immediate, all-consuming needs and desires of our child, and perhaps also of our elderly parents. At the same time, the future creeps in unexpectedly. As parents we may identify with our own parents, but also realize, poignantly, that our parents' long past stretching back generations means a shortened future, a life coming to an end. In a parallel manner, while children evoke a sense of beginning, they also hint at a future in which we will not be fully a part of as this generational chain continues without us. This transgenerational continuity may be exalting, furnishing an enhanced sense of belonging and an illusion of transcendence; but it is also dislocating, throwing us into a heightened awareness of the finite horizon of our and our family's lives. Children insert us in a temporal frame of beginnings but also of endings. Somewhat ironically, in becoming a parent, continuity and belonging flips imperceptibly into a haunting spectre of final things. Melancholy, as much as generativity, forms the unconscious background, the taken-for-granted condition of parental subjectivity.

This dialectic of beginnings and endings, of generativity and loss, is uniquely layered and may form a recurring horizon of daily life for many gay fathers. Unlike his straight counterpart, though, the experience of a new life, that of the son and becoming a parent, are weighted in distinctive ways. Becoming the father of a son may consolidate a conventionalized status as an adult man, but also elicits memories of his own childhood, some of which he may have wished to forget or felt that he had somehow left behind. Inevitably, a new father's memories of his own childhood are stirred up, and, in a manner of speaking, made alive again in the present. The protogay child he was is now back in play; the new gay dad finds himself living side by side with his protogay childhood. Unwanted, perhaps dissociated childhood experiences may flood him such as not having had the parents he wished for, not being the son they wanted and that he wished he was, not being known and loved for all of who he was, and not being able to express, not even at times feel, his confusion, shame, and fury towards parents who could not love him if they were truly to know him. Alongside joyful and ecstatic moments, the birth of parenthood may then trigger the too-muchness of a childhood gripped by absence, insufficiency, abjectness, and loss; this too may be part of becoming a new gay father.

In a further cruel twist of fate, the new father knows, even if it's not thought, that his ambiguous status will be borne by his son. If a protostraight son: will he not wonder, perhaps wish, as his father did as a protogay boy, that he had different parents, in this case straight one's? Will the son resent his gay father(s), as perhaps they did their parents, for having to carry the burden of their otherness? And, will the son, much like his parents, have to bear this difference in silence or, if his distress is expressed, be burdened, much as his parents were, with a gnawing sense of guilt for the hatred of the very parents that provide life and love? If it be a gay son: will this young boy raised in a heteronormative world resent his parents for being viewed as different and lesser? Will he resent and at times loathe his parents and himself for the burden of forever carrying the scar of otherness, indeed a double scar—his own and that of his parents? Will he not feel, as perhaps his parents did as protogay boys, the need or the expectation to be perfect in order to redeem himself but also his parents? This tangled web of contradictory, ambivalent, anguished feelings is also what is brought into life as the son of gay fathers.

If the birth of a child makes it possible for straight parents to entertain a fantasy of transcending the past or self-reinvention, this is decidedly more difficult for gay parents. There is no clean slate, no wholly new beginning for the latter. In negotiating with hetero-centric medical personnel and agencies during conception and the birth process, gay parents cannot avoid being thrown back into a familiar unwanted experience of lack and otherness. In the very moment of becoming a parent, the gay parent feels the jolt of discontinuity and is drawn into a space of otherness and a drama of inside/outside—once again haunted by the spectre of the closet.

But also, the new son, as the gay father knows, is not and will never be unburdened by his parents' otherness. There can be no fantasy of birth as a tabula rasa; no uninterrupted ecstatic beginning. The parent knows that his experience of discontinuity and inside/outside will inevitably be the fate of the son. As a child of gay parents in a heteronormative culture, he will know that his family lacks a "social mother" and that this difference is culturally marked as unwanted and undesirable. Noah Glassman (2014) evokes the melancholy that accompanies gay parenthood:

> Before becoming a father . . . my initial focus had been on our child-yet-to-be, his potential losses in not being raised by heterosexual birth parents—especially a birth mother, in a culture that so often constructs narratives of a mother's fundamental, innate capacity to soothe, nurture a baby and young child. . . . I [also] wondered about our son's birth family, their loss of him, and how this [loss] would be woven into his and our relationship with them over time.
>
> (p. 164)

The child, and the parent, forever knows and lives with the cultural insufficiency and apartness of gay parentage. This young boy, and the parent too, cannot not know this exiling from the taken-for-granted, from the continuous flow of the inside; he will eventually have to think and speak, time and again, that his family is a constructed, non-normative one, morally and socially suspect by some and that this one fact will be with him—and with his parents—always. Discontinuity, apartness, and loss circulate endlessly, imperceptibly, between child and parent; every jolt of apartness by the child is a wound felt by the parent. Such dislocations fill daily life in each hour of each day of each year, without end; the child, straight, gay, or otherwise, is reminded by friends, teachers, doctors, TV, and the internet that his family is not *the* family, that he is forever outside of the norm, always part of/a part from; this is a new beginning but also already a lack, a loss, an anticipation of an ending, at least of innocence or the illusion of continuity and belonging. Melancholy wraps itself around the inner core of the gay family.

Even if post-closetedness is an available position, there is no beyond the closet that's once and for all, no living without the grip of anxieties of difference and an inchoate sense of absence and loss. No matter how out, prideful, and normalized a life lived in a heteronormative order, no matter how much one is post-identity, queer or inhabits a homonormative enclave, there is no escaping feelings of suspect difference, absence, perhaps shame, and a longing for something hard to name (Halperin and Traub 2008, Love 2007). Still, this longing for a seamless continuity and belonging, for an unmarked personal and familial status, persists. Poignantly, Steven Botticelli (husband of Noah Glassman) speaks of the power of a culture of redemption, of the quest for a fully realized, transparent presence that grips so many gay men, as it did him. Knowing the suffering of growing up a protogay boy, he feels, as a parent, the pounding desire to leave behind the past as it's saturated with abjectness and so much unprocessed guilt, grief, and rage. As a father, Steven gravitated to a redemptive fantasy:

> Parenthood provides a perfect vehicle for such redemptive wishes, as it may foster the fantasy of getting to be the perfect, omnipotent parent . . . who, in tending one's child, attempts to repair the damage done to one's childhood self through the deficiencies of one's own parents. . . .
>
> (2014: 170)

This fantasy of becoming the "perfect parent," repairing oneself by protecting one's child from the life-altering injuries of the closet, is too easily punctured. Sharing an afternoon with his son in a playground, he can't but wonder whether other parents would worry if they knew he was gay. "Fatherhood it turns out provides no rescue or respite from such introjections, indeed just calls my attention to the presence of something I didn't know was there" (p. 170).

No doubt, all parents harbor a redemptive hope that their child will not experience their specific agonies or will at least avoid the wounds and burdens that were part of their own growing up. For a gay parent this redemptive hope is twofold: to protect one's son from the psychic and social ravages of homophobia and to reimagine one's own suffering childhood as if one had parents like oneself, parents who would have suspended the closet at least in the protected space of the family while preparing a path to a fully available life. Perhaps it's the drive to normalize or to be included in the stream of continuity and belonging as a valued part of the generational chain (Bataille 1986, Bersani 1986). It is, though, an unsustainable illusion. Children, like their gay parents, will experience a difference that marks them as not fully belonging, as bearing a sense of lack and loss. There is no stepping outside of being an outlier, no forgetting you are a child of parents who are never just taken-for-granted; you, and your parents, can never not know that you will occupy a psychic space of regret and a longing whose very desire elicits this disillusioning sense of absence and otherness.

Afterword: Oedipus in gay families

As part of the shift in gay life from the shadows to public recognition, gay-standpoint analysts contested the heteronormativity of psychoanalytic theory. At the center of this challenge was the reexamination of Oedipus.

These analysts sketched a gay Oedipal path, at once "normal" and tragic. They asked: how to narrate Oedipus from the standpoint of a protogay boy living in a heteronormative social order?

This query presupposed, reasonable enough at the time, heterosexual parents. But, in light of the appearance of new gay families, analysts have begun to rethink Oedipus. How do families with two same-gendered parents—setting aside gay families with multiple parental figures (sperm carrying mothers, egg carrying mothers, sperm donor fathers, potential partners of each of these quasi-parental figures)—alter the logic of Oedipal negotiation? To date, there is scarce clinical material available, but some analysts have offered conjectures.

In a Winnicottian inspired reflection, Barbara Waterman (2003) draws on his gendered notion of being (as female) and doing (as male), so richly used by Chodorow (1978) and others, in delineating a conventional heteronormative gender dichotomous developmental model. Citing broad changes that have brought women into the workplace and men into a deeper engagement in the family, Waterman notes that the parental modalities of being and doing are increasingly de-gendered:

> Over the past few decades with many fathers. . . . attaching to their infants and becoming involved from birth in helping the baby grow into the child the couple envisions . . . *being* and *doing* have become less gendered, each mother or father falls on a continuum relative to these two orthogonal dimensions of parenting.
>
> (p. 60)

In particular, gay fathers have entered into "the motherhood constellation;" they facilitate a maturational process through engaging in "primary maternal preoccupation," fostering an environment that makes possible a secure attachment and providing self-structuring through attuned mirroring and effective modes of containment (p. 62).

Waterman's view that "gay families . . . are a fertile ground for the creation of new parental roles no longer predetermined by gender or by biology" remains within the framework of legitimating gay parenting (p. 73). While similarly endorsing the de-gendering of parental functions, Geva Shenkman (2016) rethinks the meaning of Oedipus in a gay family. The Oedipal drama is said to pivot around

> the taboo against incestuous relations with a parent, irrespective of gender, which inhibits libidinal satisfaction. From this perspective, any parental authority may represent the taboo that gives rise to the complex. Consequently, psychoanalysis would not concentrate solely on the mother or father figure, but . . . the nature of the relationships among the three members of the triad. . . . In other words, in the case of a gay couple, one of the fathers might represent the prohibition that arouses the complex [or] . . . one side of the parent might be identified with the taboo whereas another side remains in the classic role of object.
>
> (pp. 588–589)

From this perspective, Oedipus is a process of individuation inaugurated by a prohibitionist injunction. The gendered status of the parents and children move into the background as the focus is the dynamic of sexual exclusion in a triadic configuration.

In a parallel manner, Toni Vaughn Heineman (2004) views Oedipus as inaugurated in the developmental shift from the dyad to the triad, regardless of the gendered status of the parent[s]. "Triangulation is the pivotal developmental phase of psychoanalytic theory" (p. 103). For Heineman, however, Oedipus is imagined as a potential space in which a child, in experiencing the parental couple as an independent adult world, struggles with the tensions of being inside and outside or belonging and exclusion:

> His parents inhabit the world of adult, genital sexuality—a world that is closed to him. . . . Along with this blow to his self-esteem, he must also come to terms with the immutability of generations—he will always be a child in relation to his parents.
>
> (p. 104)

If the triad can avoid collapsing the tensions in the Oedipal space, thereby retreating into separate dyadic units sustained by a closed projection/introjection dynamic, exclusion from the adult world makes possible the discovery of a world composed of singular sexual and social selves, identical but also different from each other. Oedipus may open to "a capacity for reflection—about the world around him and the world inside him" (p. 104). In short, it is the pathway to an internally and interpersonally differentiated world of subjects and intersubjectivity.

Each of these analysts are at pains to make plausible the claim that the gender of the parent[s] matters less in the Oedipal drama than the breakup of the dyad and the shift to a dynamic, tension-sustaining triad in which a child experiences exclusion but also individuation (mentalization, separation, intersubjectivity). Moreover, triads, they contend, do not require an actual third since children engage different parts of a parent or identify with non-parental adults, real, virtual, or phantastic, that function as a third (Heineman p. 106).

We wonder though: is this claim of de-gendering too quick, too unequivocal? It's one thing to argue that "good enough" parenting practices are not gender exclusive or are available to parents of varied genders, but another to assume that, in practice, parenting isn't gendered and isn't experienced by a child as gendered in cisgendered and heteronormatively coded ways. The subjectivity of gay fathers, like straight one's, is no less formed under conditions of heteronormativity, and their fathering practices still occur in a culture that is homophobically saturated. How does this implicit, procedural heteronormativity (Stern et al. 1998) enter into the dynamics of gay—or lesbian/trans*—parenting and into the child's experience of parenting?

Similarly, in the desire to legitimate gay—or queer, lesbian, trans*— parenting, to shift the focus from the sexual or gender status of the parent to the structural, processual aspects of parenting, we wonder whether this doesn't resurrect abstractions such as "parent" and "child." Aren't parents, as feminist analysts early on insisted, always situated or positioned in multiple ways as gendered, sexualized, raced, classed, and so on? In this regard, it's perhaps not enough to speak of gay fathers or gay sons, but to concretize or individualize these terms. Is the parent and child gay in the sense of post-gay or hyphenated gay or queer? These specificities surely matter in the treatment room; but shouldn't they also figure in the ways we rethink Oedipus and beyond?

Notes

1 Needless to say, this work has been paralleled by equally far-reaching psychoanalytic revisionism by lesbian-identified or affirmative analysts such as O'Connor and Ryan (1993), Domenici and Lesser (1995), Schwartz (1997), and Magee and Miller (1998).

2 Signs of change are dramatic. Consider:

* Marriage is still overwhelmingly preferred by Americans, but it is now considered a personal choice. In 1960, high marriage rates were the rule across racial and class divisions. For example, 61 percent of black Americans and roughly 70 percent of Americans without a college education were married. By 2008, the percentage of adults who were married dropped from 76 percent (in 1960) to 52 percent. And, class, race, and age differences stand out today. In 1960, there was little difference in marriage rates between those that graduated college and those that didn't (76 percent vs. 72 percent). In 2008, the figure dropped to 64 percent for college graduates compared to 48 percent for those with a high school degree or less. Among black Americans, 32 percent were married in 2008 compared to 56 percent of whites. The drop in marriage rates is equally startling among young adults. In 1960, 68 percent of all 20 year olds were married; today its just 20 percent (Pew Research Center 2010). And, while young unmarried Americans report a likelihood of eventually marrying (but just 53 percent), researchers note, "more than four-in-ten (44 percent) millennials say that the institution of marriage is becoming obsolete. . . ." (Wang and Taylor 2014). In 2012, one in five adults 25 and older, some *42 million Americans, have never been married.*

* Cohabitation has become a path to marriage and a legitimate alternative. Roughly 25 percent of never-married Americans ages 25–34 live with a partner. For a significant number of young Americans, cohabitation is preferred. A Pew Research Center report "finds that after one year, about three-in-ten young adults get married, 9 percent break up the relationship and 62 percent continue cohabiting. By *the third year*, nearly six-in-ten (58 percent) married, 19 percent broke up *and 23 percent remained in the relationship* (Parker and Wang 2013). And, as many researchers have documented, it is the least educated who are not marrying (Cherlin 2009, Copen et al. 2012).

* The rise of singledom. In *Going Solo*, Eric Klinenberg (2012) reports that 22 percent of American adults were single in 1950, accounting for 9 percent of households. "Today, more than 50 percent of American adults are single; some 31 million adults—live alone. . . . *People who live alone make up 28 percent of all U.S. households, which means that they are now tied with childless couples as the most prominent residential type—more common than the nuclear family. . . .*" (our emphasis, Klinenberg 2012: 4–5). Moreover, singledom stretches across all age groups—"the majority, more than 15 million, are middle-age. . . . The elderly account for about 10 million . . . [while] young adults between eighteen and thirty-four number more than 5 million, compared to 500,000 in 1950, making them the fastest-growing segment of the solo-dwelling population" (p. 5).

* The uncoupling of parenthood and marriage. In 1960, some 5 percent of children were born to unmarried women. In 2008, the number has climbed to 41 percent (Pew Research Center 2010). Among single parent families, the fastest growing segment is *never-married women*. In 1960 they numbered just 4 percent; in 2011, they make up 44 percent of single mothers. These mothers have been, and still are, disproportionately young, black or Hispanic, lack a college degree, and are more likely to be poor compared to previously married single mothers, who tend to be white and college educated (Pew Research Center July 29 2013). For example, in 2008, 52 percent of black children were born to unmarried mothers compared to 27 percent of Hispanic and 18 percent of non-Hispanic white children (Pew Research Center Oct. 18, 2010). Unmarried, however, does not necessarily mean being single. Up to one quarter of poor single mothers were living with the biological father at the time of birth. And, as of 2010, some 60 percent of births to unmarried mothers were occurring within cohabiting relationships, compared to about 41 percent in just 2002 (Curtin et al. 2014). However, since 2008, researchers have documented a significant decline, some 14 percent, of children born to unmarried mothers, in particular among young women of color (Miller 2015). Simultaneously, out-of-wedlock births among mostly white, educated women between 35–39, have increased 48 percent between 2002–2012 (Curtin et al. 2014).

* The new salience of multigenerational families. *Some 25 percent of Americans live in multigenerational households—more than those who live in nuclear families* (Pew Research Center Nov. 12, 2014). In 2012, some 57 million Americans, almost 20 percent of the population, were

living in multigenerational families (Frey and Passel 2014), double the number who lived in such families in 1980. Historically, aging kin accounted for a considerable number of these families. Today, about a quarter of all adults between 25–34 live in such households, compared to 11 percent in 1980. This trend is occurring across racial and ethnic lines. Roughly 14 percent of non-Hispanic whites, 27 percent of Asian Americans, and 25 percent of blacks and Hispanics live in multi-generational households (Frey and Passel 2014).

* Non-normative families: blended, interracial, lesbian/gay/trans, non-residential, and polyamorous. Consider blended families. In 2013, some 40 percent of new marriages in the United States included at least one partner who was previously married. Forty two million Americans have been married more than once, up from 22 million in 1980. Some 8 percent of newly married Americans have tied the knot for the third time. And, some 20 percent of children in America reside in blended households. They grow up then with at least one stepparent and at least two kin networks.

Blended families are one sign of a broader transformation: the trinity—marriage, lifetime commitment, and monogamy, so tightly bound for generations, has been split apart. Today, each of these core components of marriage can be individually evaluated (do I want to marry? stay in a relationship? be monogamous?). Marriage no longer carries the social and moral force of being compulsory or the only legitimate intimate arrangement. Similarly, while most Americans seem to aspire to a lifetime intimate relationship, the reality is closer to "serial monogamy." Simply put, Americans move in and out of committed relationships with greater ease—whether married or not, short-term or long-term, with or without children, straight, gay, or otherwise, and whether co-residing or not.

In short, *diverse, changing, and inventive family experiences are the new normal.* For better or worse, family and intimacy, has become a site of personal and social experimentation (Frank et al. 2013, Golombok 2015, Rosenfeld 2007). As many of us move in and out of intimate and familial relationships, we experience different kin, circulate in and out of being parents, and add or lose spouses, partners, lovers, children, and friends. For children, this new reality presents a historically unique familial dynamic: growing up in a changing family environment. Today, it is no longer just immigrant or low-income children or children of divorced families, but children across virtually all social categories that experience living in multiple families, changing parental or quasi-parental figures, adding and losing siblings, cousins, grandparents, and other emotionally significant adults.

Chapter 4

Authenticity

Men's struggle to live an ethical life

"I may omit some facts ... or make errors in dates, but I cannot be deceived about what I have felt. .... The real aim of my *Confessions* is to make known precisely my inner state, in all the situations of my life. It is the history of my soul that I have promised to give. ...."

(cited in Williams 1985: 174)

Writing in the 1760s, Rousseau aimed to carve out a sphere of "inwardness" that would be the object of an exhaustive ethical struggle to know and be oneself (Trilling 1972: 24–25). Some two plus centuries later, listen to the TV self-help evangelist Dr. Phil:

The authentic self is the you that can be found at your absolute core. It is the part of you that is not defined by your job ... or your role. It is the composite of all your unique gifts, skills, abilities, interests, talents, insights, and wisdom. It is all your strengths and values that are uniquely yours and need expression, versus what you have been programmed to believe that you are supposed to be and do.

(McGraw 2001: 6–7)

It is for good reason that many scholars consider Rousseau's *Confessions* an inaugural text in the making of a modern culture of authenticity (Guignon 2004, Starobonski 1988, Taylor 1992, Trilling 1972, Williams 1985). For Rousseau, to know and be your true self was a necessary condition of being known by others. Yet, despite monumental efforts, Rousseau felt grossly misunderstood and in ways that upended his daily life. Rousseau struggled with what Lionel Trilling (1972) called the problem of "sincerity." How can we forge sustaining bonds between citizens if we cannot trust that the other's actions faithfully express their stated intentions? Or, how do we conduct ourselves with good will if we cannot assume that the other is who they claim to be and they mean what they say?

Rousseau undertook an experiment. He would lay bare his soul as honestly and frankly as he could. He would be relentless in excavating layers of feelings and desires that were at the core of his existence but resisted discovery and clarity. He'd be ruthless in bringing to light the good, bad, and ugly parts of himself, so that there could be few doubts about who he really is. His very soul unearthed and honestly presented, others would surely know him; bonds of trust and civility would be restored.

Sadly for Jean-Jacque, he was mistaken. His relentless efforts at self-revelation, from his *Confessions* (1782b) to *Reveries of a Solitary Life* (1782a), proved futile, indeed generated scandalous forms of misrecognition. Modern social life, he concluded, inevitably corrupts and subverts the desire for transparent communication and civic uplift. In particular, sincerity is undermined by a society that fetishizes social distinctions and by a commercial culture organized around the artifice of decorum, social roles, and civic politeness.

Despite his bleak outlook, Rousseau anticipated another cultural project that would become the cornerstone of romanticism and modern Euro-American culture: the quest for authenticity. Guided by a relentless honesty and a desire to know and be oneself became for Rousseau and, especially for German and English romantics, and eventually for many people across Euro-American cultures, the highest calling of humankind. The project of authenticity was imagined as deeply personal and intimate, even if it ultimately required recognition by others; but also, this ideal preserved a thread that connected it to Christian and secular traditions that imbued the immanent with transcendent significance. To discover and become one's true self was to find a link to a wider cosmos. For Rousseau, it was the idea of nature that furnished a sense of metaphysical order and moral coherence; for romantics and idealists it was a notion of God or some cosmically ordering spiritual principle or a theistic notion that flattened but also ennobled life by its exquisite design.

For many Americans in the 21st century, a transcendent arc framing the project of authenticity has been abandoned or receded into the background. Better yet, whatever metaphysical meaning authenticity has is today a matter of personal conviction. The heart and soul of the American culture of authenticity is personal, the here and now; meaning is immanent. Authenticity is an individual chosen path aimed at discovering and becoming the unique person that you are. This concept stipulates that each of us has a specific way of being, which speaks to our unique vital impulses, core disposition or temperament, and capacities. It is not that we are each absolutely distinctive in every way; rather, each of us is an irreducibly singular expression of humankind. Knowing, cultivating, and expressing our unique humanity is what it means to be authentic. It is an ultimate or transcendent value for those in this cultural universe. Contrary to Rousseau and European romantics, as we read key strands of American culture, the quest to be authentic does not necessarily put us in opposition to society. We are social in inextricable and generative ways; our own unique genius may be innate but it is elaborated in the context of our embeddedness in social worlds; and, it is only with others that we can fully express who we are and become the person we are meant to be. And yet, the social world also threatens to seduce or colonize our personal lives for social ends, rendering our lives false and inauthentic (Guignon 2004).[1]

Authenticity carries an ethical imperative: to be true to oneself, to live a life that expresses who you are (Taylor 1992: 15–16). To live authentically is to be in a state of perpetual ethical struggle. The seemingly quotidian aspects of life, the innumerable feelings, wants, desires, and thoughts we daily experience are occasions to struggle with being one's true self; there can be no let up, no stepping outside of an ethically infused life. Like our Protestant founders, for whom daily life was replete with signs of one's cosmic fate (e.g. signs of a predetermined fate for Calvinists), the quest for authenticity renders the ordinary transcendent.

Authenticity is not a matter of knowing, validating, cultivating, and expressing every feeling, wish, want, fantasy, or desire. Not everything that occurs in our interior lives is vital and integral to who we are. We are compelled to sort through our psychic life to figure out what is real and true. Authenticity burdens us with an imperative: to sustain a focus on internal life in order to differentiate the vital and generative from the superfluous and the burdensome, the true from the false. This heightened inwardness is never ending; we relentlessly battle with self-doubt; we exhaustively examine our inner lives and choices to ensure we're on the right path. Authenticity imposes a disciplinary norm to cultivate a practice of inward reflexivity; as an ongoing self-practice it is ironically, given its egoistic and self-indulgent public rendering, a form of ethical mindedness and purposefulness that works its magic through disciplining body and soul (Taylor 1992, Trilling 1972).

Ethical struggle extends to our interpersonal life (Safran 2016). Social worlds make demands, impose expectations, and tempt seduction and a loss of self-possession. Conformity rewards with status and myriad pleasures and perks. As we participate in social institutions, from marriage to family, work, school, and church, we inevitably step into well-defined roles; we surrender to normalizing norms and beliefs that define and regulate our public selves. A challenge is issued: am I being myself or the self expected by others? Have I chosen a form of existence to express who I am or to reap advantage? Have I unconsciously bent to social expectations and normalizing regulations? In short, as an ethic commanding one to be true to oneself, the imperative to be authentic creates a life that has its own kind of integrity and moral purpose that rubs up against social artifice.

The point we wish to insist upon is this: authenticity is not about doing your own thing or being okay with yourself or letting it all hang out. Rather, authenticity is an ethic—a moral ideal, demanding and disciplining: to live as a true self, each day, alone and with others. It is an ideal that inspires and generates forms of life; it compels one to struggle with the mundane as a site of moral significance; it infuses moral meaning into daily life. Far from endorsing a "do as you please lifestyle," authenticity enjoins a disciplining, at times exacting but also transformative ethical life. It's relentless ethical-mindedness recalls the great religious cultures, except its theodicy is immanent. At its center is the imperative to be true to oneself and to choose to live a life of integrity a principled life accountable to oneself and others (Sartre 1984).

The neglected ethical life of men

The feminist sociologist, Francesca Cancian (1980), argued that American ideas of romantic love have been feminized. From the 19th century on, the key features of the arguably dominant American construct of love pivoted around such stereotypically feminine notions as emotional communication, other-directedness, and an ethic of care, sacrifice, and devotion. This construct may have given women an arena of authority in patriarchal America, but it also made them responsible for love and reinforced stereotypes of women as spiritual and moral and men as instinct-driven and egoistic. In this cultural universe, love and intimacy became the proving ground of true womanhood, often foreclosing wider aspirations for a public life; for men, it was a potential threat to masculine authority and a site of anxiety.

In a parallel way, to the extent that the ethical sphere has been culturally associated with empathy and care of the other, it too has been feminized. Ethical mindedness becomes a "woman's sphere," creating a space of potential empowerment but further narrowing women's legitimate participation in a public world stereotypically imagined as driven by self-interest and power. As public figures, men would then be represented as either amoral or ethical in a very narrow way, for example, defending individual autonomy and rights. In this cultural universe, men's quest for authenticity is understood in a decidedly thin moral vernacular, as centered on a personal striving for self-and-world mastery and individual accomplishment, which also ground their claims to moral and social authority.

Historically, there's been a reluctance to see American men as fully ethical figures. As part of the Victorian legacy (Barker-Benfield 1976, Bloch 1978, Cott 1977, 1978, Degler 1981, Kerber 1988, Smith-Rosenberg 1986), narrowly phallic tropes portray men or "real" men as driven by sexual and aggressive instincts aimed at self-aggrandizement (Barker-Benfield 1976). Their lives are said to be centered in the public world of rivalry and hierarchy where rightness collapses into power. Men are to nature as women are to culture, as second-wave feminists argued (Lamphere and Rosaldo 1974, Nicholson 1986). And, if nature is an arena of competition and dominance, men would not then be imagined as ethical selves at their core.

Shifting to a psychoanalytic register, if we read Freud from a masculinist perspective, the id is the generative life force. It is an instinctual drive for pleasure, indifferent to its object apart from discharge, and constrained only by libidinal capacity and social artifice. While the id is universal, for men it is aggressive and outward oriented whereas for women it's a zone of receptivity and incorporation. Left to its own accord, the male id dominates and destroys, leaving a trail of blood and disorder. Under patriarchal law and the moral sway of women, men are regulated. Civilization is then built on the male id's sublimation and on feminine domestication.

Post-Freudian thinkers have challenged the nature/society binary. The self is said to be thoroughly social in two senses. First, the self is object driven or aims to attach and connect to others. Second, we internalize significant others who become part of who we are. Still, even in this socially oriented psychoanalytic view, a gender binary associating men with narcissism and "doing" and women with other-directedness and "being" has been normalized (e.g. Winnicott 1989).

In the 1970s and 1980s, the work of second-wave feminist psychoanalysts such as Chodorow (1978) and Dinnerstein (1976) sought to account for the persistence of a male dominated binary gender order. At its root, they argued, was the ongoing reality of women as the primary parent. Because women mother while father's retreat into the shadows of the family, girls sustain their gender identification with their mothers, including their feminine relational orientation; and, in a heteronormative context, their sexual desire shifts to men. Hence, women become ethical hetero-relational selves. By contrast, men establish their masculinity by dis-identifying with their mother's femininity while identifying with the self-centered, achievement oriented, competitive public self of the father. Men sustain their attachment to women but as sexual objects and indeed, their sexuality—erasing any traces of femininity—is performance-and-pleasure oriented. This doesn't mean men are without an ethical sensibility. As Gilligan (1982) argues, drawing heavily on difference-based feminism, men's ethical sense pivots around autonomy, for example, a morality of individual rights, which complements a masculine culture of self control and world mastery; by contrast, women enact an ethic of care—empathic and other-oriented.

By the 1980s, a difference-based feminism found widespread support among second-wave feminists. In particular, in debates over pornography, S/M, and sexual violence, prominent radical feminists such as Kathleen Barry (1984), Susan Brownmiller (1975), Andrea Dworkin (1976, 1981), Susan Griffin (1978), and Adrienne Rich (1977, 1980), framed men as driven by a desire to dominate and control women, to objectify and demean them (Echols 1990, Rubin 1984, Seidman 1992, Vance 1984). Being a man meant subjugating women, thereby neutralizing the threat of feminization. For many of these feminists there was a direct line from a masculinist culture of misogyny to everyday violence against women. Misogyny was built into the masculine phallus. In a context of heightened division and acrimony in the women's movement, a gynocentric feminism that drew rigid boundaries between the two genders, rendering men's phallus as the source of women's oppression, offered a rally point for women's solidarity and political mobilization.

Since the 1990s, many feminists have challenged this binary thinking. In particular, poststructurally informed theorists (Butler 1990, Fuss 1989, Sedgwick 1990, and Spelman 1988), and intersectionalists such as Bell Hooks (1991), Patricia Hill-Collins (1990), Audre Lorde (1984), Cherrie Moraga (1983), and Gloria Anzuldua (1987) offered complex, layered constructions of gender. A third-wave was launched that deconstructed identity and imagined gender beyond the binary; gender multiplicity was stipulated as a new ground on which to critique heteronormativity and gender binarism, including a gynocentric feminism. In psychoanalysis, this third-wave of feminist queer theorizing found expression in the work of, among others, Aron (1995), Benjamin (1995), Dimen (1991), Harris (1991), Goldner (1991), Layton (1998) and a revisionist psychoanalytic theorizing of masculinity (Corbett 2009, Diamond 2009, 2017, Fogel 2009, Moss 2012, and Schiller 2010b). Gender was constructed as a site of plasticity, heterogeneity, and agency.

Yet, difference-based feminism, with its harsh and sometimes reductionist critique of men and masculinist culture, hardly disappeared. In the past few years a popular feminism has found a public voice. In response to a heightened public awareness of workplace harassment, child abuse, domestic violence, and campus rape, men have often been narrowly portrayed as predators—violent, narcissistic, and misogynistic (e.g. Hernandez and Rehman 2010, West 2017, Wurtzel 1999, Valenti 2016). For example, in her bestseller, *Sexual Object* (2016), Jessica Valenti conflates growing up as a girl with "getting molested by a family friend, . . . [having] rape and abuse passed down. . . . abusive boyfriends . . . strangers fondling me on subways . . . the neighbor pervert who masturbated visibly in his window" (p. 10–11). As girls become women they can anticipate "living in a culture that hates them" (p. 15). Violence is said to be at the heart of American masculinist culture. "Men get to rape and kill women and still come home to a dinner cooked by me" (p. 15). Indeed, "violence against women is at epidemic levels in the U.S. Sexual assault, intimate partner violence, harassment and stalking are part of many women's daily lives. Violence against women is so common that it's become a normal part of our living and it's being committed by 'normal people' (i.e. regular guys)" (p. 64). Valenti's explanation of men's violence: boys are raised "to be tough, to quash their feelings, and even to be violent" (p. 190). As for heterosexual intimate life, woman can expect more of the same. The author of *Bitch* (Wurtzel 1999), states:

"I live ... in a world of exhausted tired single mothers at the mercy of men who overworked them and underpaid them, men who forgot to send child-support checks, men who forgot they had children ..." (p. 44). And, in case your male partner doesn't work you to death, abandon you or neglect child support, his love will take away your dignity and worse. "For a man to claim ownership of you, for him to really assure you that he wants you for his possession, he must mark you, bruise you ... and imprint you, brand you ... with his violence" (p. 330). Men once again are represented as the amoral counterpart to the ethical woman.

Partly in reaction to feminist critiques but also incorporating parts of this critique, a men's movement and a new sociology of masculinity and men has offered more nuanced accounts (e.g. Messner et al. 2016). Its cultural voice though has been far overshadowed by big corporations and a leisure and entertainment industry that is still dominated by phallic masculinist imagery and norms. As we see it, then, a current of popular feminism has aligned with powerful institutions and popular culture to perpetuate the iconography of the phallic man and the continued feminization of ethics. But, do men's actual lives resonant with such representations? Or, has the feminization of ethical life contributed to the cultural misrecognition of men's experience?

Juan and Joseph

Juan was troubled by feelings of loneliness and anxiety about his future. This Puerto Rican man was born and still lived with his disabled mother in a poor neighborhood in the Bronx. Growing up, he rarely saw his dad, as he left the family when he was three. His few relatives were scattered across the city or lived out of the state. He rarely talked or saw them. He had few friends growing up. During our sessions, I could feel the weight of his aloneness. Even his words, spoken in a monotone with little affect and a still, unexpressive body, felt burdened by his loneliness. His deadening stillness echoed in me. He rarely looked at me; never expressed neediness though I felt a hunger for tender affection. He never asked about me; never solicited my participation; never made an explicit demand on me. He did though regularly express gratitude for listening, for being patient, and for the few comments I would offer.

On the surface, Juan presented a portrait of the phallic man: emotionally contained and detached, self-sufficient, and resistant to doing relational work. He aspired to have a successful career, to marry and be the breadwinner of his family. His conventional masculinity was, however, belied by his inner life; but you would never know this unless you had sustained access to it.

Juan's story is sad but moving, at times even inspirational. Despite his insistent separateness and muted emotionality, I was drawn to him, hoping against all odds that he'd somehow find a path to a less bare and burdened life.

Growing up, Juan felt different. It wasn't so much that his father was an alcoholic and exited the family early in his life; nor was it that he was poor or non-white or on Medicaid; this was the norm in his world. Rather, Juan was never "one of the boys." He was not muscled, not aggressive, not an athlete, and not a ready-to-fight guy. He described himself as sensitive and a little cerebral; his peers viewed him as "slow." I thought Juan was deliberate in choosing his words and putting sentences together. There was an intensity to his focus on articulation, an obsessiveness, and perhaps a certain woodenness to his speaking style that I'm guessing was in stark contrast to the sharp, sometimes playful, sometimes cutting tongue valued by his peers. From elementary to High School, Juan found himself mostly alone. He invoked phallic tropes to explain this. "I was not an athlete, not muscled and really strong—that's the kind of man others like, and want to hang out with."

Since his mother worked until he was 14, he was often alone at school and at home. In his early 20s, Juan found a zone of comfort in the church. Neither his mother nor Juan were religious, but church members embraced him. No doubt they felt his aloneness and neediness. Older church members took him under their wings, treating him kindly. Sometimes, they would bring him sweets; they encouraged him to join their Bible studies group. Juan didn't show much interest in this or, for that matter, the theology of salvation; but he went to the church several days a week, volunteering to do whatever chores were needed. It was a place that accepted him. He felt a kind of kinship but it wasn't always clear to him exactly what it was.

As I got to know him, I began to understand what drew him to the church. He felt a deep affinity to its ethical culture. By that I mean less the religious teachings of the Christian faith than the way its members treated each other. In particular, they looked past an individual's ethnic or racial or socioeconomic status or whether you were attractive or popular.

Instead, they assumed the dignity of each individual, respected each other, and judged their lives based on whether you were kind and aspired to live a "good" life. This ethical mindedness resonated with Juan.

Now, a Nietzschean might argue that he was embracing the "weak" man's moral code as an act of resentment and revenge, a case of the "transvaluation of values." That is, Christian values are embraced as a way to claim moral superiority in a culture whose dominant masculinist ethos would deem him a loser. But this perspective assumes that stereotypically masculine values are and should be the baseline of judgment, an assumption that is itself an expression of power. Alternatively, an analyst might reasonably argue that Juan's embrace of a quasi-Christian ethic was a defense against feelings of inadequacy and perhaps, a reaction formation protecting him from his own aggressive desires that were frightening. Whatever the origin story, as Max Weber might have said, his ethical values and vision infused his life with significance and provided a moral framework to live a meaningful life. But living an ethical life also made demands on him, generated tensions between competing values and between his moral ideals and his psyche.

Truly, Juan would have a rough road ahead of him. At 16, he became the breadwinner, as his mother went on disability. When I saw him, at 28, he was in his fifth year of college but had completed less than two years' worth of credit. Yet, his ambitions were considerable. He wanted to be a writer and journalist, to learn languages and study different cultures. But between work, taking care of his mother, and a crowded daily life involving laundry, shopping, and cooking, he lacked the time and focus for his studies. Moreover, his plodding style put him at a disadvantage. He struggled with many classes. His slow pace pained him greatly. I had grave doubts that he would ever complete his degree. But in session after session he would talk in great detail about his hopes for a middle class life that would give purpose to a present filled with denial and deferral. This dream helped get him through the tedious, often unforgiving present.

But Juan didn't just want to get by. Daily life was approached as an ethical arena. Juan thought hard about what "kind of man I am and will be." He puzzled over how to bring his values and moral ideals into his lived experience.

Juan would come into sessions with lists of virtues and values that made up his ethical universe. Central was being a good person. For example, one list included "being kind, considerate, gentle, compassionate, humble, thoughtful, and not hurting others." Another list spoke to what a good life might look like: "being independent, marriage, a good dancer and singer, have more friends, be learned, patient, non-judgmental, taking care of mom, reaching out to others, especially dad, church members, and some friends."

But living day to day in a principled way was not easy. For example, a co-worker, a hot-tempered aggressive man, at times would be belligerent. One time he got angry with Juan—shoved him, suggesting a readiness to fight. Juan did not want to hurt the other or be hurt. He preferred to resolve the conflict peacefully, respecting the other while also respecting himself. He decided not go to the manager, which could jeopardize his co-worker's job. Instead, Juan relied on a much-respected older co-worker to negotiate a peaceful resolution. Juan felt proud; his conduct reflected a core ethical value, being a nonviolent, caring, and responsible person. Or, consider a conflict Juan experienced between his obligation to take care of his mother in their small studio apartment and his desire to live on his own. He could not imagine leaving her alone, but neither did he wish to forestall an adult life. His mother was only in her mid-50s. Despite having a girlfriend, he chose to continue to support and live with his mother. He hoped that at some future date he could afford a larger apartment, allowing him to care for his mother and to live with his girlfriend.

Small acts of generosity and caring, hardly noticeable, if at all, from the outside. What the other sees or feels with Juan is containment, separateness, and impenetrability. Yet, these actions speak to an internal life that, though well hidden, is alive with an emotional and ethical intelligence and with a will to render his life morally coherent and purposeful, despite overwhelming social and psychic disadvantages.

In many ways, Joseph was the antithesis of Juan. White, 26, and from a two parent, middle class suburban family. Moreover, in contrast to Juan who was slight and conveyed a gentleness, Joseph was sturdy and confident in his body, as we would expect from someone whose hobbies were bike riding, surfing, and rock climbing. Joseph seemed like a leader, someone you immediately feel, as I did, the desire to look up to, defer to. He inspired confidence; one trusted that he would make the right decisions.

It was hard to pin Joseph down for our initial appointment. He kept delaying. After several weeks, we met. He said very little. It was clear he didn't want to be here; there was tension in the room. The very setup of therapy assumed he needed help and would be reliant on me, a slight, intellectual looking older man. I felt his detachment and possibly contempt; it seemed painful for him to look to me for help. In fact, he didn't explicitly ask for help. It was left implicit, never stated in the almost two years I saw him. We sustained the fiction that he was not really dependent and needy, that ours was a market type transaction, rather than a nuanced asymmetrical relationship.

Joseph was a man of few words; very little emotion was communicated. He barely talked, a few sentences followed by silence. His silence felt like a kind of power. It made me feel as if I was dependent on him. He seemed rock solid in his immovable silent body. I knew that I would be talking more than I wanted. He would respond if and when he wanted. A few words offered, then a steely look, as if daring me to meet him in this zone of silence. He read me right. I was uncomfortable with the silence. Joseph was taking control, mastering this space and me. I deferred and often assumed the dependent "feminine" position. I would be the one who would make connections, draw him into the room, if he chose to. He was in charge. So, it went until he terminated because a job took him out of New York.

Joseph spoke of being unsettled; he always felt in transition. He moved around a lot—Ohio, Rhode Island, Florida, and now New York. He wanted to plant himself somewhere, here, in the city, in a job, in a home, preferably with a partner. But he had already signaled that he was in transition here too; he was here and not here, never quite invested in us. For some phallic men they cannot fully embody the present; they withhold, detach, disinvest, and dissociate, all ways to refuse vulnerability and dependency. Such men are restless, on the move, only partially available, already elsewhere. Joseph had just begun yet he was already gone. I felt it; I also knew the feeling.

Silence was power for Joseph. It demanded respect, it was a statement of self-sufficiency; it forced the other, at least me, to be uncomfortable, ultimately respecting him as a force, a power over me. I was in a sadomasochistic drama. He claimed power and didn't want it circulating. I often felt like a part object, some part of him he could not own, perhaps his neediness, his wish to be dependent, his insecurity and longing for connection. If I probed too much or asked to many questions, he would grow irritated, letting me know I would not be allowed to penetrate. Only he penetrates; a signature of the defended phallic man.

But, I also knew that silence was not always comfortable for Joseph. His father was a talker. He would go on and on, refusing pauses and interruptions. Joseph learned to just let him go on; he would protect himself from the endless stream of words by silence; it was a retreat, a refusal to be penetrated by his father, but also a silencing of him. Silence/silencing became a relational template. For example, in the face of a sometimes screaming and punishing High School soccer coach, Joseph retreated into silence; no complaints, no outward protest. When I asked why he would say that speaking up would only make matters worse. He learned that silence would eventually silence the other, or at least defuse and neutralize their verbal assault; it would render others uncertain, confused, often less powerful. But, Joseph could not fully elude feeling small, dependent and not recognized in his silence. He may have tried to disavow such feelings but they lingered. Yet, instead of narcissistic injury fueling a paranoid rage, his psychic suffering was reworked into an ethical mindedness that pivoted around empathy and kindness. In effect, he transformed his own injury into a psychic imperative to not hurt and disrespect others as he himself felt at times. Through an ethic of care and compassion, Joseph reclaimed disavowed self-states—dependency and a longing to be cared for and belong. It was his way of staying connected to such feelings without upending the sort of seamless masculinity that he publicly embraced and that gave him a sense of security and purposefulness. A relational ethic of care was his way to reclaim femininity.

Joseph never questioned his parent's love. It was difficult for him to be critical or dwell on their shortcomings. He loved them dearly and it was important to be a good son. He called and visited regularly, despite the three-hour plane ride; at times he hosted them in New York. What mattered was being in their lives in vital ways and they in his.

Joseph accepted that his father was averse to showing or communicating feelings; but he never doubted his love. He and Joseph did things together, built stuff, fixed things, and shared a love of sports. Tenderly, Joseph told me that his dad could fix anything. Joseph acknowledged that it was hard at times to see his mother silenced, talked over by his father. But, she was no wallflower; she was as much an athlete and lover of sports as his father. And, over the years she claimed a singular voice in the family. Sports, whether as players, spectators or fans, were a shared, bonding activity in the family. His parents attended all his games and dinners were filled with talking and joking about players, games, referees, and coaches. Sports talk also was a way each was present in emotionally expansive ways, taking in and being taken in by the other, and feeling a playful, loving connectedness.

There was one special way Joseph lovingly connected to his family. He cooked for them. Joseph's passion for cooking linked him to his mother, who loved to cook. They would share recipes. For holidays, Joseph cooked something special for his family. Through their shared passion for food and sports, Joseph forged an intimate bond with his mother based both on doing (cooking and sports) and being (emotionally sharing, mutual support). At times, Joseph would turn to her for advice about relationships; and, she would often look to Joseph, rather than her husband, for emotional support.

Feeding others was one way he offered himself and let others take him in; it was a way to be kind and generous, a way to stay attached to dependency needs through caring for the other. From time to time, Joseph would bring me food and some of our most vital and connecting experiences were about food. The room became enlivened, full of play; Joseph found an articulateness rarely claimed with me.

In the course of our work, cracks appeared in his hard surface. He experienced me as a man who could fill the space with words, but also be restrained, respectful, and invite him to co-mingle our words and thoughts. He began to find a voice, one that had his mother's emotional resonance; power began circulating between us.

Late in the second year of therapy, Joseph got involved with Jenny. She was "cute, worldly, community oriented, an athlete, very expressive; she grows herbs, organic food, something I'd like to learn to do . . ." He especially liked that she was "empathic and really smart. We are really good together; we laugh, play, and talk about our feelings, about our wants, fears, family. . . . There's a lot of touching and tenderness. We are constantly processing." After some months, they committed to each other. But, Jenny wanted an open relationship. Initially, Joseph wasn't sure. He wanted to get to know her, to see who they are with each other. Gradually, he began to rethink intimacy. "We shouldn't have to be intimate with just one person. There are many sides of me. One person can't satisfy all of me. . . . It seems reasonable to have multiple intimacies." At the heart of his reimagining intimacy was an ethical and social ideal: creating layers of belonging, caring, and different kinds of loving. "It's building a network of people that care; each relationship being unique, respected for what it is, and each carries its own kind of responsibilities and obligations."

I had some concerns. Would an open arrangement mean that he wouldn't fully invest in this relationship? Would this once again leave him feeling transient and unsettled? In short, would this intimate option serve as a defense? He didn't think so, but I wasn't sure. I was though convinced that Joseph was genuinely struggling to rethink intimate life in ways that resonated with him, phenomenologically and ethically. He reassured me, sensing my concerns, it's not an anything goes, no commitments, no obligations, carefree lifestyle; rather, for Joseph, it was about trying to have integrity in his intimate life, and recognizing that intimacy of whatever kind requires commitments, sustained intellectual and emotional engagement, and a network of implicit rights and duties. As Joseph said, "I have my unique relationship with Jenny reflecting who I am and she is. We're both committed to this relationship. We don't know where it will evolve. She will see others and have what they have because of who they are. If I feel jealous it's my insecurity. I will talk about what's going on with her. . . ." I had my doubts but I didn't doubt that Joseph was, to use Bollas' term, approaching relationships as a transformational object.

Authenticity as a language of ethical life

In Euro-American traditions, including psychoanalysis, the notion of authenticity coheres around the idea that each of us has a true self, a foundational, self-identical core. It is this self that many of us strive to bring to full life.

For Freud and some of his heirs, the authentic core was beneath the surface of fleeting feelings, behaviors, and social roles. There is, he thought, a psychic core that is solid and continuous. It is a natural, biological substrate—the id. Its teeming bodily-based drives are the springs of life, a life force that animates us; interacting with civilization, the id generates tensions and conflicts that engender the chief drama of our lives.

After Freud, analysts shifted the focus of action, even as many retained his instinctual metapsychology. Whether we reference British object relations, Laing's existential psychology, Sullivan's interpersonal psychology, or Kohut's self psychology, there is a view of the self as fundamentally object seeking and connecting. From this perspective, selves have a biological substratum that may indeed drive behavior and development, but we are fundamentally social. At times, this framing was a bit obscure. For example, Winnicott (1965a) imagined a true self as a biological disposition or genetic temperament that in good enough familial environments spontaneously unfolds in playful, creative ways. In the course of maturation, the true self uses the social context to elaborate its own unique personal idiom. Winnicott however continued to rely on a notion of the natural substrate as the ultimate locus of the true self.

Drawing on thinkers such as Fairbairn and Sullivan, contemporary relationalists blur the boundary between the natural and the social. Without denying a biogenetic constitution or temperament, relationalists contend that humans are socially formed. As a potentially reflective, meaning-making agent, the self is inextricably attached and oriented to others. Others don't just shape our behavior or regulate innate impulses but form part of our inner lives through introjections and identifications. Selves are then social in a deep, formative way.

If there is no self apart from social life, if humans become selves in and through social interactions, our exchanges with different people in varied contexts suggests a notion of the multiplicity of selves or self-experiences. For some relationalists, the notion of a true, singular, and unified self is an illusion (Bromberg 1996, Howell 2008). The reality is closer to that of "multiple selves" (Mitchell 1993) or "multiple self-states" (Bromberg 1996, Davies 1994, 1996). Who we are and which self is present depends on whom we are with, our shared history, and the purpose of the exchange. Each self-state has its own singular way of being and relating.

What does authenticity mean in a world of multiple self-states or assuming a protean self? To take one of the most sustained arguments, Mitchell (1991, cf. Safran 2016) made the case that in a "postmodern" context analysts need to shift from a substantialist language of a *true/false self* to a processual or formalist view of *authentic/inauthentic self-experiences*. Authenticity is defined in terms of the formal qualities of self experiences, understood contextually.

> In differentiating authenticity from inauthenticity, the crucial difference lies not in the specific content of what I feel or do but in the relationship between what I feel and do and the spontaneous configuration and flow of my experience. . . . A particular act may

feel authentic in one context and not in another. ... I feel more "myself" [when] ... I have presented my thoughts and feelings accurately and succinctly, been comfortable enough to allow myself to reveal more of my spontaneous repertoire. At other times, I feel [inauthentic or] less "myself," [when I feel] jumbled, unable or unwilling to make myself clear, too awkward or too constrained to reveal myself in anything but a stereotyped or constrained fashion.

(Mitchell 1991: 130–1)

Authentic experiences have then specific formal qualities: spontaneity, a fluid movement between feelings and behavior, experiences expressed clearly and succinctly, and a consistent feeling of "me-ness." By contrast, experiences that are overly deliberative or reactive in a Winnicottian sense, exchanges in which the flow between feelings and behavior are halting or blocked or where feelings, thoughts and behaviors seem unclear or confused, and occasions in which there is an absence of a sense of "me-ness" are indicative of inauthenticity. Such experiences would become signposts alerting the therapist to pathology or, in Sullivan's de-medicalizing language, to troubles with living.

At one level, Mitchell seems to be making what many Americans, especially psychotherapists, would likely consider a straightforward point. There's a difference between experiences in which someone acts in spontaneous, direct, clear, playful, and creative ways and behavior that is reactive and compliant or intellectualized to the point of emotional detachment.

The virtual self evident character of this distinction should give us pause, given a history of cultural norms becoming psychoanalytic truths, e.g. heteronormativity, patriarchy, binary gender norms, biological essentialism (e.g. Chodorow 1994, Flax 1996, Layton 2006a, 2006b). In this regard, we are skeptical of the claim that these so-called formal psychological and behavioral qualities are a solid ground to distinguish between authentic and inauthentic and implicitly between normal and pathological self states. Why should formal qualities such as spontaneity or fluidity between feelings and behavior be any more compelling as markers of psychic authenticity than substantialist notions? If they are stable enough to be a ground, they're susceptible to a critique of essentialism; if they are protean, in what sense can they be a compelling basis for this normative distinction?

A cursory examination suggests that these formal or processual qualities are too indistinct and unstable to serve a foundational role. Specifically, psychic and interpersonal experiences are rarely, if at all, singular and transparent in their meaning. The authentic/inauthentic binary collapses under the weight of shifting and excess meanings (cf. Goldman 2007). For example, behavior described as "spontaneous" presupposes concepts beyond its definitional boundaries to be intelligible. To wit: Is spontaneity possible without thoughtfulness and purposefulness? If it lacks "mindfulness" wouldn't it be illegible? And if spontaneity were infused with intent and therefore reflective, why would this make such behavior inauthentic? Indeed, wouldn't spontaneity without consequentialist deliberation be dangerous? Furthermore, doesn't spontaneity as play or creativity assume rule boundedness as a condition of its possibility (Frankel 1998)? And finally, can't spontaneity be creative but also defensive, perhaps protecting against anxieties associated with committing to personal ambition or collective projects, both of which demand deliberation and deferral?

Or, consider "accurate or succinct" thinking and self-expression as signs of authenticity. Doesn't a one-dimensional cognitive emphasis on clarity and mirroring truths also, as poststructuralists have argued, evacuate contradictory and perhaps disturbing meanings or flatten out ambiguities and ambivalences? Doesn't clear, accurate expression erase or marginalize evocative, poetic expressions that thrive on emotional and intuitive and metaphorical kinds of truths?

Similar problems attend to so called inauthentic experiences. Its archetype being accommodative behavior, which can mean deferring to another's needs, seeking approval, managing others views and judgments, avoiding conflict and instability, and so on. Yet, accommodation cannot so easily be flattened into compliance (Winnicott 1965a), submission (Ghent 1990), traumatic forms of identification (Frankel 2002), or pathological accommodation (Brandchaft 2007). For example, such behaviors may fulfill a sincere desire to belong, to be liked and accepted, to create a safe space in order to be truly known; it may be a way of taking care of and validating the other and, as such, an act of moral sacrifice or generosity, or an act of deferral as a condition of participating in a collaborative effort or achieving a collective goal. Without minimizing the traumatic roots and repetition of some forms of accommodative behavior, we don't think its convincing to collapse its multivalent meanings, in particular its ethical register as an act of deferral and its role in forging connective bonds. In fact, Mitchell recognizes that our lives are shot through with consequentialist thinking and accommodative behavior. But this awareness didn't lead him to reconsider the categorical status of the authentic/inauthentic binary (1991: 133). This was perhaps an act of bad faith (Sartre 1984), a reluctance on Mitchell's part to draw the compelling conclusion: the complexity, polysemy, and overdetermined character of meaning renders the authentic/inauthentic binary arbitrary and muddled, hardly warranting a foundational psychoanalytical status (Goldman 2007).

Mitchell's case for associating authenticity with formal psychic and behavioral qualities strikes us as another instance of a normative argument masquerading as a psychoanalytic truth. Spontaneity and fluidity and creativity and playfulness are *values* shared by many Americans today, especially those in the professional class. As two therapists who share these values, we think a case can be made that these formal qualities are preferable to say rigidly inflexible and compliant behaviors. However, we prefer that psychoanalysts whose work is infused by such values fully own what in fact they are doing, namely, engaging and shaping the moral life of clients in a way that reflects their specific ethical viewpoint (cf. Jacobson on Bollas 1997, Safran 2016). As we see it, there's no way around the ethical mindedness of therapeutic practice (cf. Drozek 2015, Layton 2006a, Rozmarin 2007, 2010, Scarfone 2017, Strenger 2014, Suchet 2010, Wachtel 2014). As long as we operate with some language of preferable human experiences, as long as we deploy a vocabulary of normality and pathology or health and sickness or well-being that inform therapeutic action, we are acting as ethical subjects. By disguising ethical regulation in a descriptive, quasi-medical language, we are endorsing an authoritarian form of regulation, since a medical language references a decidedly small community of potential ethical subjects. To use Mitchell's criteria of authenticity, let's be direct, clear, and articulate about the ethical presuppositions of our practice. This implies that *our clients are no less ethical subjects*. In this regard, a challenge we face is to avoid reducing their sincere struggles for a good life to psychological adaptations or defenses and to explore with them the ways their pursuit of a good life creates psychological tensions, but also experiential possibilities.

Russell

Russell felt like a fraud. It wasn't so much that he lied or pretended to be other than who he was, but he withheld and avoided. Still, he often felt inauthentic. But what did that mean?

Russell came to see me 5 years ago. He had been feeling dead-ended after finishing college some 3 years prior. He was world-weary at 25, weighed down by feelings of self-loathing and haunted by suicidal thoughts.

Russell felt the weight of other's expectations as demands. No matter how much he wanted to be with friends or family or fellow activists, social engagements imposed expectations and entailed responsibilities; he was sure he'd fail to live up to them. Whether it was the "demand" to show up on time, to say the right thing, to meet other's standards of being smart and likeable, or to tolerate disagreeable or insensitive things said or done, social ties felt bruising and often just "too much."

Close relationships provoked considerable anxiety given their heightened expectations, e.g. regular communication, consistent availability and responsiveness, and meeting obligations. Anticipating failure weighed heavily on him, filling him with shame and a pervasive sense of worthlessness and self-hatred.

It wasn't so much that he worried about presenting a false self; rather, he feared living an unprincipled life, one that was fraudulent and lacked integrity. To be late or to cancel an appointment, to fail to do what was agreed upon or to not respond to a telephone call or a text message hurt others and impugned their dignity. Inauthenticity felt like an ethical lapse.

Russell struggled with how to negotiate social life without compromising his and others' psychic and ethical integrity. Given his current psychic state, he reasoned that perhaps it's not right for him, or fair to others, to enter into friendships or intimate relationships. "I cannot allow someone to be dependent on me because I can't be there for someone in a sustaining way. And if I cannot be there for others, I cannot expect them to be there for me. It's not fair. It's wrong. It's just not right." If he cannot live up to the ethical obligations of a friendship or intimate bond, if he cannot be consistently reliable and considerate, how can he expect other to be respectful and available? To enter into relationships, knowing what he does about himself, would be insincere, an act of bad faith. Still worse, he would be forcing the other to compromise their integrity by his inability to treat them as integral ethical subjects. Given his inability to be an effective ethical agent, Russell felt at times that he should avoid allowing anyone get too close to him.

Russell's troubles with living were simultaneously psychological and ethical. Doubts about his psychic capacity to be available and consistently responsive to the other triggered a moral dilemma: can I commit to the baseline ethical conditions of a social bond, such as meeting the responsibilities and expectations of a relationship and respecting the other's integrity? And, sustaining ethical integrity felt like too much psychically; it was as if every expectation, every obligation, no matter how minimal (answer the phone or a text, confirm a meeting), triggered psychic paralysis and a punishing self-loathing.

Russell rarely initiated social contact. If others reached out to him, it triggered a dilemma. If he didn't respond or declined an invite, the other would likely feel hurt, perhaps rejected. He would then be responsible for their psychic injury. Their reaching out to him, which rendered them vulnerable, meant that his response was necessarily an ethical one. If he agreed to connect, however, he would put himself in a position to be hurt and to hurt the other; any social engagement drew him into an ethical drama, which he anticipated would inevitably bring social and moral failure and leave him with a sense of betrayal—of the other but also of his own ethical integrity.

He considered two alternatives. First, he could withdraw. At least he would not hurt or disrespect the other and not violate his or their integrity. But being alone was burdensome. Moreover, to choose an insulated life was another kind of betrayal—of the person he wanted to be and the sort of life he at times envisioned for himself. Or, he could share his psychic and ethical struggles around participating in the social world. To those who mattered, he could speak frankly and with a raw honesty of his terrible anxieties and struggles in being with others. This was a risky strategy, as it would compel him to be vulnerable in unprecedented ways. Still, it was a way to be in the world in an ethically minded way. By allowing others to know him, they could then make their own informed judgment about whether and the extent to which they wished to be in his life. Russell's ruminations on being with others may have been triggered by aspirations to be true to himself. Yet, authenticity was in no small way about maintaining his ethical integrity—about being the person he aspired to be and living a life that he considered "good;" this included respecting the dignity and integrity of the other.

At times, the struggle to be authentic can get uncoupled from its ethical core. At such moments, the demand to be real and true to oneself betrays a narrow and potentially hurtful narcissism.

Russell related an incident that speaks to this narrowing of authenticity into psychic release. One evening, he found himself with casual friends. The conversation was honest and engaging. Then it shifted. His acquaintances began sharing personal matters, voicing discontents about their intimate lives. Abruptly, they turned to Russell, expecting a similarly personal account. He felt uncomfortable. "They started asking me all sorts of personal questions. . . . I steeled myself, thinking 'You don't get to know who I am and what I'm feeling just because you want to.'" He experienced their probing as a demand; it felt intrusive while bearing the force of a cultural imperative: transparency as an act of authenticity. He resisted, but took leave of these acquaintances feeling a bit humiliated but also furious, as if he was betraying their trust by not obeying the imperative to "be yourself, to share yourself." Russell thought, "what right do they have to presume an intimacy and expect a transparency they haven't earned?" He was enraged that casual friends could expect to know personal things about him before they really knew him, before he knew them, and before he could feel assured that his disclosures would be understood and respected. Their probing, unconsciously driven by a culture of authenticity, created a dilemma. To share would have been read as authentic but this imperative underscored the Achilles heel of this culture: a failure to consider the ethical conditions making credible the quest for authenticity. Russell chose not to share. His acquaintances had not earned the right to know; their relationship had not evolved to a point that warranted intimate knowing and could sustain the ethical obligations such knowing entails.

The ethics of intimate life

Between the 19th century and today, the sociocultural context of intimate life in the US has changed dramatically. Central to this transformation has been the retreat of the state from regulating many areas of private life along with the expansion of rights in many areas of personal life. This has yielded, however unequally and incompletely, greater personal freedom.

It wasn't that long ago that we could speak of a racial state: a state that perpetrates racial inequality, for example, by enforcing racial segregation, excluding or limiting voting rights based on race, outlawing interracial marriage, and so on. Similarly, until recently, the state could be described as a "straight state." It enforced the closet by criminalizing same-gender sexual behavior and spaces where "homosexuals" or genderqueer selves associated such as bars, clubs, and cruising areas, and by policing non-normative gendered practices such as cross dressing or transvestism (Canaday 2009, Eskridge 1999). Likewise, until well into the 20th century, the state was a patriarchal state. It enforced institutionalized male privilege by, for example, recognizing men as representing the entire family or by extending veterans rights and social security benefits primarily to men (Cott 2000). The state effectively rendered non-whites, non-straights, and other non-normatively gendered selves and women either uncivil outliers and/or subjugated quasi-citizens (Alexander 2007).

In the course of the 20th century, the state shifted from a racial, straight, and patriarchal one to one that was still implicated in racism, heterosexism, and sexism less by official legislative and judicial policy than by not fully protecting non-whites, non-straight, and non-cisgendered selves from discrimination, harassment, socioeconomic deprivations, and cultural degradation.

In the past few decades, there has been a third shift: the state has extended legal protections to areas of personal and civil life that have made possible an expansion of individualization for more and more Americans. The official dismantling of state enforced apartheid, for example, the integration of schools and the full extension of voting rights to non-whites, the criminalization of rape in marriage and sexual harassment in the workplace, and the end of sodomy laws and the legalization of same sex marriage, underscore the role of the state in creating personal and civic spaces that allow considerable decisional autonomy (Cohen 2002, Seidman 2013, Singer 1992).

We are all too aware, especially in the era of Trump, that these developments remain contested and are reversible. We also understand that there are many other ways in which the state continues to sustain hierarchies, e.g. its severe weakening of the welfare system, its failure to guarantee healthcare to all, the underfunding of schools in low income neighborhoods, and on and on. We're cognizant too that there are non-state social forces, from political parties to social institutions and cultural formations that contribute to the maintaining of hierarchies, and these are key sites of power and contestation. We're mindful, as well, that a

Foucauldian might object to our account of the "liberalization" of personal and civil life: what about the internalization of forms of regulation that are linked to identity discourses and normalizing norms? We don't deny the power of disciplinarity, but don't believe, as some Foucauldians seem to, that this negates liberalization; rather it creates tensions, sometimes generative ones, as Foucault seemed to believe. Furthermore, alongside liberalization is a cultural dynamic of "individualization." Many Americans today recognize the normalizing power of standardized identities; some embrace them, for example, endorsing black or gay pride or true womanhood, but others refuse to be constrained by these disciplining statuses that dictate behavior and misrepresent the complexity of our experience. Deconstructive currents among feminists, queers, antiracists and others speak to a revolt against identity-based normalization (Butler 1990, 2004, Fraser 1997, Fraser and Honneth 2004).

The upshot: the liberalization and individualization of personal life presents an opportunity and challenge: how to regulate personal life? Nowhere is this more evident than in the sphere of intimacy. Since at least World War II, romantic intimacy has become an arena of personal choice. Normative scripts stipulating heterosexuality, sex coupled to love and marriage, marriage wedded to co-residence, monogamy, and family-making have been challenged; each of these aspects of intimacy are today matters of personal negotiation and choice (Giddens 1993, Seidman 2013, Stacey 2011). In short, as intimate life is less rigidly and seamlessly normatively scripted, each of us must evolve our own ethics of intimate life (Cohen 2002, Seidman 1992, 2013, Weeks 2007). While individual-ization in the sphere of intimacy has raised anxieties of anything goes or hedonism run amuck, Americans have been fashioning variations of a relational ethic. In two vignettes we wish to explore the dynamic tension between psychic and ethical matters in intimate life.

Zai and Jimmy

An incident with a girlfriend prompted Zai to seek treatment. In the heat of an argument, he pushed her and was on the verge of hitting her; instead, he put his fist through the wall. He was sickened by this show of violence, and confused.

Zai was a 24 year old, soft spoken, socially aware Chinese-American. At the time, he was working on a master's degree in the humanities; he was well versed in feminism and the critical race literature. He fancied himself a kind, playful, compassionate man who respected women and was committed to an egalitarian ideal of intimacy.

In the course of a four-year treatment, Zai went through a series of romantic relationships—each with women of integrity, each approximating an egalitarian ideal, and each lasting 6–12 months. He also struggled, to use his own word, with "cheating" or having sex with other women. What did this say about his psyche but also his ethical mindedness?

Elizabeth was the kind of woman Zai admired and imagined he might someday marry. "She's considerate, self aware, good, kind, non-judgmental, and she thinks I'm smart and cute." She easily melded into his wide friendship network. Zai also found her sexy, but he didn't pressure her to have sex. As they dated, he asked if she was ready for sex. And when she was, he wanted to know her erotic likes and dislikes. She preferred sex that was tender and playful, not performative or act oriented. He obliged her, sacrificing his own more adventurous desires. The latter found an outlet in jerking off to porn, which was okay with Elizabeth. After a few months, they committed to each other. Zai was smitten by her genuine sweetness and goodness. He was though troubled by a sense that she expected him to be unfailingly nice and agreeable.

Losing touch with himself by accommodating to the needs and wishes of the other was a focus of our work. His parents were first generation immigrants. They were anxious about doing well and fitting in. They had high expectations for Zai who was smart and socially adept. He was their "golden boy." He tried, but routinely came up short in this regard. For example, Zai was initially excited about music lessons, which his parents arranged. Gradually, as with other pursuits (e.g. writing and school), he lost interest and passion, disappointing his parents. As our work progressed it became clear that a pattern of underachievement and a certain detachment spoke to a resentment towards his parents. His wants and needs seemed marginalized by his parents' expectations that he do well, as if his success eased their anxieties about fitting in. This organizing pattern continued into adulthood. Excitement and high expectations in school, relationships, and jobs would gradually pivot into a loss of interest and purpose, as Zai would coast on his smarts and agreeable personality.

He didn't want this pattern to play out with Elizabeth. He needed to be honest with her. "We need to be real with each other." Zai decided to let her know that he can be depressed, and sometimes bitterly judgmental.

Despite his efforts, the relationship seemed to lose an edge of excitement and passion. One evening, hanging out with a girl friend, they landed in bed. He wondered: "should I tell Elizabeth? It's a one-time thing, and we just played with each other. It would just hurt her to tell her." He didn't. Some months passed and he realized that there was something missing between them. He spoke with Elizabeth. "I'm someone who struggles with loss, death, depression, pessimism . . . and you don't seem to. . . . At times it makes it hard to connect. . . . There's a part of me that feels left out of the relationship. It makes me feel alone." He ended the relationship. For Zai, being authentic meant sharing deeply personal experiences and trying to bring himself fully into the relationship; but it also involved committing to an ethical idea of a relationship as a zone of honesty, sincerity, and integrity. It was unclear to me, and to Zai, whether breaking up with Elizabeth was a case of repeating a pattern—initial excitement, high expectations followed by declining passion and withdrawal. But it was clear to both of us that he was struggling as well to sustain his sense of ethical integrity in his intimate life.

During an 8 month period of being single, Zai discovered the world of escorts. I could understand why this would resonate: condensed excitement and no room for routinization. Zai was drawn to the novelty of sex with different women; he felt desirable and sexually potent, something he doubted at times. But, as a feminist, he anguished over whether it was right to pay for sex. Would he contribute to exploiting and demeaning women? He reasoned that since he paid them well and the specific sex acts were consensual, and because "he would treat them as whole persons and respectfully," he could "do this without guilt." But there was a further ethical consideration. "I don't want to do this often. This is not the person I want to be." Zai reasoned that "true, its minimally exploitative and I'm respectful of the woman. Yet, I still feel bad . . . because this is not what a good person would do. I want to be a good person."

While still single, Zai and his good friend Megan had sex; they were partying and a little drunk. Afterward, he felt guilty because she had been dating someone. "Yes, Megan chose to be with me but it didn't feel right. I felt I was betraying her boyfriend . . ." Struggling, Zai related that a good friend was having an affair with a married woman. "I am not sure what I should feel about that. I feel uncertain as to whether I'm too relaxed about accepting his behavior. Is that really okay?" Zai wasn't sure, but he was clear that he didn't feel comfortable being in a moral zone of indifference or collapsing ethics into the rule of impulse and desire. "I want to be a good person, to do the right thing, to be considerate, not hurt others. . . ." He wondered: "Do I have a sturdy moral compass?"

Single life came to end when he met Min. She was "smart, big hearted, kind, non-judgmental . . . a good person . . ." For the first 6 months their relationship sailed along; they enjoyed playing video games, listening to music, dancing, eating out, movies, and sex. Then, things got bumpy. There was tension, fights. She felt too needy, too demanding, and at times shut down when he shared his feelings. He resented that her needs and wants were always center stage. Frustrated, arguments would sometimes get heated; Zai would berate her. She would feel shamed and fall silent. He felt mortified, as if he were an abusive man. He doubted his own integrity. "I'm not sure whether I'm good enough for her. . . . I feel like I abuse her with my yelling . . . I don't let up. Its hurtful." Zai took on all of the blame and responsibility for their troubles, stripping her of agency; the exacting standards he imposes on himself took its toll: "I'm bad." He seemed to be reproducing the disappointment he believed his parents felt as he failed to live up to their expectations; his defiance cost him—disapproval and a harsh self-judgment.

Zai considered ending this relationship. "It felt terrible. I hurt her and me." Yet, he didn't want to end things. Instead, he decided to be honest with her about his own anxieties and struggles, hoping that his candor might enable her to be more open. "I talked to her about . . . my anxiety about masculinity, being smart enough, sexually potent, attractive. . . . I spoke of feeling jealous of other men in her life. I told her how bad I feel when I yell at her or don't let up when we argue." Teary-eyed, he said to me, "I struggle to be less perfect. I try to be the best I can, to live with being imperfect but not use that to justify being bad. . . . I want to be a good person." Through a series of conversations Min and Zai seemed to get back on track.

Then, some two months later, Zai confessed he cheated. Should he tell her? "I think it's okay; it was consensual, a one-time thing. I'll never see this girl again and after all I'm good with Min. . . . If I can forgive myself then I can forgive her for her stuff. I think it will help me be even better with her, nicer, kinder. . . ." But Zai was troubled. He knew why he cheated. He was drawn to the novelty, the excitement of being desired; he felt big when he was with other women. Could he really give this up?

But he was even more troubled about what cheating said about his moral character. "I don't want to be this type of person. I don't want to betray others' trust. I care about her. I want to be honest." Maybe he should tell her. "She deserves to know, to know me, all of me. It's what we're about. If I don't tell her she will not know the real, full me. I will have deceived her and then I can't respect her or myself." Yet, "If I tell her she would be hurt and likely destroy our relationship. I don't want this . . . [And], if she didn't breakup with me, could I still respect her?"

Zai considered a third option. "Sometimes, I feel I should just end it. I don't deserve her. I have too many secrets, too much guilt, and this has eroded our trust. I don't know if I can respect her because what does it say about us that I cheated? And, how could I respect her if she's okay with this? Can I trust myself to not cheat again? Maybe I'm just not ready for someone like Min." At this point, Zai wondered about his capacity for intimacy.

Notice: cheating interweaves a psychological and ethical dynamic. Zai is drawn to the psychic novelty and excitement of cheating; he feels big, potent as a man, but also knows it may be a way to avoid intimacy, to sabotage a vital romantic bond. And, not least, cheating seems to be part of a re-enactment: he expresses resentment toward the other by disappointing and hurting them, but this betrayal reaffirms his own badness or unworthiness. When pressed about his cheating, he declared, "I feel like shit, I don't deserve to be with a woman like Min." But the temptation to cheat and then seek redemption simultaneously speaks to his struggle to be an ethical self: "Is cheating in itself bad? Am I doing the right thing in telling or not telling her? How much do I tell? Is the telling itself another facet of injuring the other? Underlying such concerns is an ethical ideal: "Am I being a good person, the person I want to be?"

Zai's psychic dynamic might have driven him to end the relationship, but ethical considerations prompted him to try to save it ("I don't want to hurt her, I can be kinder knowing I'm imperfect, we care deeply for each other"). Alternatively, his ethical-mindedness at times prompted him to consider ending the relationship ("I'm not good enough, I disrespected her, I broke the trust between us, I betrayed her and my integrity"). He wondered: "Until I am capable of sustaining intimacy in the terms I value, which includes monogamy, perhaps I should either refrain from such relationships or enter into them in an honest open manner." This, too, would put pressure on him psychologically to be vulnerable, to access a wide range of his feelings and desires, and to risk loss. What seems clear is that intimate life is not, for Zai, reducible to psychic impulses or a drama of desire and domination. It is where he struggles to sustain a life of ethical integrity.

Zai was a gregarious fellow; he had a wide network of friends, some stretching back to childhood. Being social was more or less written into his disposition. Yet, his worldliness carried psychic stress. His desire to make the other feel good as a way to feel good about himself triggered resentment and envy, then guilt. As much as this accommodative pattern positioned him in a state of dependency, it was also controlling—of himself and the other. Both self states generated relational tensions. His public presentation often didn't align with his inner life; he felt inauthentic and experienced a lapse of ethical integrity. But forging an alignment triggered heightened anxiety, as his psyche felt stretched and in a zone of risk. Psyche and ethics struck an uneasy balance.

Despite appearances, Zai, like many men, was not so comfortably in the world. For Jimmy, though, social life was often infused with dread and panic. Handsome and talented, Jimmy was sure, despite his extra-ordinary everyday competence and social adeptness, he would fall short and suffer mortification. He navigated social affairs by staying at a remove; cordial enough to not betray his ethical ideal of being a kind and good person but avoiding becoming the object of others burdensome expectations. He found himself, all too often, living a double life: "privately, a true self, publicly, a false self." But this compromised his ethical sense. He knew that his managed public self was psychically driven, not a matter of principle or ethical choice. Jimmy's struggle to maintain integrity with a psyche always uneasy in the world extended to intimate life. The later demanded authenticity as both a psychic and ethical state but such vulnerability evoked anxieties of humiliation, at times psychic terror; yet, anything less undermined a principled and purposeful life.

Jimmy (36) first laid eyes on Adam (32) in a club in Brooklyn. Adam was a saxophonist in a rock/jazz fusion band that Jimmy wanted to check out. After the set, Adam sat next to Jimmy. It took three beers before Jimmy could begin a conversation. They talked through the night. That was some twelve years ago. After living together for nine years, Adam chose to live on his own. They remained a couple but over time their relational status became fuzzy.

Jimmy began treatment two years after Adam moved out. He had always struggled with "shyness;" he was often paralyzed with fear, gripped by a kind of terror, as he named it, whenever he anticipated worldly engagements. He was certain that, lacking deliberate management, humiliation and a judgment of failure would follow almost any social exchange. This was especially troubling because he was also a musician.

His guardedness was apparent in our initial meetings. He rarely made eye contact; he would sit still, barely moving throughout the session; he would talk from the moment he arrived until I interrupted to mark the session's end. His talk was obsessive but stunning; words carefully selected, evocative and moving, and sentences that flowed beautifully, barely needing editing. But, Jimmy rarely paused to allow me to speak; and, in many years of treatment, he never elicited my opinion or showed interest in my personal or professional life. He was though unfailingly respectful, and generously let me know that he valued our work together.

If you didn't know Jimmy the way I came to, you'd likely describe him as a stereotypically phallic man. He was broad shouldered and physically imposing, emotionally contained, and projected an impenetrable aura of self-sufficiency. Jimmy was driven by work and creative ambitions; he was most comfortable alone, composing and playing music. Jimmy was a professional pianist in a jazz band, but also played in a chamber ensemble. But, getting to know Jimmy from the inside out revealed a layered, contradictory inner life. Moreover, in his devotion to Adam and to his band mates, in his generosity towards friends and compassion towards those less fortunate, and in his refusal to intrude or impose on others, Jimmy would more appropriately be described in the stereotypical language of femininity. At his core was an abiding commitment to fashioning a life driven by an idea of ethical integrity and purposefulness.

Adam's decision to move out didn't mark the end of their relationship. He wanted to live on his own; after all, he moved in with Jimmy when he was just 21. After a year on his own, Adam was diagnosed with an autoimmune disease. He continued to work as a freelance graphic artist, but his music career was considerably slowed. Jimmy didn't want him to move out, but he adjusted. Despite being uncommonly handsome, Jimmy didn't want to be with anyone else. But Adam wasn't easy. Health-wise, he required a lot of attention—a daily regimen of medications, many trips to the pharmacy and doctors, and he was often tired and moody. Moreover, Adam was anxious, emotionally needy, and demanding, and, despite being kind hearted, he could be harshly judgmental. As Jimmy said of him, "no one measures up; no one is good enough."

After his diagnosis, they decided to marry so Adam could be on Jimmy's healthcare plan. Jimmy bore the extra cost. He was, as well, heavily involved in Adam's healthcare; he read the medical literature, consulted alternative treatment options, accompanied him on doctor visits, and often kept Adam company when he felt anxious and miserable. Jimmy was devoted to Adam. Theirs was a rich, layered intimacy. They shared a love of music and all manner of worldly matters. They talked daily, sometimes for hours; Adam would share his distress over his health and his anguish over his stalled musical career. Jimmy listened, at times offered advice, and was an ever-hopeful voice. Growing up with volatile parents, Jimmy had learned to skillfully manage his and others anxieties. But he would only infrequently share his own personal troubles and angst; he didn't want to upset Adam. They both believed that stress aggravated Adam's health and, as Jimmy said time again, "Adam's well-being is my number one priority."

They had stopped having sex some 2 years prior to Adam moving out. Adam still loved Jimmy but no longer had romantic feelings. It didn't surprise Jimmy and it didn't significantly change their relationship. Jimmy and Adam never wanted a conventional relationship. They had experimented with threesomes, sometimes with men, other times with women. And, Jimmy knew that Adam had brief encounters, even short affairs. This didn't threaten Jimmy. He knew that Adam could be impulsive and flirtatious. Moreover, Jimmy felt reassured by Adam's confiding in him about the ups and downs of his extramarital episodes. In Jimmy's mind, he remained the constant in Adam's life, always available and serving as his emotional anchor. He never doubted Adam's love.

In the fourth year of our work, Jimmy learned that Adam had considered ending their relationship soon after he met a man with whom he carried on a year-long affair. It ended two months before Adam told Jimmy. Jimmy was stunned and deeply hurt. "He was telling me that he loved this guy and wanted to leave me." However, instead of shattering his idealization of Adam, Jimmy blamed himself. "I failed Adam in some way. . . ." It was as if Adam's affair confirmed what Jimmy already knew, his fundamental defectiveness (Balint 1992). I wondered though whether Jimmy could allow himself to think what he sometimes suspected: that

Adam was not the man he knew and loved a decade ago, and they were not the "they" he idealized.

In the course of processing this event, Adam made this "unthought known" known (Bollas 1987). He no longer thought of them as a married couple. He felt that Jimmy was too dependent on him, as if he needed Adam to need him. Adam accused Jimmy of using him to avoid staking out a fully independent life. Jimmy's dependency felt stressful and unhealthy, Adam said. Jimmy saw things otherwise. Adam projects his dependency needs on him, refusing to recognize how attached he is to Jimmy because he's uncomfortable with such needs—this would be Adam's "unthought known." Still, Jimmy was deeply hurt; it was "as if Adam was telling me that our life together was a lie, that my feelings were a lie, illusory."

Despite Adam's behavior, he continued to depend on Jimmy and nothing seemed to actually change between them. They still talked daily; still shared personal matters; and continued to rely on each other and to do so in caring ways. For all of Adam's claims to be independent, Jimmy knew the way old lovers know such things, that Adam loved him. Jimmy realized something else. He had chosen to be with Adam and continued, from day to day, to make that choice through his actions. "It feels right to me . . . It's what I want, to be with Adam, to love him, to have a joint, shared life whatever form that takes. . . . I am devoted to him, even if he doesn't always want that or knows that he wants that. . . . It's about who I am . . . I am committed to him. It's who I want to be."

Sometime after these revelations, Adam told Jimmy of an experimental medical treatment. Jimmy agreed it was promising but it was expensive and their insurance wouldn't cover it. Adam had little savings, and such an amount would seriously deplete Jimmy's savings. His musings are instructive. "I must pay for it because it's the right thing to do . . . I love Adam; he needs the operation. I want to help . . . and by helping him I help myself and us. If he's healthier than I will feel better and our relationship will be better. I want to do this for him, for us. . . . I expect nothing in return, no obligation on his part. I want to do this."

This series of events prompted a reflection that's fascinating for the ways psychic and ethical matters are intertwined: "What is my responsibility to myself and to him . . . I worry that my responsibility to Adam can become a preoccupation, overwhelming because he's so needy and I want to help him. . . . But he drains me emotionally . . . so nothing or little is left for me. But I cannot do anything but help him. It's who I am and he's the most important person in my life. But then I can feel lonely . . . exhausted, especially since he doesn't always understand me and appreciate what I'm doing and why. He doesn't always take in my giving. . . . He often feels like I'm being controlling. I guess I am a little but that's not why I'm with him. So, how do I take responsibility for him and not lose responsibility for myself?" Indeed!

Jimmy's ethical reflection raised a parallel issue for me: what was my responsibility to him? I worried that he was in an asymmetrical, non-mutual relationship, being "in control" yet doing most of the connecting and caregiving work. Should I question his devotion to Adam? Is Jimmy's unconscious need to be the caregiver or to rescue Adam a way he stays attached but also removed from his own dependency needs and longings to be cared for? Is his decision to exhaust his savings for someone who planned to leave him and who no longer considers them married an internal drama around his goodness and self-worth that perhaps should be contained and not acted on? Their relationship seemed to parallel our relationship in another way. I'm also "in control" and do most of the caring. And like Jimmy with Adam, I'm committed to Jimmy and to us. But, I've also realized that the formal frame (asymmetry and unequal mutuality) belies the fluidity of our dynamic. For example, Jimmy typically takes control of the space by deciding what's discussed and by monopolizing talk; and there are ways he takes care of me, for example, reassuring me of the value of our work or referring to comments I've made as helpful. Maybe, in a parallel way, the seemingly asymmetrical, unequal reciprocity of their relationship masks a circularity as each controls and cares in ways reflecting their unique capacities and needs. When I've queried Adam's sincerity, Jimmy reassured me that in his own way Adam is deeply invested and committed to him, to them. Ultimately, I was convinced that Jimmy knows him like no one knows him, and part of that knowing is knowing he's loved by Adam—knowing by thickly intertwined lives and by inner worlds vitally impregnated with the other; that's what mattered, said Jimmy. I couldn't disagree.

Afterword: the therapeutic self revisited

Freud and Max Weber shared a lot in common—German speaking poly-maths, pioneers of new knowledges, cultural pessimists but still ambivalent heirs of the Enlightenment. They offered though very different images of the human condition.

Weber viewed humankind as meaning-making ethical selves. In his pioneering sociology of world religions (e.g. 1993), he depicted ordinary individuals inspired by religiously based transcendent notions of moral goodness and salvation; religious cosmologies provided ethical frameworks giving purpose and moral significance to daily life, and often yielding the most unexpected social outcomes. Most famously, he proposed that those Puritans embracing a faith commitment to the predestination doctrine of Calvinism unintentionally contributed to the making of the materialist world of industrial capitalism by sacralizing this-worldly economic behavior.

In contrast to Weber's vision of the ethical self, Freud imagined a "psychological self" (Reiff 2006, 1979). He delineated a distinctive arena of life—"the psyche." It had its own structure, dynamics, conflicts, and developmental trajectories. The psyche is irreducible to the biological or the social. However much individuals or groups experience the good fortune of wealth, status, and power, they're specific temperaments in conjunction with family dynamics produce psyche's that may still suffer, often in ways that are unbearable. Freud delineated and catalogued psychic discontents and offered a clinical practice to ease such malaise. Subsequent psychoanalysts may have revised and reconstructed his ideas but have not abandoned the image of the psychological self, even if they have "interpersonalized" the field. Moreover, it wasn't just Freud who was, to use Phillip Reiff's (1979) phrase, "a moralist" but contemporary psychoanalytic practice continues to frame analysts as ethical subjects, inspired by ideas of a good life—health, normality, well-being, freedom, fluidity—and by a will to cure and heal, and, as Foucault (1997) might say, to expand the self's exercise of freedom.

Curiously, the normative unconsciousness of psychoanalysis is still for the most part unreflected upon (e.g. Layton 2006a, 2006b). Notions of normality, health, and well-being and their antitheses—illness, pathology, abnormality, or perversity—circulate widely in the analytical literature with scant critical commentary. It's not surprising then that, on the whole, psychoanalysts do not consider their patients as ethical subjects. Instead, patients' struggles are framed in terms of their "mental apparatus" or the interpersonal or relational field; if ethical concerns are addressed in the consultation room, they are understood either in terms of the analytic frame or in the narrow language of the superego as a regulator of impulses and drives. For the most part, analysts have not theorized and do not clinically address the ways their patients struggle with aligning ethical commitments with psychic dynamics.

Is the parallel between the analytical abstraction of the ethical from its core conception of the psychological self, and the popular cultural construct of men as either narcissistic or minimally ethical, merely coincidental? Arguably, to the extent that psychoanalysis has been and continues to be informed by a certain masculinist culture, it marginalizes and minimizes ethical considerations and reinforces the feminization of ethics. In fact, some feminist analysts such as Chodorow (1978) and Dinnerstein (1976) and Donna Elise (2001) reproduce the man/woman, narcissist-egoistic/other-directed-ethical binary. At the same time, other feminist relational analysts such as Benjamin (1988), Flax (1990), and Layton (1998) have sought to bring ethical considerations into the heart of analytical thinking and practice, for example, in the form of an ethic of mutual recognition.

We are pressing a straightforward point: just as our practice as therapists is ethically informed, so too is that of our clients. Like us, they are ethical subjects. Their psychic struggles are informed by and implicated in ethical commitments. What would it mean for us as ethical subjects to begin to address our patients as ethical subjects?

Note

1 The project of authenticity, given heft by the likes of Sartre and Heidegger, has been sharply contrasted to the notion of self-invention or what Foucault (1986) calls the "care of the self." Whereas the former pivots around discovering and freeing the real, true self that underlies social artifice, the latter refers to the ways selves contribute to their self-formation through various "technologies of the self," that is, rules and principles guiding the self's relation to itself. Whereas authenticity typically assumes a notion of an integral, core subject, Foucault holds that these technologies, which form the basis for the care of the self, create the self as an ethical subject. In place of the project of uncovering and liberating the self, Foucault proposes self-creation as an aesthetic act. "Sartre avoids the idea of the self as something which is given to us, but through the moral notion of authenticity, he turns aback to the idea that we have to be ourselves—to be truly our true self. [But], from the idea that the self is not given to us, I think that there is only one practical consequence: we have to create ourselves as a work of art . . ." (1990b: 262). We think the contrast is drawn too starkly. Discovering and freeing the self, as we've argued, involves a deliberate and dynamical ethical

relation of the self to itself; the authentic self is not only to be known, but to be elaborated as an object of imagination and cultivation. The authentic self may also be, in Sprenger's (2016) words, a "designed self."

Chapter 5

Between abjection and the ecstatic

The erotic lives of men

A stark, sharp-edged binary has been at the center of American culture: women as sentimental in contrast to men as desiring selves. Women are sexual but in ways that are secondary to their nature; sex is just a thread of their selves. And, while desire is present, it is softened into life giving and caregiving. Sex builds and sustains relationships. By contrast, men are stipulated as sexual in a primary and fundamental way; sex is driven by an unbounded desire; it is act-and-pleasure oriented and ultimately driven by an impulse of self-aggrandizement.

To say that men are sexual in a foundational way underscores the point that desire infuses all of their lives; it saturates their core impulses and their unconscious wishes and fantasies. Sex has a driven, compulsive-like character. It's as if men have no choice but to be sexual, to be constantly on the edge of a carnal hunger. Sexual desire animates their risk taking and world shaping practices; it propels men to bridge the here-and-now with the future and the actual with the possible; it drives their restless, sometimes frenetic movement and incessant "doing."

Men are then awash in desire. And this desire is of a particular kind: carnal, discharge oriented, and mobile across acts and objects. As such, men's sexuality is imagined as virtually uncontrollable, polymorphous, and beyond good and evil in its sheer narcissistic drivenness. It propels and hungers for relief, and edges into excess, into the ecstatic. It is this cultural collapse, at once descriptive and normative, of men and desire that perhaps explains the almost taken-for-granted association of men with seduction, violence, porn, predatory behavior, abuse, and perversity. As desiring subjects, men are at once admired for their erotic daring and intensity and feared as their very desires may leave a trail of torn and broken bodies and psyches.

A series of overlapping binaries remain at the heart of American culture even as they are increasingly contested: man/woman, narcissistic/other-oriented, and desire/affect. In a sense, this book is an effort to deconstruct and expose the unconscious cultural and psychic power and instability of these binaries.

To wit: just as it perpetuates an injurious politic of misrecognition to collapse women into sentimentality, it is reductive and, we argue, increasingly illegible to conflate men with desire. In a series of queries, we explore some of the complicated ways that social context, psyche, and sexuality interweave, generating, often simultaneously, both dread and ecstatic states.

Identity and the retreat from ambiguity

The politics of identity did not begin with the civil rights and liberation movements of the 1960s. Instead it was a response to an existing, taken-for-granted politics of identity, which, to put it simply, privileged whiteness, men, heterosexuality, bodily and mental ableness, and so on. The social movements of the sixties altered identity politics by exposing established but untheorized identity-based hierarchies. A structure of privilege organized around the unequal distribution of rights, status, wealth, and access to institutional and market opportunities was said to be based upon specific identity traits. Crucially, rights and liberation movements framed the existing identity hierarchies as social, rather than written into nature or history; they could be changed. A critical identity politic aimed at either incorporating disadvantaged identity groups or deconstructing the categorical binary foundation of these hierarchies with the ultimate intent of putting an end to these identity-based classifications.

In the arena of sexuality, a politics of identity was arguably inaugurated by the establishment of a social order of compulsory heterosexuality. This regime enlisted the government and core social and cultural institutions to enforce the norm of heterosexuality; only opposite gendered sexual desires, behaviors, and intimacies, which assumed gender binarism, were legitimate (Rich 1980, Seidman 2009, Wittman 1972). Non-hetero-sexualities were located in a space of disenfranchisement and cultural pollution; they were framed as unnatural or pathological or sinful and subject to criminalization and exile from civic life.

As we see it, such a regime was not institutionalized until post-World War II in the U.S (D'Emilio 1983, Eskridge 1999, Seidman 2004). Prior to the early 20th century, heterosexuality was simply taken for granted. In the absence of organized political contestation, there was no provocation for the state to mandate compulsory heterosexuality. It was the appearance of non-heterosexuals in urban public spaces (bars, balls, cafes, cruising areas) that spurred the state and society to deliberately enforce the exclusive legitimacy of heterosexuality and gender binarism. Ironically, this regime unintentionally provoked the rise of critical movements defiantly speaking in the name of sexual and gender otherness. Moreover, this system of compulsory heterosexuality also enforced a restrictive code of heterosexuality—one that coupled it to gender conventionality, romantic love, marriage, family, and monogamy. Accordingly, parallel to the making of gay, lesbian, bi subjects, abject forms of heterosexuality, for example, interracial, non-monogamous, or non-romantic sexualities also resisted rigid sexual and intimate norms. Compulsory heterosexuality was then a political project launched in mid-20th century US enforcing heterosexism, gender binarism, and narrow norms of sexual normality.

By the 1970s, a sexual identity politic championing social justice was mobilized by self identified gay men and lesbians. Despite differences regarding political strategies and aims, they were united by their opposition to the social and psychic conditions of the closet created by compulsory heterosexuality. In ways paralleling the ghetto and the women's sphere, the closet was said to render desire into a form of self-mortification and an oppressive social destiny (e.g. Seidman 2004, Wittman 1972). These newly formed political subjects rallied around a politic of coming out and community building as a way to fully claim and affirm their homoerotic desire and a gay/lesbian social identity.

From the 1970s on, local, state, and national organizations took shape based on community building efforts in urban centers across the country. From the beginning, there was a political and cultural divide. Some organizations advocated a politic of mainstreaming, linking justice to full citizenship rights and the end of state and institutional discrimination. Alternative movement organizations leaned on a pluralistic or a liberationist politic. The former sought recognition of a unique gay/lesbian culture as part of the American mosaic; the latter advocated a politic of social transformation, anticipating a social world where sexuality and gender would no longer be grounds for identity and social status; these radical sexual-gender subjects imagined a world beyond the hetero/homo, man/woman gender binary.

By the 1980s, rights-based movements dominated gay organizations at the local, state, and national levels. For the American public, "the gay and lesbian movement" became a rights oriented, mainstreaming movement paralleling the civil rights movements of non-whites, women, native Americans, and the disabled. Justice meant equal rights, the end of discrimination, and social incorporation, including tolerance of public forms of gay/lesbian life. After Act Up in the '80s, and the short-lived queer politics of the early '90s, a transformational sexual politic migrated to the cultural margins, flourishing in academia and on the political periphery (Warner 2002).

Underlying the politics of rights was the notion of "normalization." For gay men and lesbians, normalization meant recognition as the moral equals of heterosexuals; as such, they deserve equal rights and respect for their cultural uniqueness. Moreover, for many gay men, but less so for lesbians, normalization meant projecting themselves as gender conventional and participating as good citizens in core national institutions such as the military, the church, the market, politics, and marriage and the family. Representations of normalized gays, especially gay men, found powerful resonance in American popular culture in the past two decades. For example, in a study of Hollywood films between 1950 and 2000, Seidman (2004; cf. Walters 2001) documented a dramatic shift in the 1990's towards tolerance and respect based on images of gay men and lesbians as all-around good citizens, for example, as gender conventional and marriage and family oriented and as enthusiastic participants in a market economy. From this cultural vantage point, gays—and straights— who are gender or sexually transgressive or genderqueer or engaged in multipartnered sex were marginalized, at times occupying the cultural space of "bad citizens." In effect, normalization created elements of a new alignment between "good gays" and "good straights" against "bad" or non-normative straights and queers (Seidman 2004).

Despite social shifts marking incorporation, which culminated in the legalization of same-sex marriage, not all straight-identified Americans have embraced gay normalization. Many might be intolerant of public homophobia, but resist moral and social equality. Few Americans are prepared to surrender heterosexual privilege and compromise a national ideal that weds Americanness to heteronormativity. Still, notwithstanding its unevenness and incompleteness, a trend toward normalization and incorporation speaks to the emergence, alongside of a regime of compulsory heterosexuality, of a "politic of heteronormativity." The latter speaks to the way normative heterosexuality is enforced: less by repressive and exclusionary state and institutional practices than by local and informal networks and organizations and an implicit but still vital culture of homophobia (Anderson 2009, Dean 2014, McCormack 2012, Seidman 2004, 2009).

Gay normalization and mainstreaming have altered the broader cultural landscape of sexual identity. In particular, for perhaps the first time in American history, heterosexuality is recognized as a singular identity. Heterosexuality can no longer simply be taken-for-granted. In particular, it can no longer be assumed that the "normal-looking-and-acting" colleague or friend one works with, prays with, soldiers with, learns with, and grows up with, is heterosexual. Today, many straight Americans, like their gay counterparts, deliberately and publicly claim their sexuality as an identity.

Gay normalization has had an additional unintended consequence: many straight men experience gender anxiety. Historically, as gender non-conformity signaled homosexual suspicion, many gay men anxiously and vigilantly regulated their self-presentation. Tellingly, in the heyday of gay liberationism many gay men projected a hyper-masculinity (Levine 1998). Was this a way to claim conventional manliness despite being gay or was it perhaps an ironic performance, exposing its constructiveness? Regardless, as liberationism was overshadowed by a normalizing politics, many gay men embraced a conventional gender identity as the signature of a good citizen.

But, what of straight men? Didn't they historically fear that gender variance would elicit homosexual suspicion? Wasn't homophobia, after all, intended to police hetero-gender? Perhaps. But, insofar as heterosexuality was compulsory, straightness acquired a taken-for-granted status. In this social environment, suspect forms of gender variance were attached almost exclusively to a specific species of men—homosexuals.

However, as straight-acting gay men blend into the social mainstream, gender conventionality is no longer an unambiguous sign of straightness. Ironically, while anxieties surrounding sexual identity have lessened for many gay men, it may have increased for straight men. With echoes of the lives of closeted gays, straight men today are more deliberate about managing their sexual identity. In particular, gender non-conformity will likely trigger concern, for some panic. Straight men who are single "too long" or have little or no history of heterosexual relationships or are "too chummy" with women or gays or too fashion-aware may be suspected of being gay or not "real men." Straight men then are increasingly aware of their heterosexuality as a specific and performative identity; many feel compelled to manage it in order to secure its legibility and recognition; as such, their gender performance is under heightened scrutiny—by themselves and others, including by gay men!

As much as many Americans read gender conventionality as a marker of normality, there is simultaneously a growing awareness of its variance and plasticity. More and more Americans are living at times outside of a cisgendered heteronormativity; as they "do gender" situationally, many American men experience gender as a site of choice and flexibility. And, discourses of gender variation, once confined to queer or trans* communities or to a narrow band of academics and cultural creators, are today integral to mainstream public culture (Brubaker 2015, Halberstam 2018b, Stryker 2008). Gender has become a wobbly site to stake out a secure sexual identity; yet, it remains perhaps its chief signifier.

There is a parallel dynamic in the realm of sexuality: sex too is increasingly acknowledged as socially constructed and a site of variation and mobility (e.g. Davies 2015, Diamond 2008, Frommer 2000, Harris 1991, Sedgwick 1991). For example, straight men and women are no longer surprised to find themselves desirous or fantasizing about being with same-gendered partners (LaMarre 2016, Ward 2015). Indeed, many straight-identified Americans experiment with same-gender sex (Anderson and McCormack 2015, Anderson and Robinson 2016, Diamond 2008, Ward 2015). And, it's no longer mindboggling when lesbian-and-gay-identified individuals find themselves in the unlikely embrace of opposite-gendered mates, while sustaining their same-gendered desires and identities (Franklin 2017, Nestle et al. 2002, Rupp and Taylor 2013, Wilchins 1997). But also, some lesbians and gay men "become" straight as they "transition," while straights may become gay, lesbian or queer as they or their partners undergo bodily reconstruction (Nestle et al. 2002, Serano 2016, Sojka 2016). And, many young Americans are simply abandoning rigid categories of sexual identity, some preferring odd sounding terms like heteroflexible, genderqueer, trans*, pansexual, Questioning, or asexual (e.g. Murphy 2017, Rupp and Taylor 2013, Savin-Williams 2006, 2016). They object to reducing sexual identity to gender preference, and some sound off against all identity labels for inevitably flattening or reductively misrecognizing their sexuality, which many youth today understand as person-and-context dependent or simply a zone of heterogeneity and excess.

Straight men are then enmeshed in a web of contradictory gender and sexual meanings and politics. They are under pressure by an iconography that still normalizes a seamless heteronormative masculinity. Ironically, this gender normativity is today, at times, endorsed by a culture of gay male homonormativity that invokes heteronormative gender tropes to redeem claims to normalization (Duggan 2003). This gender normativity is policed by pathologizing and polluting transgressive gender and sexual practices. Yet, queer subjects are claiming their own voice in the form of public representations championing gender and sexual variation and choice as signifiers of enlightenment and liberation. Gender and sexuality are then burdened with layers of contradictory meanings and normativities. If not more thickly policed then in the past, they are surely carriers of excess meanings and affective and moral resonances. Accordingly, for many Americans, gender and sexuality demand more individualizing efforts to sort out issues of desire, identity, and intimacy.

Philip

Philip, a 39 year old, white, carefully groomed and dressed, and pleasingly open-faced retail manager settled onto the couch of my consulting room. In response to my greeting, "Hello Philip," he replied, "Actually, it's Phil. . . . Or Philip, too, I guess. . . . Or Philly. . . . Take your pick . . . any one is fine." Then, 20 minutes into our session, he blurted out, "You know . . . I'm sorry . . . but . . . I've been thinking . . . everybody does call me 'Phil' . . . except my family . . . they call me 'Philly' . . . even though I *hate* it. . . . What's worse is they *know* I hate it. . . . But, secretly, I've always preferred 'Philip'. . . . It's a good name . . . don't ya' think? Is that okay?" I agreed, " 'Philip' is a good name." "Well," he said, "You may be the only one that's ever called me that. . . . Why haven't I ever asked anyone to call me that?"

In this initial session. Philip informed me he had read about me in a NY Times Magazine essay on "conversion therapy." He was intrigued by my early struggles with sexual identity; it was what prompted him to call. Already apparent, the issue of identity, specifically sexual identity, would stay front and center.

Philip narrated a history, starting as a young boy, of obsessively thinking he might be gay. This thought haunted his teen years and continues to this day. At one point he painfully confessed, "The thought that I might be gay never leaves my mind . . . and it terrifies and disgusts me! When I read about you in the Times, I couldn't imagine myself being *you*: married . . . having a child . . . realizing I was gay . . . losing *everything* . . . I'd want to die. . . . Oh God . . . *ugggh*! (a visible shudder). I apologize. . . . I didn't mean to offend you." As the months became years, I learned that, given his homophobic association of being gay with being effeminate, his sexual anxiety was inextricably linked to a deeper sense of shame about his status as a man. To ward off such doubts, Philip would often embrace a rigid identity as a hetero-masculine man.

Philip had consultations with other therapists in years past. In each case, it was after he read an article highlighting their specific insights into working with seemingly repressed or closeted gay men. In each instance, he aborted treatment because he wanted to know, unequivocally, whether he was gay or straight, and none could absolutely confirm either.

Philip's story reawakened early struggles with my sexual identity. Like him, I desperately wanted to be "fixed." But, unlike him, I went to a psychiatrist knowing I was gay and hoping he'd make me straight. Sadly, I had the misfortune of finding an analyst who, for five anguished years, sadistically tried to do just that. But that was in the 1960s! Philip, some 5 decades later, has sought therapists who would confirm or disconfirm that he might be gay, a dreaded, abject identity in his view. His life felt stalled until he could know the answer. I was struck by his desperate need to be recognized as a straight man. I wondered whether his anxieties weren't so much about his sexual and gender identity, but, rather, about reconciling his deep investment in heteronormativity as a marker of normality and goodness with an unruly inner life whose desires and identifications were troublesome. But why such intense anxiety, and why such desperation to be recognized as a straight man while living in a metropolitan environment that has normalized varied desires and identities?

Like all of us, Philip's internal life was filled with multiple, contradictory, and shifting desires and identifications rooted in varied attachments. Philip was aware of a gentle, kind, and accommodating part of himself, manifested in an easy going, friendly, and considerate way with others. But this self-state often made him uncomfortable as it evoked feelings of not being manly, which he read as a possible sign of being gay.

This part of Philip was in conflict with a narrow phallic masculinity that found expression in his preference for power suits, slick-backed hair, a preoccupation with monetary success and social status, and a tough-minded conservatism that was short on compassion. His phallic self could be relentless in its ridicule of the sensitive Philip. "You're unmanly! You're different! You're weak! You're GAY!" At such moments, he spiraled into shame and panic, which triggered an almost reflex-like embrace of a hyper-phallocentric masculinity, as if to reassure himself of his normality. But this put him at odds with his own internal life, and so his embattled inner state continued.

Philip grew up in a middle class family in Detroit. His father, an attorney for a small law firm, "was always working and hardly ever home." He describes him as distant and unemotional, a workaholic, passionate about sports but showing Philip and his mother little affection. "I never remember being hugged by him or his giving my mother more than a peck on the cheek. He would boast, 'I show my love by being the man of the house and the provider for this family.'" As Philip eventually realized, though, his father was something of a frustrated underachiever, as his mother needed to work to sustain their upwardly mobile aspirations. Still, his father claimed to be the *man* of the house, the breadwinner and moral authority who masked his shame for underachieving by his boisterous all-knowing attitude and his bossiness. No one, least of all Philip, ever challenged him.

His father would routinely spend weekend hours watching sports on TV. Philip was derided for his disinterest in sports. "He rejected me because I wasn't masculine enough" and would humiliate him in front of his mother by calling him a "crybaby" or a "sissy" or a "momma's boy." His mother's response to this ridicule—and to his lack of affection towards her—was to collude with Philip: he needed protection and they both craved recognition; an enmeshed relationship was forged. She smothered him with tender affection and sought to comfort him as her "sensitive boy," telling him "you're not a roughneck like the other boys, my little Philly." Philip was torn. An adhesive attachment (Kainer 2014) to his mother, and her validation of his gentle, receptive self, provided a tender loving bond. Yet, in this anxiety-filled atmosphere of overprotection and dependency, Philip felt even more the sting of his father's emasculating ridicule, instilling in him the beginnings of self-doubt about his gender and sexual identity. But to embrace his father's narrow phallic manliness threatened his deep attachment to his mother and to the gentle tender qualities that were embraced by her. And, given his father's seemingly impossible yardstick for gaining his respect and love as a man, Philip's attachment to him risked becoming an object of repeated narcissistic injury. What Philip perhaps did not yet realize was that his mother unwittingly echoed the same stinging message as his father: he was a different kind of boy, not normal, not like others. She just sugarcoated the message and wrapped it in a hug, but left him without a clear sense of himself and facing huge impediments to fully individuate. By the time our work began, Philip oscillated between a state of homosexual panic and a resolve to present as a rigidly straight man, a determination that continuously rubbed up against a messy inner life.

Despite a gender conventional and straight presentation, Philip cannot easily see himself in gender normative terms. Of course his family background weighs heavily on him. Then, too, there were the childhood taunts that remain seared in his psyche. Throughout his schooling he was bright and made friends easily. But, in the schoolyard, though not a sissy or girlyboy (Corbett 1993, Ehrensaft 2007, 2011), his being awkward and thin-skinned made him a target for bullying. He recalls being tormented by his peers, at times using the same humiliating words his father used, but adding "Silly Philly" and "Philly Cream Cheese," and "gay" and "faggot" to the taunts. Did others see something in him he couldn't yet see? He was sure they did. Adding to his uncertainty, Philip acknowledged having conflicting feelings toward the schoolyard bullies. "I was frightened of these macho tough guys . . . but I was also attracted to them. . . . to their swagger. . . . I wanted to be like them." At times, Philip would conflate his heightened gender identification with these "macho tough guys" with a desire for them. He began to feel that they saw through him the way his father did. He worried, did they see a truth: he was not really a masculine boy, but instead its antithesis, gay?

Philip's confusion continued into young adulthood, except the site of doubt and panic shifted from the playground to dating. "I was terrified of approaching girls . . . especially if they were pretty and popular and attracted to the macho football player types. . . . I wasn't like those guys, so what could they possibly see in me?" He rarely dated, but continued to be drawn to these manly men, at once envious yet also wanting to be them—or was it wanting them? Self-punishing judgments as not measuring up triggered panic attacks. "My inability to tough it out and go the distance," whether it was dating, pressing for promotions, or standing up to his father, were, in his eyes, indelible markers of a failed masculinity and, he suspected, his secret homosexuality.

Long stretches of our work focused on Philip's belief that he was repressing his true identity He desperately wanted to know he wasn't gay, that he was a real man, but his "sensitive" side seemed to mock this wish. And, there was a long history of being pulled towards masculine men. Was this just an identificatory love that was transferred from his phallic father to other manly men, which he confused with sexual love? After all, he wanted to be like them, be recognized by them and be part of their world. Yet, the line between identification and desire is blurry.

Although a long-term relationship had eluded Philip, he occasionally hooked-up with women. He grew animated, however, whenever he spoke of participating in heterosexual sex parties. Often, several men pleasured the same woman; at times, two or more men's cocks would inadvertently touch as they simultaneously fucked, and it was not unusual for another man's hand to make contact with parts of Philips body, though there was never explicit sex. Philip admitted being excited by the close proximity of these very masculine men. Though never acknowledging any sexual desire for them, he could not deny being super-turned-on during these erotic episodes. This troubled him. I wondered though whether his excitement might be less homoerotic than an experience of a merging gender identification making him feel powerful and desirable? He was again confused, and his response was to reduce such uncertainty to a matter of questioning his sexual identity; he could not tolerate the blurriness between identification and desire, and the messiness in the linkages between his desires, identifications, and a social identity. Instead, multiplicity and fluidity frightened him; it elicited homosexual panic. He responded by taking flight from this internal unruliness embracing a rigidly cisgendered straight identity.

Given his insistent homophobia, I struggled both to understand and respect Philip's considerable investment in a straight masculine identity. While such social identities can serve to defend against a more fluid internal life and intimacies (Corbett 1996: 458–459, Prager 2013), they can also anchor a sense of security and psychic coherence. Being part of a straight middle class world filled Philip with feelings of normality and pride. And, as Foucault might have said, Philip's identity made possible varied kinds of relationships and experiences; it provided him with codes of conduct ("technologies of the self") that he could use to care for himself and elaborate a life that is recognizably his own. Yet, as Philip came to learn, there was a cost to this normalized identity: a range of desires and forms of relating to himself and others were not only inaccessible and foreclosed, but stirred up heightened anxieties and dread. In particular, as he collapsed conventional masculinity and straightness, and a seamless straight masculinity with being a man, such desires at times evoked sexual and gender panic. The dissonance between his identity and his desires and identifications constrained but also haunted him, causing considerable suffering.

Philip gradually formed an idealized transference; he began to experience me less as a feared gay man then as someone who is married to a man, someone who is a parent and grandparent, someone who can be competent but also playful and, most importantly, someone who cares deeply about him and whom he cares about. As being gay was less fraught, Philip could relax the stranglehold that his identity as a straight man had on his inner life; he was able to occupy a wider range of feeling and self states. In a recent session Philip mused, "You know I used to be terrified I'd be like you. . . . Now I'm trying my damnedest to be like you."

Phallic troubles: the struggle to redeem manliness

When Simon and Garfunkel sang "I am an island I am a rock . . . and a rock feels no pain," they echoed a view many Americans hold about men. In the face of anxieties of vulnerability, men are said to retreat into a detached, self-sufficient pose; their anxieties masked by a fierce independence which protects them from potential humiliation but renders men unable to fully feel and be truly intimate.

Psychoanalysts have their own origin story of boys becoming rock-like. One such narrative speaks of loss and defense. In this telling, young girls sustain a rich identification with their mothers and, in a heteronormative context, are pressured to shift their desire to their fathers in order to achieve "normal" womanhood. In this trajectory, daughters have the full support of parents and society. The boy, however, must make a sharp break from the mother in order to protect against the threat of internalizing a too-solid feminine self-identification. But the mother-son attachment is powerful, and, to make matters worse, the father is often absent and unable to provide an emotionally secure masculine identification. Reeling from the narcissistic injury of his mother's prioritizing her love of the father and by experiencing a father hunger (Herzog 2001), many boys navigate individuation by adopting a seamless phallic masculinity. In this account, boys embrace masculinity as a defense against experiencing the double loss of the mother—as an identificatory and sexual object—and the longed for but unavailable father or, in the case of a boy's homoerotic longing, the proscribed eroticized father. Boys protect themselves by becoming self-exiled islands, impervious to loss and hurt; their surrendering of a certain intimate capacity compensated by joining their fathers in a world of powerful men. Donna Elise (2001) calls this state of impenetrability that boys and men enlist to fortify a fragile male psyche, the "citadel complex."

From this perspective, the notion of phallic masculinity pivots around two conceptual couplets: narcissism/omnipotence and impenetrability/penetration. Phallic masculinity is said to presuppose a certain omnipotence: the world is mine; my sense of entitlement is expansive; I know of no limits to what is possible and the other, whether a subject or nature or an inanimate object, is there for me to use to project myself into the world. I know others only as they relate to my self-needs, as part of my own expansiveness, as part-objects, and as a condition of my self-validation and aggrandizement. Phallic masculinity then is said to be narcissistic as it denies the independent subjectivity of the other. To the extent that it refuses reciprocity, it admits the other only as an object to reflect back on itself or to be penetrated, but the phallic self is itself impenetrable. Self-states coded as feminine, for example, being vulnerable, dependent, and receptive, are projected to women or to "lesser," failed men, especially gay men.

Critics have raised doubts about this account. For example, Corbett (2009a) argues that phallic narcissism does not necessarily extinguish the other. "What about the positive valance of phallic aggression? How might we consider the pleasures of phallic narcissism for subject and object alike, including the paradoxical manner in which as narcissism opens out it both expands and excludes the other" (p. 219). In the arena of sexuality, many men use the surface of the body as a space of erotic display and playful provocation. Their phallicism is experienced by themselves *and others* as an erotic object to be desired and an occasion to elicit and explore sensual pleasures. While not discounting the ways phallic narcissism can be defensive, Corbett invites us to

> consider how narcissistic stances can be seen as fantastic bids toward relationship: invitations toward complementary bigness, invitations towards competitive bigness . . . the quest for the self-confidence of mastery (to be distinguished from domination), the wish to grow, the longing to create and find a corresponding excitement and desire in another, along with the practice of elastic play (roles are made, roles are traded) that affords fantastic recognition.
>
> (p. 213)

From a developmental perspective, Michael Diamond (2009) argues that phallicism is indeed narcissistic as it pivots around self-expansion and a desire to penetrate and dominate. However, in boys' ordinary development, phallicism blends into a broader standpoint of "genitality." This underscores a psycho-sexual position in which "penetration in the service of mastery, potency and authority is integrated with the needs for connection and attachment. Phallic urges are present . . . but . . . are transformed into more aim-inhibited and object-recognizing forms" (p. 27). In the realm of sexuality, genitality signals that

> [heterosexual] men yearn not only for the pleasures of penis-in-vagina, but also to enjoy being penetrated, having ones' testicles stimulated, experiencing pleasure through the use of their mouths, and fantasizing as well as engaging in a variety of sexual practices that are too easily societally pathologized. . . . Penetration and receptivity, as well as intrusion and inclusion, are the hallmarks of genitality.
>
> (p. 27)

Building on these revisionist views of phallic narcissism, we argue that the conventional psychoanalytic view of phallic masculinity as organized by a rigid binary logic of impenetrability/penetration is one-sided and arguably speaks to a defensive position. As we see it, the masculine phallus crumbles or wilts without recognition; furthermore, recognition presupposes a self that has the capacity to extend or project outward into the world in a legible and authoritative manner. But this dynamic of recognition renders phallicism precarious. Analysts have failed to theorize phallicism as a site of anxiety and precariousness.

Phallicism involves outwardness or a desire for a worldly presence in order to warrant its claim to authority. Whatever else it is, the phallus is world-making; that is, it's about marking the world and being seen, felt, and heard as a desiring, ambitious world-inhabiting subject. Paraphrasing Sartre, the self projects itself into the world at once being world-and-self-forming. The phallic self's narcissism implies a demand to be responded to, to be recognized and deferred to or allied with. But this very demand is fraught with a double anxiety: the risks of phallic projection and the refusal of recognition. The threat is real: the crumbling of the phallus and an ordeal of public humiliation.

Phallicism pivots on the imperative of self-projection; but this risks psychic immobilization in the face of daunting expectations that men be visible and command admiration and deference. Phallic paralysis may mean being stuck in a state of *containment*, that is, in a desire deferred, in an incapacity to extend into the world as a generative force. Suspended in a state of unrealized desire is a kind of impotence. The "contained" masculine self may try to pose or "pass" as phallic; but, instead of assuming this posture as iconically manly, we believe it's a potential suspension of manliness, threatening to slide into feminization and worse, in its passivity and impotence, into a stereotypically abject form of homosexualization.

Phallicism is perhaps redeemable as containment in contexts where men can take-for-granted women's deferral and deference. This speaks to social environments in which women's lives are centered in the private realm, as wives, mothers, and caregivers, and, as indicative of their subordinate status, they are expected to do hetero-social relational work as acts of deferral and deference. In this context, a state of mere containment—silence, invulnerability, detachment, and impenetrability— is a legible and compelling signifier of masculine authority. But, in social contexts where women are fully engaged worldly subjects, which includes a refusal of deferral and deference based solely on gender, men's pose of containment indicates less one of masculine authority then a wobbly, insecure state of an anxious defensive masculinity.

Instead of containment and impenetrability redeeming masculine authority, instead of serving as a semiotic marker of phallic power, in post-Victorian settings this standpoint often threatens men with forfeiting their manliness. A state of ongoing containment may slide into passivity, masking an anxiety around projection and worldliness; as a pose, it may become a thinly disguised state of vulnerability, concealing anxiety and a paralysis of will and, as such, is potentially marked as stereotypically feminine.

A faltering phallicism can be stalled in the sheer act of being seen, a pose of narcissistic display. Suspended in containment, the self adorns or stylizes its surface with the markings of masculinity (e.g. muscularity, bulk, hardness, swagger) as a way to pass as fully masculine. And while such a pose of containment may indeed be redeemed as masculine, it can also slide, once again, into an anxiety of the masculine turning feminine. Display or becoming an object of adoration and desire risks feminization. Without pivoting into a generative worldliness, narcissistic display risks turning into its opposite, femininity or abject homosexualization. Today, containment and masculine display is often less a defense against femininity than a mask disguising an anxiety of lack and insufficiency, a paralysis of male will, a stalled, faltering phallus.

It is then only as desire is elaborated into a world-marking-and-inhabiting-state that the phallus is truly redeemed along with a recognized manliness. The latter pivots on moving from potential into actuality; it's the doing, the risk taking, and the adventures in world-and-self-making, that give the phallus authority and allows a masculine self to command admiration and authority.

But what does it mean for men to claim the phallus as an act of self-projection and world-making? In some psychoanalytic, feminist, and masculinist discourses, the male phallus is imagined almost exclusively in the language of penetration. This concept is often understood in terms of masculine conquest and domination. Psychoanalytically, Klein's (1957) notion of greed comes to mind. Whereas envy fantasizes denying the other's good fortune by destroying the other or attacking the signifiers of recognition, greed is a wish to penetrate the inside of the other, scrape it clean, and empty the very soul of the other.

More recently, Elise (2001) has argued that phallic masculinity has a dual dynamic: establishing impenetrability (the phallus "as a fortress of emotional self-sufficiency") while relentlessly, indeed compulsively, penetrating the other. The masculine self is opaque to the other who is ruthlessly used to expand and inflate the power of the male phallus. In Elise's view, men stake out their masculinity by establishing "an impermeable bodily and psychic boundary—which makes possible the ability to penetrate without the availability to be penetrated" (p. 499). As she sees it, many men are locked into this compulsory psychodynamic logic. To sustain phallic masculinity, men must dominate and penetrate women while also rendering other men inferior, thereby validating their phallic status. "A boy learns that, to be a man, he must be the one to penetrate as long as it is assumed that this does not include the father. . . . [or] any adult male. . . ." (p. 510). This masculine gender logic is "most apparent in the preoccupation that some [heterosexual] men have with sex as penetration of the woman and as very little else" (p. 519). Indeed, "the penis is imbued with magical qualities of power as the organ of penetration" (p. 507).

This view of penetration and its conflation with masculinity is misleading. Penetration can indicate an attitude of wonderment, a curiosity to explore and examine, and an openness to know and be known (Schiller 2010a, 2010b). One critic of Elise notes that to penetrate is " 'to permeate; to imbue, to cause to feel; to move deeply, as to penetrate with grief and to reach mentally; to understand; to grasp the hidden meaning of.' *These latter definitions evoke intersubjectivity, empathy, and attunement*" (Wyrem 2001: 537, see also Kaftal 2001: 544).

Interpersonally, we can think of penetration as a desire to know the other in a deep and expansive way, to know something of what their experience feels like; to penetrate is to be willing to learn about the other in all the ways they are like and different from us. As such, to penetrate is to risk a fuller knowing of the other, which may call into question one's perceptions of the other, but also potentially challenge one's own sense of self.

There is a reverse side to penetration: it suggests surrendering to the other, allowing oneself to be taken in, held, and known by another (Corbett 1993: 137, 2009a: 219, Ghent 1990). In penetrating another, in knowing the other inside out, one is also opening oneself to being known in similarly intimate ways. In this state of being engulfed, the penetrator is penetrated. We experience and know the other as someone who knows us in a deep way; and through the others knowing us we then can know ourselves in perhaps a different way. In other words, we experience ourselves through the way we experience ourselves in the other. In penetration we become aware that each party has a vital presence in the others internal life and each experiences themselves and the other through this interpenetration.

Rather than being narrowly conceived as an act of mastery or a narcissistic obliteration of the other, penetration can be a condition of intersubjectivity (Geist 2008, 2009, Knoblauch 1996). It makes possible recognizing and caring for another in an intimate way, knowing another from the inside as well as the outside. It speaks to a formative experience of inwardness that has often been exclusively associated with women (Fogel 2009, Slochower 1999). From this perspective, the notion of penetration assumes porous boundaries, a certain psychic fluidity and a life lived in as rhythms of penetration and being penetrated.

To achieve this intersubjective, layered connectedness, each self must be sturdy enough to resist anxieties of formlessness and self-dissolution and of being colonized by the other. As penetration resembles mutual surrender (Ghent 1990), it is ultimately an act of trust as one allows another to be a formative presence in one's interior life. It assumes a willingness to know and be known and a capacity to be cared for and to care for another, as they are exposed and vulnerable in their mutual engulfment. It also assumes a capacity to identify with the other enough to be compassionate without collapsing into the other. In that sense penetration makes possible a deep intersubjectivity and an ethic of caring.

A question that strikes us as compelling and rarely asked is this: why is claiming the phallus so difficult for so many men? In our clinical work, we have been repeatedly surprised at how many men struggle mightily to be phallic subjects. Many men feel they have failed or fallen short in fully occupying a phallic position. The pressure is intense: a cultural landscape obsessively focused on the doings of men, proving their bigness and displaying their triumphs (Corbett 2009a, Chodorow 2015).

All too frequently, observers, including psychoanalysts, confuse the normativity of masculine phallicism with men's actual lives. Sadly, men themselves often fall prey to taking what a real man is supposed to be, understood in hyped-up phallic terms, as a yardstick for their actual lives. Many men are gripped by a dread, even terror, about their inability or insufficiency to redeem a phallocentric construct of manhood. Overwhelmed by the anxiety of failure and lack, some men invest in a hypermasculine surface and a mystique of containment and display hoping that it will be misrecognized as embodying a phallic masculine ideal. Many will feel trapped, immobilized by their inability to get beyond containment and display, what Faludi (1999) calls "ornamental masculinity." But this pose of phallic masculinity often covers up intense fear and shame; and perhaps nowhere is the drama of phallic masculinity more clearly played out then on the stage of the erotic.

Chris

"Trump's not afraid to take power. I am!" With a mix of shame and an assuredness that edges into something like bravado as he ironically declares his unwavering investment in failure, Chris signals his state of ongoing phallic paralysis. He intends, I think, for me to feel his failure, to share in it, to experience the collapse just as he does. But in its sadomasochistic pleasure in announcing his—and my—failure, after 5 years of intensive analytic work, he inadvertently betrays himself; his "success" at failure underscores his phallic capacity. Even as he experiences phallic "triumph," albeit in the service of failure, he still resists claiming it, and if he does it's as a form of masochism confirming his utter failure as a man. For Chris, the underlying telos of phallicism is domination. "Displaying or expressing too much of me is harmful. . . . I fear . . . dominating others; I'll harm them and myself." If only one of us can be phallic, and phallicism equates with domination and destruction, his default position is to surrender power to the other in order to preserve his "innocence" or experience moral compensation, as Fairbairn might say, as an injured party, but one he knows to be insincere and itself a sign of defeat. But this submission fills him with resentment and envy; ultimately, frightened by the implicit phallicism of envy, he retreats into despondency and emasculation. For Chris, phallicism, whether as sadistic power or submissive envy, cannot be fully owned.

Growing up, Chris was overshadowed by his older brother, John. Although a poor student with apparently little ambition, John was a star athlete and popular with the girls. His rebelliousness and charisma claimed center stage in this solidly middle class family. John shared his capacity to occupy an expansive, clamorous space in the family with his mother. "Mom" was the chief breadwinner, the legislator of house rules, a champion of a can-do, achievement ethos. Despite family recognition of his smartness—graduate of an Ivy college—and his creativity, "Dad" was more of a background figure. Socially adept but emotionally opaque, as if he bore a burden that was unstated but known in the family, dad suffered a lifetime of his own mother's punishing judgment: enormous potential unrealized. No doubt, shame and rage bubbled just below his amiable surface and emotional reserve. From time to time, his father, unaware, enacted a drama of mortification with Chris as his victim. Perhaps temperamentally ill suited, Chris was also burdened by his mother's hope, again unstated and likely unaware, that he redeem her ardent wish for a crowning success by one of her men. Neither he nor I ever doubted that his was a loving family—caring and compassionate; but also one that left him haunted by self-loathing and suffering an abiding sense of failure. "It was hard to hate them, so I hated myself. I was bad, not ok."

Still, Chris managed well enough through most of his school years. Not a star athlete but an enthusiastic soccer player; not a string of girlfriends but a steady girl in High School; but also a straight-A student and an actor in school and community theatre that garnered him considerable admiration in the family and beyond. I was curious about this seemingly discordant part of this introspective, cerebral guy. "It felt natural, easy; I rarely memorized lines; I would learn them in rehearsals, at times improvising during performances." His final High School performance was a 45 minute monologue. "I went on stage not really knowing the lines; I was incoherent at times, really winging it. It was embarrassing but the audience didn't seem to notice." Chris never acted again. "I had no ambition, never thought about pursuing it." Perhaps, but I wondered, did he sabotage his final performance, making a failure out of what could have been a triumphant moment? He didn't disagree. He was unable to fully occupy his performative demand for recognition and admiration; instead, he surrendered power to the audience, who, he perhaps believed would deliver what he felt he deserved—public mortification for his hubris.

Chris's introduction to sex was fairly ordinary for a white middle class straight suburban boy raised in the 1990s. Fantasies of girlfriends, stolen moments with Dad's porn, the secret excitements of masturbating, and a High School girlfriend with whom, against the wishes of his parents, he had sex, including fucking. But, alongside the "everything seems normal" surface was an erotic fantasy world that filled him with intense excitement, but also with dread and shame. Sex was never talked about in the family; bodies were always covered. Mom and Dad rarely displayed erotic desire; and a heteronormativity that stipulated heterosexual dating, marriage, romantic sex, and monogamy was seamlessly woven into family life, unstated but known, a certainty needing no comment.

He never doubted his straightness, but there are many ways to be "bent." For example, at the age of 8, and in a mood of erotic playfulness, he tried on his mother's bra and panties. He fantasized being with a sexy woman; it turned him on. Unfortunately, his mother discovered her missing undergarments. She confronted him and in a scolding tone admonished, "never do this again. I froze. I felt scared . . . small, silenced and shamed." For many years after, "I felt that sex was wrong. I stopped masturbating." I never doubted Chris's account of this event as a heterosexual fantasy, but I wondered about its gender take away. With a crumbly and depressed father, and a powerful take-charge mother, would Chris associate the phallus with his mother and, if so, how would he negotiate a gender identity? Would he retreat from the maternal phallus to claim a masculinity that would be over-identified with the wobbly phallus of the father?

In High School, Chris experienced his first girlfriend, Andrea. Andrea wasn't easy. She was demanding. "I was afraid to disappoint her, afraid if I refused her demands she would get angry, leave me, even commit suicide." She wanted Chris to be there for her, whenever she needed him; mostly he complied. He was often unhappy in the relationship. "I couldn't be myself." But, Chris was excited by the power of Andrea's desire. "She wanted me and I could make her feel better. . . . It felt good to be desired and . . . wanted. I also liked being touched, receiving oral sex. . . ." Still, the sex was anxiety-ridden, as Chris feared disease, pregnancy, and censure if his parents learned of his behavior. In his senior year, Andrea faked being pregnant and threatened suicide. Their sexual relationship became public, embarrassing his parents and humiliating Chris. In our initial consultation, he described this episode as traumatic.

In his first three years of college, Chris did not have sex. Still, he seemed okay; he did well in his studies, made friends easily, and enjoyed living away from home. He took his senior year abroad in Amsterdam. His thoughts often turned to sex. "I hadn't had sex for 3 years . . . I was terrified. I had performance anxieties. . . . Sex felt too intimate." After a night of drinking, he hired a sex worker. Initially, he felt "cool, confident as a man." This feeling quickly passed into repugnance. "I felt guilty, shame as if I was dirty, disgusting, infected. . . . I could never share this with anyone. I'd be abandoned. . . ." Chris spiraled into a depression that continued to this day, some 7 years later.

In an effort to interrupt his bleak, deflated state, Chris moved to NY to join Occupy Wall Street protests and to pursue graduate studies. These were thrilling times; he felt expansive and impactful. A year in he dropped out of radical politics and abandoned his studies. It felt too much—too demanding, too exhausting, and futile. The initial exquisite moment of phallic projection crumbled, landing him in the consultation room, deflated and filled with self-hatred and envy.

Two years into our work Chris met Helen, a smart, ambitious, and caring woman. They began a relationship soon after. Chris felt an "honesty and frankness that was rare for me." He worried though. "I don't want anyone to need me. . . . I can't deliver." But Helen felt similarly toward Chris and her tender, inviting and "menschy" spirit quieted his anxieties. Then too, Helen's living in Boston established an emotional boundary that eased his anxieties.

Once again, Chris surrendered power. It was Helen, always, who initiated contact, expressed an interest in seeing him, and made arrangements to be with him in NY. Chris would acquiesce to her desire, even if he didn't want to see her. "When she wants to be with me, even if I don't want to, I can't say no. I don't want to hurt her. . . . I feel an urge to comply." Resentment and envy of her agency manifested in withholding behavior, routinely interrupting their bonding.

This dynamic infused their sex. Though Chris experienced sex, for the first time, as splendidly lustful and enlivened by their mutual affection, it often pivoted into an asymmetrical power dynamic. Chris's priority was first and foremost to please Helen. "Satisfying her is my pleasure." What he most wanted was her to desire him, to want him, but when she expressed this desire it felt like a burden, as if his wanting her to want him and her wanting him was "too much," triggering his emotional withdrawal and a stinging coldness. He was, he knew, punishing her for her naked, willful desire for him, for the power it wielded over him, for making him feel needy but also hungry for more. But what was less clear to him was that he was also punishing himself for his own desiring of her to desire him. The "too muchness" was both the phallic narcissistic force of his desire to be desired and Helen's emphatic desire. In the face of the anxiety of phallic desire, his and hers, Chris retreated into a punishing passive aggressive resentment, itself masking a projection of himself as a phallic agent. But even the phallic gesture of resentment was in the end too much; it often prompted a retreat into an abject submission and emasculation. Chris was locked into an asymmetrical quasi-sadomasochistic drama.

Helen encouraged Chris to break from being submissive and from his passive/aggressive behavior by assuming more responsibility in their relationship, including in their sex. He struggled. Her very desire for him to be more dominant felt burdensome. "I'm aware of being submissive and resent it. She asks me to be more dominant but it's not easy and her request feels like a burden, provoking another act of submission." What lay behind this phallic anxiety? "She says 'take me over,' 'possess me' . . . but I'm ambivalent, scared. I find it sexy but too much responsibility, too risky. . . . I fear hurting her." You see, Chris was turned on by fantasies of aggressive sex. "I fantasize about grabbing her hair, forcefully penetrating her mouth, cumming on her face. . . . She becomes like some object for me. . . . I just want to choke her, slap her. And, I want her to like it . . ." This fantasy felt exciting but also horrifying. In such moments, he likened himself to the angry straight white fascistic and misogynistic men he detested. Worse, he envied their full throttled will to power.

Anxious and unsettled by his aggressive fantasies, Chris would embrace a reverse fantasy centered around submission. "She wants me to take her over but I often want her to take me over, for her to be on top . . . to experience being desired by her. I want her to claw, scratch, and to attack my cock with her mouth, with her body, ride me not so it would hurt but to feel her want, her need for me." But just voicing this desire was too much. "In reality, I cannot ask for what I want sexually . . . I can't. I won't. I just want her to take over. . . . I don't want to be responsible . . . for anything. . . . Sometimes, I feel like I'm going to explode or collapse." Chris often felt stuck in an insatiable, twisted carnal desire that excited but also repulsed him; his stuckness confirmed his abject, emasculated state as a man.

Lately, Chris speaks of a growing awareness of absence and loss, a mourning for a (phallic) life not really lived. "I have no sense of achievement or even possibility. I'm mired in loss, bitterness, miserableness. . . . A self without a story; a job I hate (as a waiter); and a loving relationship but unsustainable." He's stalled in a state of phallic containment. "I'm jealous of people who have enough confidence to act and be active. I'm uncomfortable about being seen, doing. Why do I stop? I guess fear. I'm not really up to the task. . . ." At times, Chris invokes and embraces smallness. At least, he says, small persons have a shot at being cared about and attended to. When I ask if that's also possible if you're big, he's not sure. "I guess you can get cared about being big, but its fraught, difficult, a lot of work and you can fail, sexually fail. But being small you can get attention. . . . Someone will have to pity you and take care of you. . . . Maybe being big has other rewards. You get love and care and other kinds of satisfactions. . . . Big persons get their own worth from themselves; small persons get their worth from the other."

The poetics and politics of desire

In the past few decades, there has been a significant rethinking of psychoanalytic views of sex. In the 1980s and 1990s, relationalists critiqued Freud's biologically based drive theory and psycho-sexual developmentalism. They offered an alternative foundational idea: the socialization of desire. Sex was said to be relationally formed and in fundamental ways about attachment and individuation or boundary marking and power (e.g. Davies 2004: 394, 404, Frank 2013).

More recently, responding to a perception that sexuality or, more to the point, the carnal or erotic aspect of sex has been marginalized or domesticated in the relational canon, a new wave of theorists have offered a return of sorts to Freud—not to the language of drives and discharge, but to the pleasure-seeking libido and to a polymorphous perverse desire that crosses normative boundaries as it explores a wide range of possible acts and objects (Dimen 2003, Rundel 2015, Saketopolulou 2014, Stein 2004, 2008). These theorists remain relational; as a site of meaning and affect, sex is shot through with the other; still, eros underscores a desire that is intensely bodily, phantasy based, and generative and transgressive (Saketopoulou 2014, Stein 1998, 2008). In this regard, Rundel (2015) frames

> sexuality as driving the psyche to dedifferentiation, not as a form of regression but . . . a mode of experiencing with tremendous power in the present tense. It is . . . a feeling of a falling away of boundaries, of limits, of separation, and into an experience of union and largeness. . . . This helps to account for the . . . ways it [sexuality] manifest[s] in extremes, in states of desire and ecstasy and obsession, that pull us toward our outer limits.
>
> (p. 628)

This perspective favors phenomenological accounts that attend to the ways sex impacts on the psyche that are irreducible to the interpersonal dynamics of attachment and relationship-building.

From a Foucauldian (1980) vantage point, shifts in psychoanalytic thinking are part of a Western culture obsessed with writing desire into a new language of sexuality. And, as Foucault insisted, this discursive outpouring is integral to a disciplinary social order. But Foucault (1990a) also understood disciplinarity as perhaps more unstable then is often assumed. Discourses of sexual normalization (e.g. sexology, psychiatry, psychoanalysis, demography, sex manuals) prompt counter-normalizing dynamics or, if you will, "queer" possibilities. Every effort by Freudians or sexologists or the sexual reformers of the early 20th century to embed sex in heterosexual marriage and norms of romanticism and companion-ship, thereby underscoring its "higher" moral purpose (e.g. family making or character building through deferral and discipline), paradoxically elicited erotic imaginings that found a voice in a grammar of illicit, unruly desires.

Consider the proliferation of a wave of popular sexual advice and medical literature in Victorian America authored by doctors, health advocates, moral reformers, purity crusaders, and feminists. Contrary to the stereotype, Victorians were not anti-sex; instead, they viewed sex as a powerful, potentially beneficent force. It could not and should not be denied but neither should it be given free reign. It should be confined to marriage, but not as its foundation. Sex had little to do with love. Indeed, sex was considered dangerous as it threatened to unleash a carnal desire that would debase and destroy the moral-spiritual core of love and marriage. Legitimate sex should be focused on procreation, though erotic pleasure as a secondary affect was acknowledged as contributing to the procreative function. Ideally, marriage was to be based on ethical-religious values, the good character of each spouse, family-making, and clearly delineated dichotomous gender roles that installed patriarchal authority. What about love? Victorians contrasted "true love" and romantic love; the former pivoted around the moral and spiritual kinship and psycho-social complementarity of men and women; the latter was based on fleeting desires and lust. A marriage based on true love, and one not contaminated by lust, stood as the aspirational ideal of at least white middle class Victorians (D'Emilio and Freedman 2012, Lystra 1989, Seidman 1991).

A sea change occurred in early 20th century America. In their battle against aspects of Victorian culture, liberal reformers embraced a forward-looking sexual ethic as part of a vision of social progress. By coupling a sensual, erotic sexuality with personal well-being and success in love and marriage, progressive reformers aimed to discredit Victorianism whose sexual ideas were not only associated with social backwardness and ill health but were said to underlie the rising tide of abortion, divorce, prostitution, and homosexuality. Reversing the Victorian ideal, progressives made sex into a privileged sign of love, a marker of true love. A mutually fulfilling sexualized love became the indispensable basis of a successful marriage. By framing sex as a core part of love, they inadvertently legitimated the eroticization of sex. That is, if mutual sexual satisfaction is the foundation of love and marriage, the erotic aspects of sex assumes a heightened moral significance (Seidman 1991, 1992). At the same time, against sex radicals who questioned marriage, they defended the Victorian view that sex and romantic love were only legitimate in a monogamous heterosexual marriage.

The popular sex advice literature of the pre-World War II period provided how-to guides to becoming knowledgeable, skillful, and playful erotic agents. Based on a medical-scientific understanding of the erotic zones of the body, ordinary Americans would be able to effectively give and receive sensual pleasure as a way to express love and consolidate a stable, companionate marriage. This advice literature detailed a world of erotic zones, sex acts, positions, and carnal enhancements using lighting, music, smells, and role-playing. Moreover, against Victorian representations of the passionless moral woman, they were viewed as erotic citizens fully capable of giving and receiving sensual delights as acts of love. Mutual erotic pleasure was legitimated or rendered into a moral act as a way to love and secure a stable marriage (Seidman 1991).

This wave of sex advice literature, popular medical texts, marriage guides, and popular sexology and sociology promoting a sexualized love and an eroticized sexuality, as part of a new ideal of companionate marriage, was wildly popular. Progressive sexual discourses shaped the cultural context that made Kinsey's volumes on men (1948) and women's (1953) sexual behavior into bestsellers in mid-20th century America. Let's be clear. We are not saying that Americans actual sexual practices mirrored these new sexual ideas, though surveys through the first decades of the 20th century document significant changes (Seidman 1991). Rather, a culture of eroticism was taking shape in the mainstream alongside of, and in tension with, a Victorian one.

As reformers sought to normalize a culture of sexualized love and eroticized sexuality, they did not anticipate a dramatic unintended consequence: the legitimation of eroticism as a source of pleasure, play, self-expression, communication, and well-being apart from love and marriage. This development was at the heart of the so-called "sexual revolution" of the 1960s. Sex as an erotic experience, reformers and radicals argued, need no higher moral purpose such as marriage or family-making. While the pill, reproductive rights, relative affluence, extended adolescence, and so on made this "revolution" possible, discursive enticement and legitimation followed quickly in the sexual ideas of the counterculture, the women's and gay/lesbian movements, the radical theories of a Herbert Marcuse and Norman O. Brown, and the sexual libertarianism of popular publications such as the *Joy of Sex*, *The Secret Garden*, *Playboy*, and *Our Body, Ourselves*. Hippies, feminists, gay and lesbian liberationists, playboys, and libertines embraced an eroticized sexuality that no longer needed to be contained exclusively in contexts of love or marriage (Seidman 1991, 1992). Eros was unleashed, producing what Foucault called "laboratories of sexual experimentation" (1990a: 298), except that where Foucault was thinking of gay bathhouses, the new laboratories were the bedrooms of more and more ordinary Americans.

The debates and conflicts around abortion, gay rights, recreational sex, single motherhood, and divorce evidence an abiding ethical division in America. Do specific sexual desires and practices have an inherent moral significance or is their meaning and import entirely a relational negotiation? The former leans on a "morality of the sex act." Sexual desires and acts in themselves bear a moral significance. Some desires and acts are inherently normal, good, healthy, and right; others are simply abnormal, bad, unhealthy, perverse, sinful, and wrong. Is homosexuality or sex without love or single motherhood or sex work or non-monogamy wrong and bad (sinful, unhealthy, pathological, symptomatic)? Or, is their moral significance wholly dependent on the contextual meaning agents assign to such desires and acts? Stated otherwise, is sex to be understood as embedded in a moral context in which there is a more or less coherent classification of good and bad, right and wrong, healthy or pathological? Or, is sex best situated in an aesthetic context and, as such, sexual choices are matters of personal taste or lifestyle? Of course, ethics still informs sexuality via the nature of the relationship. For example, should sex be exclusively between adults and what counts as consent? But this is a minimal, formalistic ethic resonant with an aestheticizing of the domain of sex (Segal 1994, Seidman 1997, Weeks 1995).

In our view, these broad shifts in American culture form the wider social context for grasping changes in American psychoanalytic thinking about sexuality. Relationalism didn't just free itself from Freud's drive theory but from a Victorian culture that constructed sex as fundamentally a biological drive, bearing an inherent moral meaning and purpose, and one that coupled normality to heterosexuality, love-based marriage, family making, and monogamy. By contrast, relationalists insist that eros is about meaning, not drive or discharge, and that it often bears psychic and relational meanings that exceed a narrow normativity (e.g. Hirsch 2009). However, there remains a residual moralizing: many relationalists continue to draw a dividing line between the normal and the pathological or the healthy and the perverse, even if the moral yardstick is less the sex act per se than its psychic and relational meaning (cf. Chodorow 1994, Dimen 2003). Against this residual Victorianism, and against relationalism's overdetermination of a socialized desire, the new theorists attend to the carnal aspects of sexuality and situate sex more squarely in the sphere of aesthetics, without abandoning an awareness of its ethical and political significance.

Eroticism fixes attention on bodies, desires, acts, fantasies, scenes, pleasures, and experimentation. Eros is said to be unruly and excessive or transgressive as it is driven by bodily excitations and unconscious desires and phantasies. As such, it is in tension with normativities that stipulate not only the appropriate gender or race or class of a sex partner but scripts a normalizing logic of sex acts, positions, and trajectory. Indeed, as Stein (2004, 2008), Saketopolulou (2014) and others (e.g. Blechner 2005, Dimen 2005, Rundel 2015) argue, it is a desire that exceeds normative scripting that gives it its passion and boundless, potentially self-shattering excitement, but also its underside of distress and abjection. It is less desire as discharge, but as occupying a liminal space where psyches and bodies mix with intense fantasies and excitations, and where selves surrender to unnameable pleasures, that make possible peek or "limit experiences." In transgressive sex, selves can feel that they are unraveling and opening up to unintended psychic and interpersonal possibilities. Referring to Foucault, his biographer writes:

Through intoxication, reverie, the Dionysian abandon of the artist
... an uninhibited exploration of sado-masochistic eroticism, it
seemed [to Foucault] possible to break ... the boundaries separating
the conscious and the unconscious, reason and unreason, pleasure and
pain—and, at the ultimate limit, life and death—thus starkly revealing
how distinctions central to the play of true and false are pliable,
uncertain, contingent.

(Miller 1993: 30)

As we see it, this new theorizing is directly linked to gay and queer culture
and is informed specifically by queer perspectives, in particular, the
work of Bersani (1986, 1987, 1995), Butler (1990), Foucault (1980),
Hocquenghem (1972) and Sedgwick (1990). Indeed, we don't think it's a
stretch to suggest that much of this new psychoanalytic work is informed
by, even driven by, queer-identified analysts such as Botticelli (2010),
Corbett (1993), Dean (2014), Gonzalez (2013), Guss (2010), and Hartman
(2010). This is hardly surprising. Gay men and queers, the latter including
transgendered and genderqueer folk, have since the late '60s pioneered
the elaboration of cultures of eroticism that validate a transgressive eros;
in bathhouses, backroom bars, sex clubs, porn, apps, and cruising areas,
gay men have explored every possible way bodies can yield unimaginable
pleasures and ways of using eroticized bodies to innovate modes of being
and relating. It is not only that some gays and queers have embraced
polymorphous perversity, but for the past half century they've produced
discourses and representations that mark such eroticism as liberatory (e.g.
Altman 1971, 1983, Califia 2000, Rubin 1984, Samois 1982, White 1980,
White and Silverman 1977). In other words, a queer culture of erotic
experimentation is institutionally embedded and culturally valorized,
shaping particular types of sexual subjects. Are their counterparts in
straight culture? No doubt, but it strikes us that it's perhaps only in
gay and queer life that eroticism is deeply woven into the ordinary
fabric of personal and public life, and that it's an unapologetic part of
mainstream life.

As much as we're excited about the current effort to offer psychoanalytic
elaborations of a culture of eroticism, at times some of this work abstracts
desire from social dynamics. It's as if in the throes of erotic liminality, or
in the longing for the continuity of being or dedifferentiation, or in the
quest for ego shattering erotic episodes, we are witnessing a pure psychic

experience—as if these forms of eros aren't already and always bearing social meaning, If this is an unstated claim, we are doubtful. Moreover, the psychic meaning of such peak erotic experiences is often emptied of everything except this transgressive psychic altering experience. Again, we're doubtful. With these two caveats in mind we turn to Alexander.

Alexander

Alexander was often on the edge of collapse: overwhelmed and panicky as his sense of self felt blurry and crumbly. His environment regularly failed him, upending Alexander in ways that infused ordinary life with dread and high anxiety. A missed dental appointment, his mother's stubbornness, an unpaid bill, or an off-putting remark by a friend would aggravate and enrage him, often triggering a profound sense of dislocation.

In a typical session, Alexander would talk about some event that was upsetting—for example, a friend demanding attention but showing little interest in him. After circling round and round trying to figure out what he actually felt and how he could and should have responded, he would often ask if I experienced something similar and, if so, how I felt and dealt with it? It was as if narrating my reality allowed him to know and regulate his experience. He didn't trust his perception of reality; he was unsure of the appropriateness, even the realness, of his own emotions and thoughts; and, he would often puzzle over what would be appropriate behavior. It was if he needed to see himself in me in order to know what he felt and if it was okay. By identifying with me he was able to locate himself and feel contained. Alexander's sweetness and vulnerability, along with a driving hunger for an expansive life, made it easy for me to serve as an idealizing and containing self-object (Kainer 2014).

Alexander grew up in a poor, heavily Latino section of the Bronx. Abandoned by his father as a young child, this 24 year old mix of a Costa Rican mother and a Chilean/Greek father was raised by his single disabled mother. In many ways, she was dependent on Alexander for emotional and financial support. He was devoted to her; they enjoyed movies and dinners together; he worried endlessly about her health and well-being; he loved her dearly.

But mom wasn't easy. Living in a small studio apartment, she watched TV late into the night, despite Alexander's wish for quiet in order to read and relax. But he never doubted her love, even if she didn't really understand her slightly built, sensitive son who preferred books to sports and worried about his looks but not about being popular. Yet, it meant a lot to Alexander that his mother accepted that he was gay, even if she didn't want to know much about this aspect of his life.

I thought that her narcissism made it difficult for Alexander to see himself in her in ways that made him feel seen and special. Instead, he saw what she wanted and needed him to be and he would too often mirror that self as a condition of feeling loved and good. Unable to easily find a place in her psyche, except as the devoted son, he struggled to secure a solid sense of identity and belonging. I think he found a holding space in his mind (Corrigan and Gordon 1995), in the books he read and in the ideas he entertained that seemed to lift his life at times into a sublime place. My academic background facilitated his identification with me; indeed, it enabled him to experience an identificatory love as well as a powerful idealizing transference.

In the face of environmental disappointments, Alexander often felt unanchored. He would be gripped by an intense unsettling anxiety, which defended against experiencing the psychic roots of his sense of dislocation, namely the trauma of his father's abandonment and his mother's narcissism. In the grip of high anxiety, Alexander would lose himself in distractions, intellectualism, obsessiveness, and somatic preoccupations. Anxiety would also move him to attach to idealized figures such as therapists, teachers and professors in order to locate and contain himself. Such attachments served him well, as grounds for building a coherent, sturdy self. However, to the extent that his anxieties drove him into a heightened a hyper-idealization, I wondered whether such identifications also protected him from really knowing and experiencing himself in a fuller, more real, way.

In the course of our work, Alexander's bookish, cerebral disposition led him to pursue graduate studies. His drive and smartness yielded scholarships and opportunities to study abroad. He also hoped that he could forge a coherent sense of identity and belonging in academia and in the idea of being a global citizen.

University life, especially at the elite institution he attended, was fraught for him. Many of his fellow students were wealthy and cosmopolitan; he didn't easily fit in. He often felt unrecognized and unknown. He gravitated to cultural studies classes and peers. But here too he found a milieu that was challenging. It was, he complained, often hyper-politicized: personal life, especially for a gay person of color, was often read in over-determined political terms. Every desire, opinion, action, and relationship was weighted with heightened identity-based political significance. Instead of feeling free and secure in the life of the mind, academic politics at times left him anxious and, once again, unmoored.

Like many of today's youth, Alexander came out early and did not experience the traumas of past generations. By 16 almost everyone in his family and among his peers at least knew and were tolerant. Being gay was one of the few things he was sure about. However, living as a gay person caused him considerable grief. His body was not the body he wanted. He was not tall enough, not muscular enough, not handsome enough, not stylish enough, and most importantly not white. As a dark skinned, somewhat nerdy, heady, gentle sort who lacked confidence and the resources to stylize his surface to be "gay cool," Alexander felt undesirable and squeezed to the margins of queer life.

Lacking a boyfriend, Alexander used *Grindr* to find sex partners. He had a specific type: 18–25, muscular with six-pack abs, handsome, and white. As someone whose world view was queer, feminist, anti-racist and anti-colonial, he was anguished, at times disgusted, by his desire for such an iconic symbol of white male colonialism. Still, desire trumped politics, even if it left a large psychic footprint of shame and guilt.

Despite many rejections, such men would from time to time agree to sex. Alexander would go to their apartment. Typically, he would suck their cocks; when they came, it was over. No reciprocity. He never asked, they never offered. His description of these sexual encounters struck me as stark and bare. Alexander though would describe them as often glorious.

Sex began with the initial contact made via texting and the resolve to meet. If the fellow was as advertised, just seeing and being in his presence felt thrilling. Alexander would savor every word spoken as he watched him undress; Alexander would typically remain clothed. He would touch and kiss him, everywhere; in such moments, he would begin to lose his sense of apartness. Alexander would slowly take in his cock, caressing it with his lips, engulfing it deep into his throat, drawing out the process while his hands never ceased gliding across the other's naked body. The boundaries between him and his white beauty would blur. As he felt the other's muscles tense, then release as his cock emptied its fluids into Alexander, he would become the other. "Feeling him explode in me,

I really felt that I became him; I was part of the white world; I became beautiful." Sometimes Alexander would jerk off during the act but mostly he'd prefer to just watch this naked Adonis go limp, content and oblivious to all but his spent desire. Reciprocity was not the point. It was the fantasy and the experience of identification, of losing himself by becoming the other, that rendered this sublime.

These iconic white men represented everything Alexander imagined he wasn't: beautiful, desirable, entitled, worldly, stylish, moneyed. As he explained, when he was simply in their presence he didn't just want them, but he felt like one of them; and when he was in the throes of desire he became them. "It's like I want them, to possess them, to be associated with them, so I can feel good, beautiful, and sexy." In such moments, he was no longer part of the nearly invisible army of the dark skinned, lower-class colonialized and ugly mass who service the white masters. Unfortunately, such transcendent moments passed in a flash. As he was quickly shown the door, Alexander was reminded that he's not one of them; even in moments of ecstatic merging he was aware of his otherness by the absence of reciprocity and any tenderness; he was always the Other.

Alexander split. The values and virtues of the sublime were attached to whiteness while the dark skinned mass represented the abject other. The former world is inaccessible except when he's in the grip of desire; in the aftermath of these episodes, he's filled with self-contempt, reminded of his abject status. Worse, he feels racist, as he reproduces the white/non-white hierarchy. His desire is then punishing, but perhaps, as some have argued (Saketopolulou 2014, Stein 2008), suffering is integral to ecstatic erotic experiences, but such sublime moments are never without abjection and melancholy.

Alexander cannot see these white beauties as psychically and socially complex figures struggling with their own agonies. He cannot know that their idealized virtues and status as hyper-agentic is, in part, an expression of his own racist colonial imagination that stipulates that only whiteness, pure and seamless, can be sublime. In this racist imaginary, only dark skinned folk are abject and racked with miseries and indignities. His ecstatic eroticism is illegible without understanding that he has internalized a racist colonial iconography; his transgressive sexuality is wedded to a fiercely retrograde politics. And he reproduces this racism in his self-hatred, in his demeaning of the dark skinned other. Sadly, Alexander's self-mortification is reinforced by a thread of left identity politics that renders every desire and fantasy politically significant. It's as if his very desire is then made to bear the responsibility for the perpetuation of a history of white colonial racism.

Afterword: anxieties of phallic collapse

The phallus circulates across genders; it can be claimed by men, but also by women—and non-cisgendered people. Phallicism is a position that one moves in and out of or assumes or surrenders depending on the context. It speaks to a desire to explore, to take risks, to be world-inhabiting-and-making; its outwardness can extend into a will to dominate and master while its inwardness might fold into a standpoint of imperturbability and self-sufficiency. Most of us move in and out of this position. However, for individuals for whom this position is consolidating and controlling, it may make for triumphant acts of self-and-world-making but also pivot into a narcissism that leaves one painfully alone and restless as well as denying others' subjectivity and agency. Hence its instability: world-making but also world-shattering.

Men have been subject to a fairly severe normativity: the imperative to be big, sturdy, successful, and powerful. But because men live their lives, as we all do, in multiple spheres (sex, intimacy, family, economy, culture, etc.) each involving varied capacities, and because men will always encounter others who are bigger, stronger, more successful, and smarter, they are bound to experience phallic deflation and suffer self-mortification. The dread of phallic wilting and collapse prompts many men to save face by assuming a pose of containment. To disguise their doubts and vulnerabilities, to avoid being exposed as less than real men, some enact a phallicism that pivots around impenetrability, cool detachment, and self-sufficiency. But, again, this gender idiom is also a site of heightened anxiety, often masking crippling fears and a psyche racked with a pervasive sense of inadequacy and perhaps fraudulence. No matter how big, triumphant, and powerful, there is no escaping anxieties of deflation and impotence; these hidden pockets of deep shame may be masked by a hyper-phallic performativity, but this locks men into a separateness and aloneness that can be unbearable.

Despite varied heterosexual experiences, a steady career that provided a solid middle class life, and a fairly seamless masculine surface, Philip was racked by self-doubt about being a real man. His temperament and desires didn't always align with a rigidly cisgendered heteronormative ideal. He was troubled by a pull towards manly men. He would often conflate his intense identification with sexual desire; and given his homophobic identification of gay men with femininity, this collapse prompted anxiety about his gender identity. Then, too, his strong identification with his mother, in a context of his father's hypermasculine normativity, rendered his gentleness and quiet sweetness, especially in the absence of "buddies" and interest in sports, into markers of a failed masculinity, triggering homosexual panic. In order to protect himself from these unruly desires and identifications, Philip sought to embrace a rigid hetero-masculine identity. But this only heightened his growing awareness of a misalignment between an unruly internal life and his overdetermined embrace of a heteronormative phallic self. Homosexual panic accompanied a rigid phallic masculinity.

Chris knew no such doubts. He knew he was straight. He felt like a man, but harbored doubts about being truly manly. His surface projected a seamless phallic masculinity: tall, thick, bearded, handsome and manly in stereotyped ways, for example, taciturn, self-sufficient, and relying on a powerful intellect to navigate interpersonal affairs. He also knew he was privileged as a white middle class, straight guy. He had opportunities denied many to achieve the conventional markers of success.

Still, Chris's internal life was at odds with his unruffled public phallic self. Narcissistic injuries and perhaps an adhesive identification with a wobbly, often deflated father impeded his inhabiting a phallic position. He retreated into a state of containment, hoping it would be misrecognized as embodying a controlled power, a readiness to do, to rival, and to dominate. The reality was the opposite: containment masked heightened anxiety, a sense of smallness, a wish to be cared for, and a retreat from the game of power. To project himself as a man of desire and worldly ambition was to inflict harm and to dominate, even extinguish the other. Only others could be phallic and that often meant "bad"—injurious and destructive. This splitting seemed to redeem him as "good," at least as long as he was "small." Inevitably though his emphatic resentment and hatred towards phallic others, including violent fantasies, elicited his own version of a hateful phallicism, which repulsed him and prompted self-loathing.

Containment was then unstable. He could barely acknowledge an implicit idealization of big powerful figures (professors, activists, therapists); yet, his raging envy betrayed his phallic dreams. In a sense, this was his dilemma. An idealizing transference, along with his love for Helen prompted a hunger for more life, a worldly desire, and made it harder to retreat into containment and surrender the phallus. Could he join the world of phallic selves while still holding onto the small, compassionate, sweet, and gentle self that I—and Helen—came to know?

Unlike Chris, Alexander could not easily pass as a phallic man by embracing a standpoint of containment. His slight, gentle. and nerdy public self, especially in the rough neighborhood he grew up, would not confer a presumption of phallic masculinity. He didn't play sports nor did he project a toughness or cool detachment; but then, Alexander was not one to retreat into containment.

Alexander's outward softness betrayed an inner toughness and a driving ambition to achieve and be recognizably worldly. He aspired not just to be an academic, but accomplished, and to be a global citizen armed with languages and an Ivy League education. In this regard, while devoted to his mother, he was prepared to pursue his educational goals even if it meant leaving New York. There was a psychological toughness and resilience to Alexander. This mild mannered, sweet fellow who took enormous satisfaction in taking care of his mother was also able to claim a phallic position, to join the world of phallic others, despite intense anxieties of whether he belonged.

In the erotic realm, he conflated phallicism with having and becoming the iconic white man. In his phantasy, through sex he would be transformed, even if just momentarily, by the beauty and sublime status associated with whiteness. But as much as this phantasy lifted and transfigured him in the heat of eros, he never escaped an edge of contemptible otherness. Perhaps, as he climbs the academic ladder he will acquire enough of a sense of phallic sturdiness that his struggles for identity and belonging will be uncoupled from whiteness, at least in his erotic life.

Chapter 6

Intimate knots

The unconscious dynamics of intimacy

In American culture, the coupling of "men" and "intimacy" is often construed as either a contradiction or men are said to experience intimacy very differently than women, to wit, more about "doing" than "being" together. Let's unpack this a bit.

Stipulating men and intimacy as antithetical typically assumes that intimacy is equated with stereotypically feminine experiences—sharing feelings, an ease with being vulnerable and dependent, caring for the other, and a longing for a thick emotional intermingling (Cancian 1980). Such traits are said to be at odds with being a man, indeed threaten feminization or worse, homosexual suspicion. From this vantage point, men are seen as capable of material provisioning and effectively managing caring relationships, but fall short in facilitating and sustaining emotionally rich, expressive intimate ties.

We might describe this representation of intimacy as "Victorian." In roughly mid-19th century white middle class America, men and women were thought to inhabit different psyches and were expected to occupy different social roles. Men were naturally aggressive, competitive, intellectual, and driven to seek power and dominance; accordingly, they would be well suited for roles as decision-makers and managers in the public sphere. By contrast, women were maternal and relationally oriented; their lives naturally revolve around domestic life, in particular, sustaining the moral-spiritual well-being of the family. In the Victorian model, men and women aspire to "true love" not romantic love. Whereas the latter is based on passion and dreamy hopes for an ecstatic fusion, true love pivots on mutual respect, shared ethical-religious values, and fulfilling divine or nature-dictated gender roles.

Intimacies might be forged, however, between individuals of the same gender. Historians have documented that men and women fashioned emotionally thick and committed same-gendered relationships. "Romantic friendships," especially between women, often involving declarations of love and commitment, were not uncommon among the white middle class (Fadermann 1991). As Victorian moralists imagined a gendered divide between the heart and mind and between the private and public spheres, there would be little common emotional and social basis for heterosexual intimacy.

If the Victorian intimate ideal peaked in the late 19th century, a new concept began to gain social appeal in the early 20th century: the so-called "companionate model." The Victorian notion that men and women were in some important respects different was sustained but reformers claimed that this difference creates the basis for a new complementary-based intimacy. For women, intimacy was about "being" or expressing their nature as empathic, nurturing, and relationally oriented. For men, intimacy was about "doing," which spoke to men as deciders, providers, and protectors. As companions, though, men and women could be sexually, emotionally, and socially complementary, forming a sturdy solidaristic unit.

Moreover, in the decades after World War I there was a growing awareness of a gradual converging of the lives of the two genders. Men and women were regularly mixing in public, for example, in higher education, in entertainment and leisure activities, including something new—dating. They were sharing more common life experiences. But, within the family and the workplace, neo-Victorian gender norms were upheld. A woman might have a college degree and work alongside men in the office, but she was still expected to assume stereotypically feminine-coded work roles, be deferential to men, and to be other-directed. Still, in the companionate model, men and women were to share joint activities, including mutual sexual satisfaction.

Both models of intimacy are, roughly speaking, anchored in a middle class, heterosexual normative experience. Women were to be the primary stay-at-home parent in a marital-based nuclear family while men were to be the breadwinners; father's functioned as a background supplement to the wife—ideally, a steady provider and the ultimate disciplinary authority. In the companionate model, boys became men by disavowing any trace of femininity while identifying with their father's idealized masculinity.

"Real men" then felt compelled to avoid or minimize sentimentalism and longings to nurture and be nurtured. Such feminine-coded traits were projected onto women, gay men, or other figures of failed manhood.

The Victorian and companionate models are still very much alive in American culture. However, in the past few decades a third construct has gained broad public appeal: the "soulmate." Intimacy is to revolve around partners exploring each other's inner life and sharing a transformative journey in which personal growth parallels growing intimate solidarity. In this model, there is an ongoing process of self-examination and expectations to share deeply personal experiences; each partner is to be engaged in practices of self-improvement while supporting the other's projects of personal growth (Seidman 2013). In principle, the closer a couple comes to a soulmate or "pure relationship" (Giddens 1992), gender would slip into the background or dramatically lessen as an organizing principle. Gender complementarity and companionship would ideally give way to twinship and soulmate status.

Paralleling these changing cultural ideals, many Americans have experienced far-reaching alterations in their psychic and social lives. In Chapter One, we highlighted the "de-gendering" of many social roles. There is a gender messiness in many sectors of public life that encourages recognition of persons as complex, highly individualized selves who cannot be collapsed into a stereotyped gender identity. If true, many men today will be less anxious about incorporating into their lives behaviors culturally marked as feminine or historically associated with women. Although many men may not be deliberately embracing femininity, or revising public accounts of their gender experience, their actual lives are multigendered.

Paralleling a de-gendering dynamic, we noted trends toward the de-institutionalization of heteronormativity. Many institutions are retreating from enforcing heteronormativity as evidenced by state recognized same-sex marriage, the constitutional repeal of sodomy laws and by similar gay-affirmative policy changes in corporations, universities, professional associations, and in the media-entertainment industry. Underpinning this institutional transformation is a dramatic cultural shift towards the normalization of homosexuality (Anderson 2009, Dean 2014, Gamson 2015, McCormack 2012, Seidman 2003, Weeks 2007). In this decidedly less manifestly homophobic environment, we expect men to express themselves in ways that are less restricted by stigmatizing associations to femininity and homosexuality. As we see it, a cultural environment is taking shape that is more hospitable to men having a more expansive, heterogeneous gender experience than in previous generations.

Paralleling these social changes have been equally significant alterations in the *psychodynamics* of gender. The parental environment is being transformed (Chapters 2 and 3). Consider a two parent heterosexual family. Today, the mother is likely a fulltime wage earner, and not necessarily in traditional women's occupations; likewise, she is engaged in all aspects of public life, from running for public office to being a cultural creator and a policy-maker. She brings into the parenting experience capacities, relational styles, values, and competences that are gender mixed. Simultaneously, many men find themselves in work and social roles that are not stereotypically masculine; more and more men are developing sensibilities and relational orientations that fall well outside of hegemonic masculine norms. Tellingly, these men are revising their ideas about manhood to include an aspiration to be equal participants as intimate partners and parents.

Many young boys today are then encountering mothers and fathers who are more gender mixed, and more insistent on claiming sexuality and gender as a field of personal choice. It's true that the lives of many Americans in the past also exceeded regulatory binary norms. But, today there is a culture—discourses, narratives, and representations—that normalize, even celebrate, this gender variation, including the idea of stepping outside of gender as a marker of personal authenticity, psychic well-being, and social progress (Brubaker 2016, Halberstam 2018b). In this environment, we would expect many parents to be hospitable towards their son's experience of multiple gender threads and their exhibiting a certain gender ambiguity (Ehrensaft 2011, 2014). The soulmate model of intimacy gives expression to these far-reaching socio-psychological changes.

In this chapter, we introduce men, all below forty, whose intimate lives evidence a gender-layered and complex character. We assume that their interior lives consist of multiple gender threads and identifications. We wonder: how are these young men experiencing intimate life? How do they negotiate the complexities of individuality and intimate solidarity?

We introduce the notion of *intimate knots*. Each of us brings to close relationships organizing patterns and unresolved conflicts that trigger relational tensions and impasses (e.g. Stolorow 2011, Stolorow and

Atwood 1992). We identify four psychodynamic drivers of intimate knots: struggles to forge self boundaries that are firm but also porous, to negotiate relationships that balance dependency and autonomy, to idealize the other in ways that are ennobling but also attuned to who they are, and to recognize the other as similar but also different.

Boundary Struggles: the dialectic of presence and absence

Many psychoanalysts believe that in the course of everyday life we experience multiple selves. Each self or self-state entails distinctive psychic ways of being and relating. Here's how Phillip Bromberg characterizes this viewpoint:

> [Self] states are the fundamental units of experience that organize consciousness and give to the human mind its unique capacity for both stability and flexibility. Because states are discrete and discontinuous, when a transition from one state of consciousness to another occurs, the new state acts to impose a quantitatively and qualitatively different structure on the variables that define [that] state of consciousness. . . . Mental health . . . might be seen as the ability of the individual to access a broad range of self-states. . . .
>
> (Bromberg 2000: 556 citing Putnam 1988)

However, as self-states shift in the course of everyday life, we also sustain an ongoing experience of spatial and temporal continuity and a sense of identity and effective agency (Kohut 1971, 1977: 177, Lachmann 1996, Laing 1960, Mitchell 1991, Wolf 1991).

Arguably, a lynchpin of the experience of psychic continuity and coherence is a boundaried self. Establishing clear-enough personal boundaries enables self-possession, which, in turn, is a necessary condition for sustaining an intimate bond. These are claims we intend to expand upon.

Clear self-boundaries make possible an awareness of being different from the other (Gabbard and Lester 1995, Stern 1985). As a boundaried self, I know that certain feelings, desires, and behaviors are "mine," not "yours." I experience myself as a psychically separate agent, impacting on others and being impacted by others. A state of boundariedness allows a line to be drawn, however fuzzy or fluid, between experiences that are "me" and "not me." Sturdy boundaries ground an inner-centeredness and solidness that allows us to feel deeply connected to others without losing ourselves. They enable us to reflect on our internal and interpersonal lives and, in principle, to purposefully negotiate rather than just react to the inevitable fluctuations and ruptures of relational life.

From an interpersonal vantage point, establishing clear enough self-boundaries is a condition of mutual recognition. If we experience ourselves as psychically independent agents, despite our connectedness, we are more likely to perceive the other as a distinct subject, both alike and different from ourselves. This awareness of two subjects opens up the possibility of each appreciating the other's humanness but also their singular individuality. It also allows us to become cognizant of the ways our narcissism or anxieties might, at times, deny or erase the other's subjectivity and individuality.

However, if self-boundaries are too hard-edged or steely, intimacy is seriously compromised. One's inner life will be unavailable or minimally so to the other; one's desires, hopes, longings, and anxieties will be inaccessible to others. If an impenetrable shell keeps the other at a remove, not only will one remain strange to the other, the other will not become a vital part of one's internal life. For such individuals, emotional availability and sustaining empathy may trigger anxieties and agonies of earlier intimate ruptures and narcissistic injuries. But without the sharing of inner lives, intimacy is impossible or terribly limited.

Confronted with a rigidly boundaried self, their interior can only be imagined from their surface. To sustain a hidden inner life, one's outer shell must not be penetrated. For example, one might retreat into a quiet, detached presence, covering up a turbulent interior; alternatively, a noisy grandiose self may avoid exposing an interior awash in shame or rage. Such self-states leave little space for the other, except as a spectator or part object. In a terrible irony, protecting vast interior territories of the self can also lead to self-estrangement. Parts of one's inner life become inaccessible not only to others but to oneself.

In this regard, post-Freudians have underscored the formative significance of parental unavailability and misattunement during early childhood. However, even when faced with a not good enough parent, the infants' survival still depends on staying attached to its caregiver. So, in the face of considerable environmental failure, a young boy confronts a dilemma: if he continues to seek parental love, he risks repeated narcissistic wounds that will cut deep into his psyche. As he matures, there may be a part of him that continues to long for a rich, vital experience of parental love, but this very desire evokes the crushing rejections of the past. Yet, protecting himself from this injurious repetition by dissociating from such longings risks losing touch with parts of himself and compromising the possibility of a vital intimate life (e.g. Kohut 1977: 136).

In his work with children, Winnicott (1965a, 1988, 1986) came to believe that faced with a failed parental environment, some children adopt a "false self" tasked with avoiding psychic injury and at times self-annihilation. As an adult, an injured self may manage well enough, even flourish in work or social affairs, but at the likely cost of losing touch with his "true self." An enlivened life of spontaneity, play, and creativity will give way to a more deliberate and reactive life that greatly limits possibilities for self-elaboration and intimacy.

Such adults may be stuck in a space of ambivalence, aching with a hunger for love but terrified by unconsciously felt memories of rejection and suffering (Guntrip 1969a). Some adults may retreat into themselves or immerse in a work-centered life or dull themselves with alcohol or drugs or sexualization to avoid thickly layered intimacies. The true self may be protected, but hardened self-boundaries will impede the forging of emotionally rich loving attachments.

In order to establish intimacy, selves need boundaries porous enough so their lives can be known and experienced by another and simultaneously experience the other as a vital internal presence (Geist 2008, 2009, Schiller 2010a: 137). Each must be understood as having a uniquely layered life and history. It's a delicate balance: we need boundaries that are firm enough to maintain a sense of self-possession but permeable enough to allow another to be psychically alive inside us.

If boundaries are too porous, the line separating selves becomes elusive. Blurry self-boundaries engender confusion as to who owns which feelings and desires. The relationship will lose its rich intimate texture as each partner struggles to differentiate and determine who is doing what to whom. Interdependence may turn into a kind of enmeshment, challenging each to disentangle the "me" from the "you." A precondition of intimacy is absent: boundaried, coherent enough selves who are able to maintain psychic independence and interdependence.

In extreme forms of blurry boundaries, selves merge. This is not a fusing that is ecstatic, but one in which self-boundaries are fuzzy to a point of being unsure where the "I" ends and the "you" begins. De-differentiation wrecks intimacy by destroying the psychic space that allows each self to imaginatively step out of their immediate experience to claim the viewpoint of the relationship as a whole. From this intersubjective position, each self can more easily tolerate and negotiate relational conflicts without the relationship collapsing into a war zone, with a victor and a vanquished (Benjamin 2004, Ogden 2004).

Boundary dynamics then can unsettle and cause trouble for intimate relationships. For example, two parties with rigid self-boundaries will be challenged to create relational spaces where they can experience an emotionally rich and fluid intersubjectvity. But we cannot assume that intimacy requires self-boundaries that are unfailingly complementary. If we favor the notion of multiple self-states, our boundaries will vary in terms of their degree of rigidity and flexibility or impenetrability and porousness depending on the social context and the relational histories, the moods, and motives of the parties present. Finally, boundary struggles are challenging because we are mostly unaware of them. Most of us, most of the time, externalize our relational troubles by focusing on, say, money or sex or styles of communication, rather than attending to the underlying psychodynamics that are at the root of these ruptures.

Daniel and JR

Daniel and JR, both 32, have been together for five years, yet each complains they often feel alone and unloved. While they both want a rich emotional and bodily connection, their boundary dynamics often lead to frustration. Daniel says, "JR won't let me in . . . he never has . . . and if I push . . . or ask him why, he shuts down or becomes angry." JR acknowledges his struggle: "I don't know how to let someone in. . . . The thought of opening myself up to someone, and to be that vulnerable, is terrifying." JR then voices his own grievance. "Our sex life sucks! I can never please him. . . . I wanna' fuck, but he wants to 'make loooooooove' (he flutters his eyelashes in a decidedly feminine way)." Daniel jumps in, "Really? You're mocking me because I want tenderness . . . some touching . . . or, God forbid, an occasional kiss instead of your *incredible*, manly cock? I want *you* to want *me* . . . not just an available orifice or a sometimes willing mouth."

For each, their struggle to be intimate stretches back to a time lost to memory. They've learned to avoid repeating early traumas by avoiding too much closeness. Both Daniel and JR have forged boundaries that at times protect them from psychic injury but also from sustaining the very intimacy they both desire.

Daniel is seemingly more accepting of being emotionally available and processing ruptures. He seems comfortable with boundary fluidity and wants the same from JR, whose self-boundaries appear more rigid and stereotypically masculine. Indeed, when JR feels vulnerable or longs to merge with Daniel, he at times shuts down or retreats into a defensive masculinity—detached and mocking.

An only child, Daniel was raised by his mother in a midsized city in the Northwest. His father left the family when he was 4. Daniel never seemed interested or troubled by this abandonment. "It's a topic that was never really discussed. I never really asked. I have vague memories of my father and some unpleasant ones, but I don't think about them, and I've never been particularly curious about him." Despite this early loss, Daniel spoke of a loving supportive home life that included his maternal grandparents and a gay uncle whom Daniel idealized. During his preschool years, his mother arranged to work at a family-owned lumber company, which allowed her to care for Daniel at home. When he started school she began running the business, eventually turning it into a successful enterprise that dramatically changed their socioeconomic status.

Daniel was proud of his mother. "In a man's business, and dealing with men who'd rather negotiate with my Grandpa, she was a dynamo and eventually gained their respect." From early-on Daniel seemed to have internalized his mother's gender hybridity and psychic flexibility. She, in turn, nurtured Daniel's gender inclusiveness. As an involved mother, and as a tough businesswoman, she concretized for Daniel a multigendered ideal and provided the psychic space to negotiate his own gendered version of himself. As a young adult, his flexible self-boundaries allowed him to find a comfort level with his sexuality and to confidently negotiate relationships.

The family dynamics of JR's early life were markedly different. Raised near Pittsburgh in a blue-collar environment, JR was the youngest of five children. There were three older sisters, one barely 11 months older than JR. As a child, JR was overweight, quiet, and compliant. The only boy, he was named after his father and throughout his youth was called "Junior." In high school he adopted the more macho "JR" but his family still calls him "Junior." As a child, he felt pressured to take on the stereotypically seamless masculine persona of his father—despite feeling that "it never quite fit." Indeed, "to this day when I go home my voice drops an octave and I'm aware of every hand gesture." JR felt compelled to disavow any expression that might be marked as feminine.

His mother, a seamstress, had little time and inclination for the connective work sustaining a close-knit family. She often used food or "sudden bursts of overbearingly intrusive kissing and cuddling" to show her love. JR alludes to a possibly narcissistic disposition. "My mother was a schemer and she was vindictive, and if she didn't get what she wanted when she wanted it, eventually you'd pay for it."

"My father," he says, "never wanted to be anything more than a bartender. He was either remote or ranting, and the only thing we seemed to have in common was a desire to be 'ambitiously unambitious.' He had no time for the day-to-day running of the house and even less time for us; and he constantly raged about both, shouting to my mother, 'It's your fucking job. . . . Leave me alone!'"

JR often looked to his oldest sister for the nurturing and recognition lacking from his parents. But with his other sisters, accommodation was typical. He acceded to their wants and wishes; and, when it came to his mother's attention, the sisters came before him. But to show anger towards his sisters or to display hurt and jealousy would be met with ridicule as unmanly. So, with his sisters and parents, JR complied, repressed his anger and struggled to dissociate from longings to be loved and loving. What one analyst calls "pathological accommodation" had become an organizing pattern for JR (Brandchaft 2007). But his outward compliance masked internal rage at withholding so much of himself in order to get the mere crumbs of a love he craved.

His mother's narcissism, coupled with his father's detachment, and their consistent misrecognition of JR, left him confused about his own needs and desires. He often fell back on a stereotyped masculinity to secure a sense of self-coherence and respect. His self-abnegating compliance and retreat into an emotionally contained masculinity to regulate himself left him feeling inauthentic and incapable of intimacy.

The apparently dramatic boundary differences between Daniel and JR continued to surface in the sessions. Daniel was seemingly more open and flexible, JR more guarded and rigid. But, over time, this binary proved somewhat illusory. It turns out that each had adapted organizing patterns that, as children, served to protect them from re-traumatization; each, in their own way, muted their desire to be loved, especially by men. Sadly, this pattern continued into the present. The intimacy each desired triggered anxieties and anticipation of psychic injury. Daniel and JR at times would regress to their childhood experience of being hurt and angry young boys. But now, as adults, each had core psychic strengths and interpersonal abilities, so they could reconsider whether their organizing patterns still served them well.

Daniel and JR enter the room and sit at opposite ends of the couch. Silence fills the room until Daniel says angrily, "I talk to you but you don't listen. . . . I just want you to hear me. . . . I want you to take in what I'm saying." After a long silence, JR says, "When you say that . . . when you demand that I take you in . . . I feel engulfed . . . trapped . . . strangled. Instead of confronting you, I stay silent and resentful. It feels like there's no 'me' . . . just this sense of two of us merging into one. It's like you're trying to inhabit me, and I'm afraid I'll lose myself . . . so all I can do is disconnect. What you said before, 'I don't listen' . . . my mother always said the same thing . . . over and over . . . 'Junior? Are you listening?' She even had my ears checked. I knew if I listened . . . if I let her in . . . I'd be swallowed up. . . . And I still feel that way. I'm terrified that I'm going to lose myself." Daniel whispers, "I just want us to be close." JR retorts, "That's always your story. 'I want us to be close' . . . 'I want you to let me in'. . . . then you blame me for our disconnection. At least I own my shit . . . what about you? Your outside doesn't match your inside. You present this calm, loving demeanor that skillfully masks a mass of anxiety, your constant demands . . . and, a bottomless chasm of hurt. Why don't you ever bring any of that into this room? For fuck's sake, your father abandoned you and you never ever talk about it. You say you have no feelings about it. . . . Bullshit! He shut you out . . . he didn't love you enough . . . and now you feel that I shut you out. . . . And you don't see a connection? I can't give you what he didn't . . . it's too deep a hole to fill."

In this session, we see how the boundary landscape does not neatly fold into the binary—Daniel/flexible, JR/rigid. Boundary struggles are typically neither unidimensional (hard/soft, rigid/fluid) nor fixed—or easily altered.

Each of us struggles in different contexts with whether to engage the other with steeled or porous boundaries or with whether to fuse and intermingle or contain and detach.

JR felt he needed to satisfy the expectations of others by denying what he felt were his more authentic impulses. Furthermore, carrying a history of self-denigration and shame, it's not surprising that a defensive phallic masculine pose proved, for a time, an effective form of self-regulation.

By contrast, Daniel presented seemingly flexible self-boundaries. Yet, as JR suspected, there was an absence in Daniel that spoke loudly to a closed off, steel encased, part of himself: a father who abandoned him. Daniel managed a seeming fluidity but at the price of dissociating from his father's desertion and feelings of being unloved. However, his unacknowledged but pressing longing for fatherly love would periodically de-stabilize his relationship with JR. Daniel's subtle but driving need triggered a self-protective reaction in JR; but his detachment was re-traumatizing for Daniel, further escalating demands that JR satisfy his father hunger (Herzog 2001). But, it was not really, or only, fatherly love that he consistently needed from JR, nor was this the kind of love JR could offer.

The impasse this couple struggled with was not that they presented antithetical boundary issues. Rather, they were unaware of the varied ways boundary dynamics were at play, and unaware of how their present relationship activated past psychic wounds and responses, which at times led to hurtful and troubling ways of relating.

Interwoven into these psychologically driven boundary struggles were also social class dynamics. JR grew up in a blue-collar world surrounded by solidly middle class neighborhoods. In his family and class culture, he was expected to publicly perform masculinity in ways that disavowed expressions of emotional vulnerability. He was expected to exhibit a consistently phallic masculine surface.

Yet, JR aspired to a more expansive life than his father and kin. In fact, his income and circle of friends had put him squarely in the middle class. But, in these environments JR was anxious and guarded, often feeling inferior and envious. To make matters worse, he was drawn to upper middle class men like Daniel.

Daniel came of age in a prosperous world of private schools, nannies, and travel abroad. He unwittingly absorbed a sense of class privilege and entitlement that was foreign to JR. Daniel was comfortable voicing his needs and making demands on others; he expected to be heard and respected.

Their disparate class backgrounds disposed each to different styles of boundary regulation. For JR, especially as he found himself in middle class worlds, interpersonal life was fraught with potential for disrespect and psychic insecurities stemming from gnawing feelings of inferiority. For Daniel, while his early loss registered the potential injuries and assaults of life, he lived with a taken-for-granted sense that the world will be responsive to his desires and ambitions; he negotiated social life with a confidence and playfulness that made him seem open and flexible.

Class status does not explain the psychodynamics of boundary regulation. For example, Daniel's flexible social style took shape in no small measure during his childhood bonding with a mother who concretized gender inclusiveness in her life as a successful business owner. And JR's more guarded self-boundaries speak powerfully to a family environment with a narcissistic and intrusive mother and an attachment avoidant father. Yet, their very different class statuses shaped their sense of self and boundary regulation.

Negotiating interdependency

Intimacy is unimaginable without dependency. The issue is whether dependency is a relational position that circulates or whether it congeals into a fixed role in an asymmetrical relationship. Intimacy is threatened then by two dynamics: autonomy morphing into a rigid standpoint of self-and-other control or a one-sided dependency frozen into a fixed role.

Autonomy stretched too far slides into a tightly bounded self-sufficiency, which undermines intimacy since so much of the self is withheld. This standpoint also pre-empts the possibility of becoming a vital part of another's internal life. It prevents one from being seen and seeing the other, and from each experiencing the other in complex, layered ways. Each experiences a separateness or an apartness that strains the intimate texture of the social bond. Autonomy sliding into rigid self-sufficiency then underscores a degree of self-containment and psychic withholding that, at best, permits intimacies that are bounded, transient, or rely on part-object attachments.

This position recalls what the British object relations tradition called a "schizoid position." Broadly speaking, this self-state is a response to grave narcissistic injuries that follow repeated experiences of a failed parental environment. The child seeks to avoid emotionally vulnerable attachments that may trigger terrifying anxieties of fragmentation and self-annihilation (e.g. Laing 1960). A traumatized self retreats into a world of internal objects or relationships, even regressing to a primitive state of extreme withdrawal (Guntrip 1969a). For such individuals, public behavior may become highly scripted, perhaps overly polite and formal or decidedly intellectualized. In some cases, the mind becomes a substitute for external objects or people as the self's chief object relation (Corrigan and Gordon 1995, Guntrip 1969a, Fairbairn 1952, Impert 1999, Laing 1960, Winnicott 1992). In such a state, one dissociates from longings for intimate forms of relatedness; indeed, the very need for intimate bonding may be "forgotten" or disassociated from or projected onto others who, in turn, become either threatening or selves to be taken cared of or rigidly controlled.

William

William, a 19 year old African-American, stepped into the treatment room anxious and unsure of himself. He had never been in therapy; nobody had in his family or among his friends. When William reluctantly told his father, he quickly disparaged therapy. His father insisted that black men should not share their own and their family's business with strangers, especially with whites who "are not to be trusted." Black men should deal with their personal troubles on their own; self-reliance was a sign of being a strong black man.

An ethic of self-reliance resonated with William's experience of loss and betrayal. His parents divorced when he was 4. His mother worked fulltime but still the family lived at the edge of financial ruin. As the oldest boy, William knew that he was not to burden his parents; he was expected to be responsible for protecting and educating his younger siblings. He was to pass on to them a culture of black pride and an ethic of economic and personal self-reliance.

Some four years later, William's parents divorced and his mother soon remarried. They moved to Indiana while his father remained in the Bronx. His stepfather was emotionally and, at times, physically punishing. William hated him, but his mother deferred to him. William felt betrayed: his mother had chosen his stepfather over him. Life was often unbearable. When he turned 12, William chose to live with his father, who he experienced "as little more than a housemate." Things got worse. Shortly after moving in, his father's girlfriend and her three young kids joined the household. William felt like an outlier. At 14, he and his father agreed its best if he lived with his grandparents in Queens. He admired his grandfather as a compassionate and politically savvy man. Sadly, he died one year later. William continued to live with his grandmother but they had a thin emotional connection. At the age of 15, he was on his own, financially and emotionally. He remained close to his mother and stayed in regular contact with his father. Friends formed a kind of parallel family.

As a handsome, smart and ambitious young man, William attracted many girls. He had, though, just one relationship lasting more than a few weeks. He thought he knew why. Women were manipulative; they used persuasion and seduction to control men.

William feared becoming dependent on a girlfriend. If he were too needy and trusting, she would gain power over him. In his only extended romantic relationship, which occurred when he was 15, his anxiety about losing control drove him to become either possessive or remote. Eventually, frustrated and angry, his girlfriend broke up with him.

William was troubled by the lack of a girlfriend in the four years since High School. He either forged close platonic relationships or pursued casual sex. At one point, William decided, "I want a girl I can have fun with, but gives me a lot of space. You know . . . doesn't demand too much, isn't always nagging or ragging on me. . . ."

The avoidance of dependence became an organizing pattern. For example, he'd been hanging out with Teresa and Keisha. Keisha wanted a relationship with commitment and day-to-day emotional and social companionship. William was attracted to how she looked as well as her intelligence and worldly ambitions. Yet, he was impatient with her sexual withholding and her insistence that she wanted to be sure about his intent and character. He complained that she's manipulative and controlling; he was becoming weary of her. By contrast, Teresa "loved sex . . . and didn't make too many demands on me."

Was William avoiding the anxiety of being dependent by sexualizing women and splitting them into friends and girlfriends? Perhaps, but I suspect that at the root of his avoidance of romantic intimacy is a multilayered experience of melancholia. William experienced a series of losses that were never adequately grieved. Instead of mourning parental figures he held onto them by attaching to idealized contemporary figures.

His first serious loss was his father, initially in the divorce and then in William's move to Indiana; but, perhaps more profoundly, in his absence as a fatherly presence. "We never did and still don't talk about anything really personal, about feelings . . . I don't feel I had a father in that sense." Freud argued that melancholia involves incorporating a lost loved one. But, internalization is not the only way to retain a lost object. The melancholic may also repeatedly search for a substitute or try to become a version of the lost object. In this regard, William developed strong idealizing attachments to older men in their roles as educators, sponsors, and public officials. Tellingly, in our initial consultation, he acknowledged wanting to work with an older man who could provide "wise counsel." Paralleling William's pursuit of a father figure he has also sought to become the absent father, for example, as a student president and a leader among social justice activists.

The move from New York City to a small town in Indiana also entailed loss. William grew up in a black neighborhood in the Bronx knowing only black friends, neighbors, schoolmates, and adults. In Indiana, he was living in an almost all white town. And, unlike his father and grandfather, his mother and stepfather were not African-American identified. For the first time, William struggled with the loss of a solid, taken-for-granted racial identity. Now, he had to try to fit into a white world that he didn't feel a part of; he struggled with feelings of racial shame and being an outsider.

In a manner of speaking, he also lost his mom in the move. She had to work fulltime and was not as available as she was in New York. And then he lost her again, and in a traumatic way, when, in his eyes, she chose her new husband over him.

His return to New York City was no less steeped in loss. There was the loss of his mother in another profound way, and a similar loss of his siblings. William now had only his father to rely on but he proved emotionally unavailable; to make matters worse, his father soon formed his own family that William didn't feel a part of. To his good fortune, William's grandfather stepped up as someone he greatly admired, but his death, just one year after joining his household, left him feeling, once again, abandoned and alone. With such a layered history of loss and betrayal, is it any wonder William retreated from dependency?

Underlying William's dependency anxieties were narcissistic injuries. William felt he was not good enough to warrant another's love; he did not feel entitled to ask for what he needed and wanted. Intimacy was entangled with unconscious memories and feelings of abandonment, shame, and rage. To protect himself William retreated into the safety of an impenetrable self-sufficiency, which, sadly, left him alone and burdened with self-doubts.

Intimate connectedness assumes mutuality and the circularity of power. As we've seen, if control and authority congeal around one partner, circularity and at times intimacy is impossible. From the other side, if dependency becomes a rigid relational role, the relationship also risks becoming an asymmetrical power arrangement. Power and submission will form the chief structural axis of a relational bond, all but squeezing out space for intimacy (e.g. Benjamin 1988, Shaw 2014).

Consider that it wasn't that long ago that gender roles were rigidly polarized. Based on their sex status, and a presumed maternal instinct, women were destined to be wives and mothers, deferential to their husbands and fathers. "Respectable" women were compelled to repudiate behaviors and aspirations that were culturally associated with men. Rigid gender roles entailed a melancholic loss of, and estrangement from, their masculinity and their homoerotic ties (Butler 1995). Under conditions of compulsory heterosexuality, ways of being and relating that fell outside of feminine heterosexuality were scandalized. Gender splitting and melancholia engender rigid role-based and hierarchical relationships that contradict the fluidity and circularity of vital intimacies.

What if, however, dependency trumps autonomy for both partners? In so called co-dependent relationships, collusion is its underpinning. Each party is motivated to accommodate by surrendering their own desires and wants; each strives to join together in perfect sync by avoiding issues and conflicts that might trigger fissures. Unlike intimacies that preserve a tension between autonomy and dependence, co-dependency is forged at the expense of individuation; intimacy gives way to a kind of relational dynamic in which individuation is threatening. What might at first glance seem like a thick intimate bond is instead an enmeshment in which self-boundaries are blurred and mutual recognition is replaced by relational fusion. The relationship itself, as Ehrenberg (1975) says, "may be used as a kind of interpersonal version of an individual defense. . . ." Each partner enables the other to avoid individuation and independence. Co-dependency may help lessen anxieties of separateness and self-fragmentation, but, at its root, it is steeped in low self-esteem and shame.

The struggle to be dependent without surrendering individuality, and to be autonomous without sliding into a schizoid-like self-sufficiency, is at the heart of intimacy. In principle, autonomy underscores a capacity to be self-directing while also being a part of another's subjective and interpersonal life. Dependency is not about surrendering autonomy, but recognizing the intermingling of lives and the necessity of ongoing negotiation of being alone together.

Idealization: ennoblement and misattunement

Idealization seems to combine a wish to be or be proximate to someone who is graced with grandeur and admired for their secular ambition and stature. It is perhaps this uneasy mix of desire and fantasy that explains the capacity of idealization to fuel powerful passions and transform inchoate feelings and longings into deeply meaningful dramas of self and social transformation. But, precisely for this reason, idealization can also trigger explosive psychic and relational conflicts and ruptures.

A standard psychoanalytic view holds that idealization plays a key role in the Oedipal drama. In this scenario, a child romanticizes a parent. It both desires the parent and wants to be or be like the parent. The waning of Oedipal hyper-idealization—with its possessive and highly sexualized dynamic—has often been understood as a sign of maturation. Life after Oedipus may not mark the end of idealization, but its domestication. Davies (2003) offers a slightly revised perspective, but the key drama of Oedipus and beyond remains the shift from idealization to de-idealization:

> For me, it is this movement from experiences of intense romantic idealization, to de-idealized, less perfect, but more truly intimate, vulnerable, and emotionally interpenetrating experiences that marks the shift from incestuous Oedipal relatedness . . . to the kinds of postoedipal relatedness that are more endemic to adolescent development and ultimately to adult love relations.
>
> (p. 5)

A parallel process is said to occur in adult romance. Initially, lovers are idealized; romantic passion and dreamy reverie transport them beyond the quotidian. Intimacy may be ecstatic and transformative. However, in time, this adoration and emotional tumult quiets down. Disappointment and disillusionment are inevitable, as the full range of each other's lives, including parts that evoke anxiety or dread, are acknowledged. If lovers are fortunate, romantic idealization is sublimated into a sexually satisfying, tender, and socially rich companionship (Mitchell 1997: 29).

Again, Davies (2003) offers an appealing revision of the dialectic of idealization and disillusionment. In good enough experiences of adult romance, there is

> a mutual relinquishing of both the idealized other and idealized self, in return for the experience of more deeply knowing and being known, being accepted for who one is, and discovering in oneself the capacity to love in spite, and because of, the other's imperfections. It is not a repudiation of the idealized, but a growing ability to hold that image of the loved other and adored self in simultaneous awareness with the more tempered, more reality, based assessment.

> (p. 11)

Davies' tempered but still enchanted view of adult romance strikes us as compelling, especially as a normative vision. We are though less persuaded by the assumption of the seemingly inevitable taming of idealization (cf. Blechner 2006, Davies 1998, Goldner 2007, Mitchell 2003, Orbach 2004). We wonder whether such perspectives don't underestimate the ongoing transformative power of idealization. Think of Kohut's argument that adults, as much as children, seek out idealized self-objects (Kohut 1977: 122, cf. Mitchell 1997). Specific persons or cultural ideals are experienced as touched with charisma and possessing transcendent existential significance. They not only soothe and comfort or inspire ambition, they infuse moral purpose into our lives and may fuel self and collective transformation. In this regard, we find resonant Bollas' view that the parent is not only transformative during childhood, but that, as adults, many of us seek substitute transformative objects (Bollas 1989). In Euro-American societies, romantic love has become precisely an arena of transformative experience (Beck and Beck 1995, Giddens 1992, Luhmann 1986). From this perspective, no matter how routinized, romantic intimacy may continue to be a quest bearing redemptive or liberatory significance.

Idealization then can ennoble intimacies and infuse them with passion and a higher purpose (Davies 1998). But, its very power suggests that it can also generate experiences of misattunement and relational rupture.

Melanie Klein (1946) understood the ambivalent significance of idealization. In the paranoid-schizoid position, we idealize specific persons; at times, to protect them against our own envious or murderous desires or against imagined persecutory forces. But, in fantasizing an unattainable ideal other, idealization can protect us from the very intimacy we desire (Klein 1957: 192–193). More recently, Slochower (2011) has similarly commented on the way idealization can:

> become thick and impenetrable, protective walls.... Affects like disappointment, anger, and rage are not merely bracketed but utterly negated, as patient and analyst [or lovers] together deny, dissociate, even obliterate, the negative.
>
> (p. 154)

As feelings are denied or dissociated, "*such [idealizing] illusions can . . . disrupt and destroy . . . intimate relationships*" (our emphasis, p. 154).

From a perspective that assumes its contradictory and dynamic character, idealizations can enrich a relationship but they need to resonate with the idealized other. For example, if a loved one possesses the idealized traits attributed to them or if their aspirations align with these idealizations, they may feel in sync with their partner's fantasies. In effect, a lover's idealization can mirror one's own internalized ego ideal. Attuned idealizations are self-enhancing as one luxuriates in feelings of being understood and admired. Such attunement is generative as it heightens the experience of intimate connectedness, even infusing it with an aura of the sublime or the ecstatic.

Yet, idealizations may be terribly misattuned. The idealized partner may not be recognized in the lover's fantasy. Rather than experiencing validation and an enriched intimacy, idealization may cast a shadow of strangeness, eliciting feelings of estrangement and misrecognition. In the throes of such misattunement, each partner feels not only not known, but devalued and minimized since each is at odds with the other's fantasy. Idealization may misrepresent and, at times, obliterate the other. Repeated misattunements may edge into de-idealization. Without the halo of adoration and specialness conferred by an idealized cathexis, each partner risks collapse into a bad object or into a cluster of disagreeable, hated traits, dispositions, and behaviors.[1] In a state of mutual misattunement and de-idealization, partners suffer narcissistic injury and rage for not embodying the partner's fantasy, indeed, for potentially representing its opposite, a persecutory, hated object. Repeated experiences of misattunement and de-idealization wreak havoc on intimacy.

As we see it, mutual idealization animates and gives to intimacy its edge of specialness and ecstatic-ness. The challenge: in the face of the inevitable ruptures and traumas triggered by inevitable misattunement and de-idealization, how to sustain and protect the power of cathected attachment, of intimate solidarity.

Barry and Bridget

When I first met Barry, he was 28, charmingly boyish, and witty. He was always in a relationship with a woman, but with whom he saw no future. His mantra was: "I enjoy relationships without commitment."

Barry is a gifted creator of large and often provocative mixed-media constructions. He is passionate about his art but less so when it comes to the business side. Of moderate repute, the spoils of success give him sufficient recognition and adequate financial security to afford him an independent, if modest, carefree lifestyle.

Early trauma, ongoing family tensions and, a string of relationships with unavailable women brought Barry into treatment. But his fundamental core psychic and social strengths, though challenged at times, were intact; treatment was progressing well.

One day, about five years into treatment, Barry plopped down on the couch, grinning from ear-to-ear, and gleefully announced, "I'm smitten! I met someone at my gallery-opening last weekend. . . . Out of nowhere, this vision walks straight towards me holding two glasses of champagne, hands me one and says, 'I'm Bridget . . . and you're fantastic'. . . . We talked into the morning about everything under the sun. . . . It's been a week and we can't get enough of each other. . . . We've been in this fog of ecstasy, unbridled passion and endless fantasy about our life and our future together. . . . Who'd a thought? Me . . . Barry . . . over-the-moon in love!"

Life-altering decisions were swiftly made. Within a matter of weeks, Bridget impulsively left her expensively furnished home, her friends and family, and a high-paying career in Chicago and moved into Barry's less urbane digs. A short time later, they announced their engagement; and barely two months later, though her father agreed to finance an elaborate wedding, they eloped.

Counter to their cautious approaches to past romances their ardor merged the two into a fantastical world of mutual idealization.

Barry, an only child of middle class parents, was raised in Baltimore. His parents were both creative: his father, "the Bohemian black sheep of his family," was "a struggling artist who loved his work" and was a loving parent. He supplemented his income by working in a small family business; Barry's paternal grandparents hoped that his father would join the company "but my Dad hated the conventional nine-to-five world and my Mom supported his dreams." Barry's mother "was a flighty, disorganized woman, with whom I never felt totally grounded. She was a "dabbler" and a "ditz," drifting from one creative pursuit to another, but focusing on none." Barry "idolized" his "free-spirited" father and "put up" with his well-meaning mother's "anxieties and quirks."

One day, when Barry was 11 and on a family vacation, he and his father went for a long walk. Upon reaching a deserted coved beach, his father tenderly revealed that he had been ill for some time. In his characteristically gentle and caring way, he told Barry that he had terminal cancer and not long to live. "At some point I remember my Dad telling me that my mother would always be there for me . . . but I couldn't take-in what he was saying . . . actually, I couldn't buy what he was saying. I remember thinking, 'my life's just turned upside down . . . and it'll never be the same again.'" His father died soon after and Barry thought, "from now on, you're on your own."

Barry's mother tried to console him but he never did feel very close to her. "This didn't change with my father's death. . . . She really tried . . . but I ached for my father's consistency and stability . . . and was intolerant of her inconsistencies and instability. . . . I just locked her out."

In response to this "double" loss, Barry voraciously clung to an idealized version of his father's life as a guide of how to live. Like his father, he sought to live his own version of a creative and somewhat non-conventional but authentic life. It was also a way to keep his father close to him. This changed when Bridget came into his life.

Bridget was raised in the affluent Gold Coast district of Chicago. Like Barry, she idealized her father. But Bridget's father was an entrepreneur; a powerful and driven man who amassed a small fortune by the time Bridget was just a child. Like her father, Bridget was independent and fiercely ambitious; this kinship created a special connection to her father. "In his eyes, I was special. . . . I was his moon and his stars." Bridget and her younger sister were boarding-schooled, but she was happiest when her father, who was frequently away on extended business trips, was at home with her, and her "gentle and kind" mother, and her "rather mousy" sister. While still in her teens, Bridget shockingly discovered that her father had been in a long-term secretive relationship with another women. Disillusioned, and no longer feeling special, her narcissistic wound eventually turned to rage; she impulsively disclosed this deception to her mother, shattering her seemingly intact family. Once her ideal of masculine mettle, she now viewed her father as a symbol of betrayal and arrogance. With her mother and sister ill equipped to handle the emotional upheaval, Bridget became a pillar of strength; but this steeled exterior masked an inner conflict over her father and a bottomless pit of rage. As an adult, and with her father now unhappily married to this same woman, she reluctantly reconciled with him. Privately, she gloated in his misery. She was left with deep scars that had an indelible impact on her trust of men.

As we've seen, idealization can enliven intimacies, imbuing them with passion and a touch of the sublime. But, if suddenly shattered, this fall from grace can have devastating consequences. Bridget, though wounded by her father, internalized many of his phallic threads. They fueled her drive to succeed and to always be in control. She detested these stereotyped masculine traits in men, but, as Barry noted, she was often drawn to men who embodied these very traits.

Both Barry and Bridget idealized their fathers, and in different ways lost them. Barry's father died but was preserved as an ego ideal. Bridget lost her idealized father, but he lived on as an important self-object. It was perhaps less their shared loss that drew them to each other than their complex feelings about their shared idealization of their fathers.

Until Bridget, Barry had relationships with woman after woman, all much younger, all beautiful, all unsophisticated. He would tell me that the relationship was over before it even started. He had never been involved with anyone who shared his world of art and ambition. If any of these women hinted at exclusivity, or expressed a desire for marriage, the relationship soon ended.

By contrast, Bridget's demeanor was self-reliant and worldly. She recognized and admired his talent. She excited him with ideas about expanding his creative visibility and client base. She joined him in a mutual fantasy: she would take over the business side of his work, something he least enjoyed, and which she, ambitious and organized, excelled at. She seemed to have embraced his friends and his easy life-style. In Barry's mind, her independence and ambition marked her as the antithesis of his mother. Through the lens of her conflicted feelings about her father, Bridget saw in Barry the same creativity and ambition, minus her father's testosterone-fueled narcissism and controlling personality.

This mutual idealization, partnered with dreams of a shared project of personal and professional fulfillment, allowed each to bathe in the reverie of an almost dream-like future. While the ordinary tasks of everyday life took a backseat, pedestrian life was infused with a romantic halo. But in time, ordinary life burst the romantic bubble.

The fantasy of a seamless professional partnership imploded as reality exposed vastly dissimilar relational styles. Bridget's manner was aggressive, impatient, demanding, and conventionally ambitious; Barry's was easygoing, spontaneous, and freewheeling. Despite the fantasy of a blend of art and business, he realized that their styles didn't mesh and their professional partnership soon ended. Both experienced the first pangs of misattunement: he felt guilty and alienated by Bridget's demeanor; she felt betrayed and enraged by Barry's lack of aggressivity. Tensions seeped into their private life. It was important for Barry to separate their personal and professional life. He enjoyed hanging out with friends or simply cooking and watching movies at home. However, Bridget did not separate the personal and professional. She pressed them to "socialize with the mucky-mucks and be part of the scene." Bridget was rubbing up against Barry's deeply felt belief that, by and large, this networking felt "superficial and inauthentic." In contrast to Barry, she thought that they needed to center their lives on professional advancement and on gaining public recognition. Any resistance by Barry was met with anger and ridiculed by Bridget as being lazy.

Idealizing fantasies need to be sustained if a romantic relationship is going to remain vital and generative. But with Barry and Bridget the mutual idealization that drew each to the other was imploding and so too was their relationship. Idealization was turning into its opposite: denigration and resentment. Bridget's ambition and goal-driven purposefulness that, Barry says, "intrigued and excited me now feel obsessive and intrusive." For Bridget, Barry's one-sided attention to the creative process and his relatively carefree lifestyle now symbolizes his avoidance of adult male responsibility. Barry's gentler, more flexible gender style, once admired, was now ridiculed as weakness and even as unmanly. Her fantasy of a companion with whom to forge a life of passion and public acclaim was collapsing.

Barry was now unsettled by a frightening aspect of Bridget's personality that went unnoticed: irrational and abrupt mood swings from rage and contempt to sadness, insecurity and shame. For example, "She often mocks me in a decidedly unmanly voice. . . . She becomes ferociously castrating," labeling his layered, expansive gendered self as "unmanly" and his work as "artsy-fartsy." She would deride Barry by saying, "For fuck's sake . . . Man up!" What Bridget didn't realize was that such attacks felt, for Barry, like assaults on his much-adored father.

Bridget would often follow such emotional assaults with pleas for forgiveness. "She'll ask over-and over-again, day-after-day, 'Do you love me? Tell me you love me,' and I reluctantly oblige. . . . Eventually, the words cease to have meaning." Barry felt misunderstood, and hatred often washed over any love he once felt. Barry found efforts at reparation futile; he felt sadness that their love was drying up.

In retrospect, we wonder whether Barry's idealization of Bridget, who served as the antithesis of his mother and a stand-in for phallic traits that were only weakly present in his father, blinded him to parts of her that were now apparent. Was Barry seduced by her idealization of him and the seemingly effective way she could take care of him that was lacking with his mother? Did he fail to experience, until too late, Bridget's driving need for him to be a successful, triumphant man? And, Bridget so much wanted to believe that Barry would be the father successor and they would be the power couple her parents weren't. In the fog of idealization, she didn't see that Barry lacked the qualities in her father that she at once detested and idealized. She also didn't recognize how at times she became her father, for example, voicing so much rage at Barry for being a failure. And, Barry, so humiliated and enraged by Bridget's punishing style, was blinded to the kernel of truth in her frustrations, his lack of business acumen and motivation, and his seeming comfort, much like his father, with the status quo.

Recognition: navigating sameness and difference

Bill and Sarah

In our initial consultation, Bill calmly related that he was struggling with Sarah. After 8 years of living together, and after buying an engagement ring, he was still unable to propose. Sarah had no such doubts: she wanted to marry Bill and have a family. But, she waited long enough. Like him, she was in her late 20s, established in a career and anxiously anticipated the next phase of her life. He needed to decide: marriage or breakup.

Sarah was Bill's dream woman. She was smart, pretty, cultured, and fun. After pursuing her for several years they became a couple. His "courtship" felt cinematic: small town blue-collar boy falls in love with a beautiful, upper middle class girl. "She was a goddess. . . . I wanted her. . . . Could I win over this woman?" Stunningly, although his love was requited, something was holding him back from concluding the final act of this romantic drama.

We explored Bill's struggle with self-esteem. His faltering confidence seemed related to the interweaving of social class and Oedipal struggles. Dad was a union guy who railed against the self-absorbed, paper-pushing, parasitic middle class. Bill recalls his father admonishing him: "Don't forget where you come from. No matter how much you strive and achieve, you're still my son." His father's anxiety about Bill's ambition expressed itself in this personal warning: "There's always someone ahead of you, smarter and better. . . . I never felt good enough." Dad's words were haunting. A life of too much ambition and material gain might cost him estrangement from his blue-collar roots and his family. Would marriage to an upper middle class woman be a betrayal of his father and his family? Would he lose his identity in a world that he didn't really belong to, as his father warned?

Bill returned time and again to one overriding question: "Is Sarah right for me? I don't want to make a mistake." Bill thought that marriage should be permanent, like it is with his parents. He didn't want to make a fateful error of judgment.

Bill steps into the room with his usual friendliness—polite and engaging. He sits down facing me. He and Sarah had another upsetting argument about what their life would be like after they were married. They would frequently imagine and fight over what their future life together would be like. What type of community would they live in and what kind of school would their children attend—private, public, or religious?

This time the conflict was about caregiving arrangements for their future children. His father's words echoed in his memory: "Paid childcare shows how self-absorbed they [the middle class] are . . . They put themselves before their children." But, Bill knew that Sarah wanted a career.

Besides, he felt that on the plus side daycare exposes children to different kinds of kids and adults. By contrast, Sarah couldn't imagine placing a child in the hands of strangers. Coming from a business owning, prosperous family, she remembered her mother saying that daycare is the choice of the middle class who don't have the means, and sometimes the interest, to do what is best for their children. Sarah would want to hire a full-time nanny. But, for Bill, that would feel like a betrayal of his core values and sense of himself. Bill and Sarah found themselves, as they had on so many value-laden issues, locked into what felt like an unresolvable conflict.

Bill agreed that there could be many advantages to having a nanny (e.g. one caregiver, consistency, less chance of contracting an illness), but he felt that Sarah just didn't get the significance of this issue for him. "That's just not who I am . . . I would feel like I was an imposter and resent her if I agreed to a nanny. . . . Sarah doesn't seem to understand that *I am* these values, principles, and beliefs. . . . Sometimes she doesn't get me. I worry, can she really accept and value who I am?" This question spoke to the heart of his ambivalence: "I don't know if Sarah knows what it means to be me." The struggle to be truly known and respected is at the center of the dynamics of recognition; anxiety over being unrecognized or misrecognized was what stopped Bill from proposing.

Although Bill's love for Sarah has been unflagging, as has hers for him, there is not an equivalence between love and recognition. Declaring love communicates many things such as the specialness of the other, a surrendering as an act of sublime uplift, and an aspiration to forge a joint life. Recognition, however, pivots around being known and appreciated as an irreducibly singular person. One may not approve of or identify with all of who the other is, but recognition assumes that your partner understands that these unique traits are what make you who you are. Being intimate then may mean loving and recognizing someone whose very being sometimes provokes discomfort—and dislike. Mutual recognition situates a relationship in a permanently grey area.

Struggles for recognition address a tension that cuts to the heart of adult intimacies: how to pursue one's own interests and ambitions while needing and desiring acknowledgement from others who also expect validation. If each of us centers on our own concerns without recognizing the other as an agent like oneself, the relationship turns into a struggle for power. By contrast, if validating the other is a condition of being acknowledged, not only would our lives be understood as inextricably intertwined, but the aspiration for mutual recognition would serve as a regulatory force in relational disputes. Mutual recognition assumes that both agents are capable of grasping that, despite stretches of another's life that may feel strange and even troubling, there are also swatches of each of their lives that are similar enough to be understood and affirmed.

The possibility and the richness of a social bond depends in part on whether each perceives the other as a separate agent, both alike and not alike. The former suggests: "we're enough alike that I can understand and feel a sense of an affinity or twinship" or "I see in you traits in myself." Sameness makes possible empathy and civility in the face of difference. By contrast, approaching the other as wholly different stipulates: "you are not me; you have feelings and beliefs which I do not understand or appreciate. I need to either avoid or change you. Your difference will lead to indifference or conflict." If one does not respect the ways the other is like and not like oneself, the other may be misrecognized either as an "Other" or as an extension of oneself. The challenge of sustaining the tension between being connected to a person who is the same and different, even during relational ruptures, is one way to frame the struggle for recognition (Benjamin 1988, 1995, 1999, cf. Fraser and Honneth 2004, Honneth 1992).

The concept of recognition needs to be concretized to grasp the role it plays in the dynamic of intimacy. For example, what is it that's being recognized? Is it our general humanity or the particular and multiple ways we are who we are? And, what is the content or meaning of recognition? Is it only the perception of the other as a "subject" like oneself. Or, is recognition, as Axel Honneth (1992) argues, multilayered, including struggles for respect, esteem, dignity, and love. Each of these experiences is somewhat different and suggests a multidimensional view of recognition. For example, dignity extends to all persons as bearers of a common humanity and stipulates general principles by which to treat all individuals. Esteem and often respect, however, are conferred because of the person one became or one's accomplishments. And, in love we recognize the other as a special person in the fullness of their being (Honneth 1992, 2004, cf. Taylor 1992).

Recognition is then a layered experience. At a very general level, there is the awareness that as human we share capacities, e.g. to think, feel, desire, to make decisions, to care for others, and so on. This abstract recognition of a shared humanity is an essential condition for intimacy but limited without also appreciating the other's singularity. As Sheldon Bach (2006) says: "The most important thing ... is not [only] to be recognized generally ... but to be known in our absolute individual uniqueness. [And], when we are not recognized or ... misrecognized, we experience shame and humiliation, but when we are fully recognized in our uniqueness, we experience gratitude and love ..." (Bach 2006: 136, cf. Bromberg 1994: 535, Shaw 2014: 9).

We need then to think of recognition as a multidimensional construct. For example, "I recognize you as a person who belongs to a particular nation or family or race, just as I do." More concretely: "like me, you are a person with your own unique psyche, social existence, and history." And, yet further: "you and I share growing up in the same historical time, in the same nation, perhaps experiencing the loss of a father, or maybe the lack of siblings; we may also share an abiding interest in art history, basketball, and global human rights." Recognizing sameness in this multileveled way underscores a sense of knowing and feeling connected to a complex, layered other.

Recognition is not possible without identification, seeing parts of oneself in the other. This makes the validation of sameness, at least in part, an unconscious process. And yet, the more sameness turns on concreteness, the more we realize that it is always limited, as wide stretches of the other inhabit a territory of difference. Recognition is always a matter of degree, but the scope of sameness would seem directly related to the depth of intimacy. If you cannot identify at all or only minimally with the other, recognition will be replaced by an experience of estrangement or, worse, subjugation or destruction. The other may become object-like, an "it" (Grand 2003) or a menacing Other (Benjamin 1999).

Alternatively, if sameness is all you perceive, the other will be misrecognized, as their singularity is denied. Intimacy would fray since self-boundaries would blur or dissolve. To avoid collapsing the other into utter sameness, individuals must see themselves in some ways like and in other ways not like the other.

Misrecognition also occurs if we fail to recognize general (e.g. demographic) and specific (e.g. biographical) differences that are highlighted against a background of sameness. At what point the failure to perceive difference generates misrecognition cannot be stated in advance.

Misrecognition is contextual. One person might feel misrecognized if their specific religious convictions are ignored or misunderstood; for another, it's their struggle with depression or growing up in a poor family that must be understood.

Bill and Sarah struggle with their differences. They clash repeatedly over relatively minor issues like restaurant or movie preferences and over major issues such as where to live (Bill-city, Sarah-suburbs) and what kind of community (Bill-diverse, Sarah-class based). Threaded through these value conflicts are core identity issues. Disagreements about what might be the best school or childcare arrangement for their prospective child are experienced by Bill—and Sarah—as failures of recognition. Thus, Bill struggles with whether Sarah can really know him if she doesn't recognize that his value and living preferences concretize who he is.

Both Sarah and Bill seem unaware of just how fearful they are of the ways the other is different. Difference can threaten to minimize or obliterate the other. And this fear, often unconscious, can derail mutual recognition by preventing each from truly understanding and engaging the core value and identity issues that divide them and drive their conflicts. Bill externalizes their differences; conflicts are to be resolved by strategies of negotiation and compromise. If they could just find the right balance between what each wants and what each is willing to sacrifice they would be okay. Of course he's not mistaken—issues that divide need to be negotiated. But their inability to find that balance after so many years suggests that deeper, less manifest divisions continue to create ruptures and psychic injury.

Bill experiences Sarah's ways of being different—from her "sophisticated" dress to her vacation preferences—as a threat to who he is. Recently, they were in an upscale coffee shop. "I wore my usual, shorts, and a tee shirt. She wore a pink button-down blouse with her collar popped. It was a preppy look and I feared people would see me like that, which made me very uncomfortable. . . . That's not who I am, and Sarah doesn't seem to get it." Even more threatening, Bill fears that deep down she wants to change him into something other than who he is and who he wants to be. In a recent session, Bill voiced this anxiety. "It's usually me who compromises, gives in to her. If I marry her I will end up accommodating to make her happy. . . . I will feel resentful and trapped . . . and I don't want to become the person she at times seems to want me to be."

Sometimes Bill worries that "she may not fully respect me, my background, who I am and she may feel superior to me." These are real concerns, but Bill is less aware of another anxiety that grips him. He believes that accommodating to Sarah means losing his authentic self. Bill experiences Sarah's misrecognition as an existential crisis.

Bill and Sarah are locked into a standoff. Each is struggling to hold onto who they are while trying to acknowledge uncomfortable differences. Each wants to be who they are with the other, but parts of who they are threaten the other. Unfortunately, instead of engaging the core differences, most especially social class, they continue to externalize them as matters of practical negotiation. Both experience difference as threatening; they fail to understand that differences can also be generative. They are, as yet, unable to consider that forging a dynamic intimate bond will mean that each will evolve into something other than who they are, without losing their ongoing identity and integrity. Until Bill realizes that change is not always a matter of loss or surrendering who he is, but an opening to unforeseen possibilities, it may be hard for him to commit.

As much as likeness, but not fusion, can validate the other and draw two people together, difference can infuse vitality. It can also challenge taken-for-granted ways of thinking and behaving. Recognizing difference extends beyond acknowledging specific differences; it is also about seeing the world from the standpoint of the other. Such encounters with otherness risk relativizing and, for some, devaluing one's own particular viewpoint and values. Yet, encounters with difference can be potentially transformative. One risks change by seriously taking into account the experience of the other (Gadamer 1975). This hermeneutic standpoint suggests a self that is non-identical; we become who we are through encounters with the other; the self sees itself in the reactions of the other; we take over something of the way the other has metabolized us; it follows that the very interpersonal process that recognizes the self also brings about changes in ourselves (Benjamin 1999, Butler 2000).[2]

Misrecognition and relational ruptures are an ongoing part of intimate relationships. Even if we recognize the other as an independent agent, the dynamics of identity and difference inevitably trigger misrecognition. For example, in the psychodynamics of projection or narcissistic grandiosity, the other becomes an extension of oneself or is imagined to want what we want. They disappear as a distinct self, and so does a vital intersubjectivity. Alternatively, if we deny any sameness, the other becomes the Other, a feared and contemptible or inferiorized figure; intimacy is rendered impossible as intersubjectivity becomes a battleground.

Mutual recognition then presents ongoing challenges to intimacy. Sameness challenges one to see oneself in the other, and risk confronting parts of oneself that are unsettling. More obviously, sameness risks a closeness, a felt impulse to merge, that can elicit anxieties of losing oneself, as we saw with Daniel and JR. And, as we've also seen, the uniqueness of the other may be exciting and generative, but it also can be threatening. One may be forced to confront less than ideal parts of oneself through someone else's eyes, exposing a less than ideal self.

Bill and Sarah's struggles with difference can be traced, in part, to their differing social class identifications. Bill's blue-collar father conflates middle class culture with a selfish individualism and raw materialism. He splits the world into the self-sacrificing, hard working blue-collar and the narcissistic, pampered middle class worlds, seemingly able to embrace only a narrow class-based sameness.

Recently, Bill visited his parents in Michigan. As usual, on the ride home from the airport, his father talked and talked, hardly allowing any space for Bill or his mother. Eventually, there was a pause. Bill had exciting news to share. He was promoted at the social service agency where he works. There was even a photo of him in the agency's monthly newsletter. His parents were pleased that he was doing well. Bill wanted more from them: to show genuine interest in the specifics of his personal and work life. But they didn't ask about these matters. Bill feels "they really have no clue what I do." Perhaps his parents are conflicted: proud of Bill's successes, but bitter and anxious because he seems to be moving into the white-collar, middle class world they despise.

Sadly, this lack of recognition is not new. Bill proudly offers that he never has doubted his parent's love. His mom has always been very affectionate, quick with hugs and loving gestures. Dad's love was a quiet, consistent presence. But often, Bill didn't experience their love as recognition, or at least as the kind of recognition he desired. "I get abstract love, but no interest at all in who I am . . . then and now."

In recent years, Bill has felt the distance set in between his parents and himself. Yet, as his emotional connection to his parents gets thinner, and despite edging into the middle class, his attachment to their class values remains thick. Frustrated, Bill has sought recognition from his colleagues and especially from Sarah. However, Sarah's ambivalence towards his "lifestyle" and value preferences, and at times her refusal or inability to "get" Bill, reiterates his experience with his parents—of not being understood and, with Sarah, of not being good enough.

Sarah's parents can be no less withholding of recognition. By disapproving of Bill, and by not understanding the depth of her love for him, they communicate that they don't get something fundamental about her. In ways paralleling Bill, Sarah unconsciously carries her mother's more conservative class and personal values; and like Bill, she often feels misunderstood as her own desires and ambitions are ignored or minimized by her parents and, at times by Bill. She, like Bill, is deeply conflicted in ways that makes it hard, if not impossible, to separate class and Oedipal issues.

Though he does not see this trait in himself, Bill believes that Sarah is too closely tied to her parents and their class values. She hasn't effectively separated and struggles with integrating her parents' conservative social values with some of her own life preferences that run counter to theirs. For example, she wants a doorman apartment, to dine at fine restaurants, go to the opera, and shop at Tiffany's and Saks. Yet, against her parent's values and wishes, she has career ambitions, commitments to social justice causes, and intends to marry Bill.

Is marrying Bill an act of class and Oedipal rebellion that will announce her psychic independence? And, has she tolerated his unwillingness to commit to marriage because some part of her is deeply ambivalent about marrying "below" her status? Similarly, would Bill's marriage to Sarah be an act of class and Oedipal defiance? Marrying an upper middle class woman may signal a rejection of his class background; does it also express a brewing resentment towards his father?

Afterword: tensions between the fixed and circulating phallus

Consider JR and William. At initial glance, JR seems an exemplar of phallic masculinity. He proudly, even defiantly, announces his disavowal of femininity and mocks Daniel's desire for tenderness and romantic intimacy. In defensive phallic mode, JR conflates eros with sex acts and carnal pleasure. He concedes his discomfort with sharing feelings, being vulnerable, and revealing dependency needs. "I don't know how to let someone in. . . . The thought of opening myself up to someone, and to be that vulnerable, is terrifying." In school he changed his nickname from "Junior" to the more macho "JR." He attempted to wear his father's mantle of phallic masculinity, and though he admitted it never quite fit he continually tries it on for size.

William, too, feels that it's not manly to be vulnerable and tender; that's not what men do, especially black men. As for what it means to be a man, he echoes narrow phallic tropes. "Being a man . . . means I'm the provider . . . I protect." When talking about women he often narrowly sexualizes them. Commenting on a recent date, "It didn't go well. We didn't have much to talk about. But, you know I spent $50 and I wanted to have sex. She refused."

The surface of both JR and William scream phallic masculinity. They are tall, broad shouldered, thick and solid, and easily assume a detached "cool" masculine pose. If you were to see them on the street, you would have no doubt that they are "real" men, exemplars of a phallic manliness. And, both of these men at times act as if only one person, one man, can claim the phallus or can fully inhabit a space of desire and authority.

And yet, JR recognized that embracing a seamless masculinity was in part defensive, protecting him from the emotional injuries he suffered by misattuned parents. He often mused how many times he wanted to share his pain of being unrecognized and treated as second best to his sisters. He spoke movingly of his stifled longings to be gently held and cared for by his parents. But he knew that showing such feelings he would be ridiculed as unmanly in his family.

Like many men, JR experienced his macho persona at times as performative; a defensive pose that was not only self-protective, but was a way to project masculine power and a kind of sexiness. Presenting as a hot, blue-collar gay guy, JR "got off" on the power of being desired by other men; we wondered whether this compensated somewhat for often not really feeling valued and loved. In his masculine pose, JR claims the phallus but also surrenders it, as he becomes the object of another desiring subject.

In this regard, JR's refusal to take on the role of Daniel's absent father is telling. It felt to JR that Daniel wanted him to fill an emotional void left by his father's abandonment. But gradually he came to understand that this expectation echoed his families demand that he always be the cool and contained manly man. JR's resistance helped Daniel realize that looking to JR for a fatherly love reinforced JR's phallicism; it didn't easily allow him to step out of that position. Gradually, as Daniel relaxed this need for JR to be a phallic father figure, there was psychic space for JR to show tender, warm-hearted relational parts of himself.

This is evidenced in a session some months later: Daniel plops down right next to JR on the couch and says, "Well . . . sex is *definitely* better!" JR retorts with a wry smile, "Why da' ya' think?" Daniel continues, "Ummmmm . . . you're *definitely* more affectionate . . . you're *definitely* more tender (he takes JR's hand and JR smiles). . . . And, with tenderness in the mix . . . and more love-making . . . I *definitely* feel more desired."

As a black man, William also felt social pressure to present a phallic masculine public self. William related to me that he had casually mentioned to some black friends that he was in therapy. After one friend left, the other confided to William: "It's just not what men do. . . . People will think there's something wrong with you, that you're weak." It says something about William both that he was so casual about sharing being in therapy and that he disagreed with his friend, as he did with his father who likewise disapproved. His response: "Should I go on feeling depressed and unhappy? I want to deal with it, and improve my life."

To further explore the tension between claiming a phallic self and allowing its circulation, consider William's experience with a new girlfriend, Teresa. He was attracted to her because she was fun and loved sex and "will give me lots of space." That was his public account—to me, to his friends, and to himself. After just two months, he was, though, emotionally absorbed in the relationship. I asked why he was so taken with Teresa. His reply was straightforward: he felt taken care of. For example, recently she baked a cake for him, for no special reason. "Nobody ever did that for me. . . ." And, on many Sundays Teresa would invite herself to his home. He almost always said okay, even though she initiated these visits. They would typically spend the day talking and snuggling together as they watched TV. Only sometimes would cuddling lead to sex, in which both William and Teresa would voice their erotic wants and expect mutual satisfaction. As William shared his romance, it was clear that it was the tender way they were connecting that was special.

Teresa was gregarious and many men were attracted to her. William often felt insecure and admitted he lacked confidence. "There are so many guys with cars or good jobs or who just look better. . . . How do I tell her about feeling insecure without her losing interest in me, or ridiculing me as 'not man enough'? He decided to tell her about his concerns as he was falling in love.

Before he could, however, Teresa began to show another, heretofore unseen, punishing and domineering side. For example, some Sundays she would simply announce that she planned to stay the night. Despite preferring to sleep alone but wanting to avoid a confrontation, he accommodated. But, Teresa could also be emasculating. Riding in a taxi, which William felt obliged, as a man, to pay, Teresa began to make fun of him. She wondered why he wasn't "all over her," trying to kiss her and squeeze her close to him. She mocked him as not a real man. She called him her "bitch" and her "girl." "I thought she was just kidding. . . . I tried to stay calm because I don't like to get angry. . . . "Teresa soon ended the relationship. Indicative of William's complicated lived gender experience, he shared these events, including the experience in the taxi, with his friends. Neither he nor they betrayed any discomfort or shame. In the dynamics of William and Teresa we see, once again, a circulating phallus.

In the case of Barry and Bridget we witness a different dynamic. Barry was the creative, playful one. He was comfortable being vulnerable. He easily accommodated to Bridget's needs and was empathic to her angst. He was drawn to people with whom he could easily share his interior life and avoided an affected manly posturing. By contrast, Bridget was driven and betrayed an often, hard-edged, even abrasive demeanor. Financial success and social recognition trumped other life preferences. Prone to mood swings, she would vacillate between a clawing neediness and a mocking of Barry's light gender footprint.

In their early idealized rapturous state, Barry was in thrall of Bridget's grit and drive; and Bridget cherished those aspects of Barry that were the antithesis of her father's ruthless, misogynistic ways. But over time, the once circulating phallus ceased to circulate; Bridget often claimed sole occupancy of this position. Barry was squeezed into a receptive, flattened out psychic space, often feeling muted and small. Their idealization of one another, now shot through with mutual misrecognition and mistrust, turned into disappointment and gradually hatred. In time, the marriage ended. As Barry lamented quite recently, "Even though she detested him, she *became* her father. . . . At first, she loved me because I wasn't [her father] . . . and then she resented me because I wasn't. . . . It was painful and sad."

Notes

1 We are grateful to David Rappaport for suggesting the notion of de-idealization and its potential link to trauma.

2 Jessica Benjamin effectively translated this hermeneutic process into a psychoanalytic theory of recognition as an intersubjective process. The logic of recognition is mutual (I am recognized and I recognize you), as both parties have a "need for recognition." This process, however flawed or short-circuited, is the way we know and form ourselves. We are formed as part of an intersubjective process of recognition that always leaves us unfinished. We can imagine the process as follows: we assert ourselves or engage in worldly behavior. The other responds and recognizes our behavior and ourselves—in gestures, words, silence; we experience their recognition. The other then shapes our subjectivity because we are now experiencing ourselves, in part, as the effect of their behavior. We metabolize the other's recognition of us, thereby altering our sense of who we are. From this point of view, the self is not a self-identical unit, but is formed intersubjectively and more an unfinished process than a fixed unit.

Afterword

A transsituated perspective on bodies and genders

In *Becoming a Visible Man*, Jamison Green asserts, "People who have bodies that match their gender identity take their bodies for granted in their process of identity formation. Transgendered and transsexual people don't have that luxury. . . . We come to understand and accept . . . our masculinity or femininity and its relation to our femaleness or maleness, but it's the body that gives us problems—it's the body that we have to deal with . . . in order to express our deepest sense of self" (Green 2004: 35). He states a truth many trans* people would no doubt endorse: their struggle is not about gender expression.[1] All of us in principle are capable of a wide range of gender expression in our appearance, behavior, and social roles. More to the point, regardless of our assigned birth status as male or female, arguably all Americans exhibit in their interior and outward lives a mindboggling blend of what our culture marks as feminine and masculine. And, as we've argued throughout this book, there has occurred a loosening, at once empirical and normative, between our sexed bodies assigned at birth and the way we manifest our gendered selves. So, female bodied women (cis-or-trans*) today manifest masculinities in their demeanor and comportment, behavior and social roles; and while many male bodied men, in particular non-trans* men, resist fully acknowledging their femininity, their attention to body image and lifestyle, to cultivating intimate relationships, to being engaged and nurturing parents, and work lives increasingly centered around service oriented tasks in collaborationist work environments, underscore the loosening grip that maleness has on men's gender expression. Still, let's be perfectly clear. Aligning sexed status and gender expression and identity (cisgendering) still has considerable normative force and remains socially and psychically compelling.

It's the cultural incongruity between the gendered meaning of their sexed bodies and their felt and affirmed gender that cause trans* suffering. It is, for example, persons assigned a female sexed body at birth but whose subjective gender falls heavily on the masculine spectrum that triggers potential trauma or crisis; in effect, the discord experienced between their sexed bodies and gendered psyche places them at odds with a cisgendered normativity. To put an even finer point on this, many trans* people experience a misalignment between a felt sense of themselves as male or female and their actually embodied, visually recognizable sexed self. In both instances, in the discord between the sexed body and the affirmed gender and between the felt and seen body or between the inner and outer body, it is the struggle around the body, as a site of saturated cultural and psychic meanings, that is the dramatic center in the lives of trans* people (e.g. Rubin 2003: 11, Valerio 2006: 193). In exploring this theme, in particular, among transmen or FTMs or transmasculine selves, we consider the ways transsubjectivity and transsituated discourses speak to the question of manhood in America today.

There is no body in and of itself; it is always saturated with contextually specific cultural significance (Cromwell et al. 1999: 32–33 and Gozlan 2016: 303; cf. Elliot 2001, Rubin 2003, Salamon 2010). In 20th and 21st century America, the body is suffused with gender meaning. The postnatal body already serves as the visual signature of the newborn's gender identity. It announces who you are, what's expected of you, and what gestures, expressions, behaviors, and statuses are and aren't available; it serves as the unconscious cultural ground upon which our lives take shape and our destiny is imagined.

This cultural ordering is at the heart of cisgendered normativity. Thus, persons assigned a female sex at birth are expected and socially compelled to exhibit a more or less seamless femininity in their personal and public lives and to present a legible identity as a woman. Cisgendering is then a regulatory order, linking psychic and social legibility with inhabiting the identities of female/male and man/woman (e.g. Serano 2016). Moreover, these sexed and gendered identities bear the markings of nature, normality, health, rightness, and godliness. And, for male bodies, especially if they manifest hegemonic masculine expressions and especially if they are white, cisgendered normativity has historically conferred on them an ideal and privileged status.[2]

Most of us make accommodations and compromises to align our sexed bodies with our gendered selves without turning our lives topsy-turvy. This is often not the case for trans* people. For many transmen, for example, their birth-assigned female bodied status puts them at odds with their internally felt and affirmed sense of gender. Transmen inhabit the contradiction between their inner, sentient sense of sex/gender (male, masculine, man) and their visually perceived gender (female, feminine, woman). It's as if living with an ongoing sense of being out of sync, in-between, or neither/nor; an embattled interior elicits a heightened un-ease inside oneself and between one's subjective reality and the way the world knows and responds to you.

In a cisgendering regime, trans* people often describe their body, a body gendered at birth, as wrong, a betrayal, as if a foreign, alienating presence (Rubin 2003: 3, 10–11, Prosser 1998: 69–78, Valerio 2006: 43, cf. Langer 2016). Typically, they feel compelled to choose: "to pass" or present as cisgendered but struggle with repeated misrecognition and a sense of fraudulence (Stone 2006) or just "show up" (Ehrensaft 2011, 2014) and risk mortification, exile from family and civic life, or worse. It is this dilemma that prompts trans* people to initially recognize their difference and, if indeed they show up, to eventually choose whether or not to inaugurate what is arguably their defining act: transitioning (e.g. Prosser 1998: 4, 63–66, 77, Rubin 2003: 138).

Transitioning is a multileveled process, bearing many meanings and expressed in a wide range of trans* trajectories (Brubaker 2016: chapters. 3, 4, 5 and Halberstam 1998b: 305, cf. Hale 1997, 1998, Hansbury 2005, Rubin 2003, Serano 2016). Let's be clear. Transitioning is rarely described as a shift from one gender to another, a crossing from womanhood to manhood or vice versa. Becoming trans* is typically narrated as a process of coming to know one's true gender, feeling its realness, bodily, psychically, and interpersonally, and ultimately deciding to live it in whatever way is possible and imaginable in the course of a life; it's about a choice to inhabit one's internally felt and affirmed gender, which for some individuals may mean claiming a more or less fixed and essential gender identity while for others occupying an ambiguous and shifting gender space (Bornstein 1994, Feinberg 1993, Halberstam 1998b, 2018, Hale 1997, 1998). In transitioning, much depends on extraneous factors such as family and peer support, finances, and access to medical options, as well as subjective considerations such as one's psychic sturdiness and openness to experience the ambiguous and changing meaning of being gendered (Halle 1998: 322, Latham 2017, Namaste 2000, 2006, Rubin 2003). For some trans* people, a seeming minority, transitioning is principally a psychological and social process, at least for a time. In this trajectory, one forges a primary cross-gender identification, for example, as a female-bodied man or FTM or transman or transmasculine person with little or no medical intervention. Instead, one relies on dress and comportment and perhaps subcultural signifiers to inhabit a trans* position (e.g. Rubin 2003: 138, Walker 2016: 139). Likewise, the imagined end point of transitioning, however provisional, is equally individualized and comprises a cultural field of enormous variation, from passing as a non-trans* man/woman, inhabiting an explicitly trans-man/woman identity to embracing a transgendered or genderqueer or agender or two-spirited status (Brubaker 2016, Cromwell 1999 et al., Hale 1997, Hansbury 2005, Stryker 2008).

With the development of endocrinology in the 20th century and the mainstreaming of sex reassignment surgery in the past couple of decades, trans* people confront a new horizon of possibility: to alter or reconstruct aspects of the body; specifically, to use surgery and/or hormones to effectively re-sex the body. It seems unremarkable at this historic juncture to observe that for the seeming majority of trans* people transitioning marks a movement centered on some form of re-embodiment aimed at realigning a sexed body with an affirmed gender. Equally unremarkable, given the current state of genital surgery, body reconstruction most often focuses on the removal of the key markers of a sexed body, breasts for transmen, penises for transwomen, adding new body parts (e.g. via vaginoplasty or phalloplasty), and re-forming the body's surface by redistributing fat, muscle, and hair and altering skin texture and voice tonality primarily through hormonal therapy. In short, through medical and non-medical interventions, many trans* people aim to fashion a visual body whose manifest sex characteristics (e.g. muscle, fat, hair, voice) and behavioral presentation align and resonate with their felt and affirmed gender (e.g. Prosser 1998: 66, Cromwell et al. 1999: 105, Rubin 2003: 152–3, Valerio 2006: 16–17, 153). Transitioning via re-embodiment underscores a key cultural fact in present-day America: given that masculinity and femininity circulate between men and women, individuals increasingly read each other's gender identity in terms of secondary sex characteristics. Rubin (2003: 152) calls this cultural dynamic, the "expressive hypothesis." "In this culture . . . we view bodies as the reflection of a gendered self. . . . From the FTM perspective, their bodies are failed expressions of their core [gendered] selves" (Rubin 2003: 182–3). Somewhat ironically, just as the body has become a site of self-fashioning, it is no less claimed to be the essential touchstone of a normalizing gender identity (Cromwell et al. 1999: 42–43, Goldner 2011: 164, Prosser 1998: 11).

As a central pathway to a personally normalizing realignment of subjective and social identity, re-embodiment is fundamentally about the desire for recognition, to be acknowledged in what is often considered one's authentic gender (Brubaker 2015: 137, Green 2004: 21, Rubin 2003: 11, 15, 175, 183; cf. Langer 2016, Lemma 2013). Trans* people also seek a psychically deep and sustaining sense of belonging and self validation— and for many this pivots on securing a sense of home in their own bodies (Prosser 1998: 82–83, 177, Rubin 2003: 8, 11, Green 2004: 7, 195). From this perspective, transitioning is prompted by a potentially traumatizing experience of bodily and psychic dislocation and homelessness.

In this reading, the body serves as more than a symbol or performative marker of gender identity. In his stunning rumination, *Second Skin* (1998), Jay Prosser holds that the very sensual materiality of the skin, the way the body holds and contains us, optimally grounding feelings of bodily wholeness and ownership, is integral to securing an ongoing sense of psychic integrity (pp. 65–67). Drawing on the psychoanalytic work of Anzieu (2016), Prosser suggests that without a vital, ongoing sense of bodily resonance and concordance, trans* people suffer a shattering of psychic coherence. Trans* struggles then are bodily but in a way that fundamentally implicates the psyche.

Briefly, as many first-person trans* narratives recount, their actual, materially available body, culturally embedded and experienced by them and others as a sexed body, is disowned or dissociated from in key ways, especially from puberty forward (Green 2004, Rubin 2003, Thompson 1995, Valerio 2006). This body is often described as a betrayal, a foreign territory, as if an added appendage is carried about, useless and intrusive (e.g. Valerio 2006: 43, Prosser 1998: 77–78, Rubin 10–11, 99, Thompson 1995: 54). This doesn't mean, however, the absence of an experience of a sexed/gendered embodiment. There is an internally felt sense of embodiment, a subjectively imagined body that is felt as more real, more resonant, more an imagined home, and more self-validating, than the visually apprehended body.

For many trans* people, this dissonance and the anxiety of bodily/ psychic homelessness is managed by relying on two modalities: "aphasia" and "phantomization" (Prosser 1998 63–66, 84–85 and Rubin 2003: 29) In the former, body parts that bear an overdetermined sexed/gendered meaning, genitals in particular, are de-eroticized, virtually de-sexed. They are disowned, as if psychically exiled into a space of absence or otherness (e.g. Green 2004: 13, Valerio 2006: 69, 214). In the latter instance, body parts signifying the affirmed gender are imagined as materially present; they are sexed and sexualized, invested with formative psychic significance and function as if they are materially real. From this perspective, transitioning is the re-establishing of a bodily/psychic home, a return of sorts to a recognizable and owned bodily/psychic space, one only previously imagined but through transitioning can be actually inhabited and lived (Prosser 1998: 82–89, Rubin 2003: 8, 11, Green 2004: 7, 195, Valerio 2006: 193).

In Prosser's account, and this is evident in many trans* narratives, there is a presumption of a subjectively felt and known body and psyche as either male or female or as a man/transman or woman/transwoman. From this perspective, there is a right or wrong body, an aligned or misaligned sex/gender nexus, and a recognized or misrecognized gender identity. But some trans* people reject the language of a wrong body. "Many female-bodied people do not and have never felt like 'a man trapped in a women's body' or as though they have 'the wrong body'. . . . 'If I have the wrong body whose body do I have and where is my body?'" (Cromwell 1999: 25). And, while many trans* people desire a re-sexed body to ground a sharply delineated exclusive sex/gender identity as a female/male, woman/ man, transwoman/man, many other trans* people approach the body as an autonomous site of meaning and experience, uncoupled or only loosely linked to a sharply defined sex/gender identity; as such, the body is poten-tially a site of ambiguous, contradictory, and shifting sexed and gendered meanings (e.g. Feinberg 1993, cf. Hale 1997, 1998). For example, taking issue with Rubin's expressive paradigm, Cromwell maintains that many trans* people approach "their bodies as containers but feel they are not confined to their bodies in expressing their beings." Thus, some trans* people "reject . . . that having breasts and female genitals mandates being women and feminine. They also reject that female equals woman equals feminine. Instead, they (some transmen or FTMs) are masculine, which equals men in spite of having the signs (female genitals, breasts, and menstruation) that dictate being female" (p. 106). Many, perhaps most, trans* people embrace a hybrid body, a mix of the body born with and a partially modified body (e.g. transmen, FTMs or transmasculine persons. e.g. Hansbury 2005: 245), while others occupy the very sexed/gendered ambiguity of their bodies and explore its capacities for androgyny or bi-genderedness or embrace its fluid movement between and beyond genders, e.g. genderqueer, transgendered, or just trans* (Brubaker 2015, Hale 1998, Lawrence-Clark 2016, Serano 2016, Walker 2016).

From a transsituated perspective, the body is constructed as a site of tension and contradiction. Instead of being something unequivocal in its boundaries, psychic meaning and gender significance, it is a field combining materiality and intentionality, naturalness and artifice and a site of unbending hardness but also plasticity. Categories such as male, female, man and woman are construed as sites of meaning-making, shifting between states of stability and transivity (Brubaker 2015: 51, 115, 139, Cromwell et al. 1999: 134, Gozlan 2016: 303, Green 2007: 187, Halberstam 1998b: 301, Stone 2006: 231, Valerio 2006: 3).

Consider then the varied meanings attached to maleness and manhood. Against cisgendered or, as Serano says, "cissexual" normativity (2016), *neither construct necessarily stipulates the possession of an actual penis.* Most transmen, to date, decide against phalloplasty but still identify as male (Cromwell et al. 1999: 116–117, Green 2007: 152, Rubin 2003: 139). On what basis do they claim maleness? For some, maleness obtains coherence as a loose cluster of bodily but also behavioral characteristics, from the contour and texture of the body and voice inflection to energy level and at times attitude. In researching transmen transitioning via surgery and hormones, Rubin (2003) found that maleness was tightly linked to the actual body. But, "what counts . . . as a male body? Is it the often-unseen genitalia or the internal glands that they do not have? Is it the Adam's Apple . . .? Is it straight hips, a particular facial hair pattern, or a deep voice? . . . These men acknowledged the range of male bodies" (p. 187–188). For some transmen, however, maleness occupies a space of ambiguity or coheres in a conceptual field uneasily situated between actual and subjectively lived embodiment. In his stirring memoir, *The Testosterone Files* (2006), Max Wolf Valerio claims to have felt male despite having a culturally recognizable female body. "For thirty-two years I lived inside a woman's body. . . . I learned to speak the language of women. . . . I was both part of their world and apart from it. . . . *Feeling male inside yet living the life of a woman*" (p. 2). Valerio knew something about himself, something he felt deeply, before he could think it, namely "that somehow I was male, strong inside my core, my center" (p. 106). Signaling his maleness, he felt like he had a cock, despite female genitalia. "After . . . giving up the idea of sex change [phalloplasty], I decided that it didn't matter. I already thought of myself as possessing a cock. . . ." (p. 322). During sex, for example, he insisted that sex partners respond to him, as he felt, as male. "I have to be seen as male with a woman in order to be aroused" (p. 69). In a parallel manner, in the course of hormonal transitioning, Jamison Green (2004) felt his clitoris change into a cock: "It came pushing out the front of my body like an engorged cock. . . . My penis started to grow—that is, my clitoris became enlarged . . . and after about a year I had a cock I could really grab onto" (p. 152). Yet, Valerio also insisted "my male identity was deep, rooted in my body" (p. 101). And, as testosterone coursed through his veins, he invoked actual embodiment as the ultimate sign of maleness: "my body is beginning to 'think,' it's a male body. . . ." (p. 141).

One point many transmen seem to insist on: maleness is not necessarily in opposition to femaleness. Trans* people typically undermine this binary as they live in bodies whose chromosomes and gonads and brain wiring represent a sexed status different from some of their secondary sex characteristics. "I . . . knew that whether or not I ever changed my body, I would always be not completely male and not completely female, even though I . . . knew I would fit in the world better as a man. . . ." (Green 2004: 190, cf. Cromwell et al. 1999: 127). Many upend the binary by claiming singularly trans* bodies:

"Female-bodied" [people] recognize that the individual was assigned as female or had a female body. Biologically, the individual's genitalia, chromosomes, and phenotype . . . are those of a female. Many may have medical interventions that reconstruct their bodies to be more congruent with their identities, *yet they never . . . have male bodies in the same sense that those born male . . . do. Instead they have transbodies or transsexed bodies. . . .*

(our emphasis, Cromwell 1999: 30, also see
Hansbury 2005: 245, Kuklin 2014: 29)

In transsituated accounts, maleness is then understood as bearing heterogeneous, often contradictory and contextually shifting meanings, underscoring "the heterogeneity of male bodies" (Hale 1997, Rubin 2003: 187–188).

But isn't the male body, if not exclusively the penis, the signature mark of manhood? Isn't it only the limited effectiveness and cost of phalloplasty that deter many transmen from genital reconstruction? Would this change if it were more effective and affordable? Perhaps, but, as trans* accounts repeatedly insist, many male-identified persons credibly claim manhood whose penises have been destroyed, disfigured, damaged, and rendered barely visible or impotent through war, illness, trauma, and aging (e.g. Valerio 2006: 321–322). This underscores a more telling point: trans* narratives have in the main challenged phallocentric constructs. The penis has been displaced as definitive of manhood (e.g. Green 2004: 152). More generally, the conflation of being a man with one-dimensional phallic masculine constructs have been contested by the loosening and scrambling of the nexus of sexed status, gender expression, and identity (Hale 1998: 322–323). To wit: some female-bodied individuals claim manhood or claim masculinity without manhood (e.g. most emphatically, butch lesbians); and, claiming maleness, regardless of being a birth assigned male or a transman, might be a basis for identifying as a man but equally as transmasculine or transfeminine. Indeed, in claiming maleness and identifying as a man, this sexed/gendered status may unfold as a seamless masculine performativity but alternatively as layered, shifting gender expressions that confound the masculine/feminine binary.

Manhood itself bears multiple meanings. For example, the very category of transman underscores a singular identification: men who are partially or wholly female bodied; men with rich, vital histories of girl/womanhood; and men, often enough, allied with femininity, feminism and at times lesbianism (e.g. Walker 2016: 120). These too are men, but of a unique kind: transmen or FTMs. Cromwell (1999), as a transman, does not "identify as a man. I identify as an 'other,' as a transman. What I've come to realize over the years is that regardless of what others think of me, whether I take hormones or not . . . for appearances sake, I am a man. But I'm not an ordinary man. Never could be and never will be" (p. 127, cf. Hansbury 2005: 245, Brubakers 2016: 72–73, 115). Like maleness, manhood is understood less as a matter of sharp categorical definiteness (as this, not that) than as a network of loosely related characteristics associated with the visual body, comportment, attitude, self definition, and social behavior which inevitably overlap with notions of womanhood and femininity (Hale 1998: 322–323, Nicholson 1994).

Transsituated discourses have pried open the category of manhood to include such mindboggling variations as female bodied men; female bodied transmen; FTM men or transmen who mix histories of female bodiedness and socialization as girls/women with partially reconstructed male bodies (Hansbury 2005, Langer 2016, Lawrence-Clark 2016, Valerio 2006); and, not least, persons assigned male at birth who identify as men; but, in each case, this gender identification begs the question: what kind of man? This situates "manhood" in a zone of near unboundaried, near incoherent variation, and hyper-specificity (Halberstam 2018: 306). This opening up of the notion of gender is perhaps defining of transsituatedness. "Transsexuality provides us with the opportunity to think gender as precarious and . . . tolerate not knowing whether it is addressing a woman or a man. . . . *[It] turns gender from a fixed premise into an open question.* . . ." (our emphasis, Gozlan 2016: 303, Halberstam 1998b: 301, 2018: 306).

* * *

As much as trans* frames the body as a field of plasticity and multiplicity, as much as it imagines the loosening and deconstruction of sex and gender categories, many narratives underscore the solidity of the sex/gender binary. Against queering threads, other trans* narratives voice, clearly and emphatically, the idea that the categories of male and female and man and woman are culturally and experientially compelling as bodily, psychic, and social spaces of identity and belonging (Cromwell 1999: 42–43). To be sure, these categories may be stretched and resignified in boundary blurring ways; still, they retain, at least today, "their ongoing foundational power" (Prosser 1998: 11). Many trans* individuals elaborate lives recognizable to themselves and others, lives whose very integrity and viability are built upon the ways they occupy being male, female, men, and women. The gender binary, and that includes a cisgendered normativity, remains a site of deep psychic and social investment.

Trans* discourses then stipulate the body as a site of ambiguity. It is claimed as a solid ground for staking out an identity and sense of belonging, a foundation upon which one can know oneself and be known. As such, it is the most stable, unambiguous, authentic expression of real gender and the true self. Yet, the body is also something to be reconstructed, indeed designed; as such, it is fungible, transitive. And, as much as it can signify a personal truth and reality, it can also be a source of betrayal and fraudulence, a site of both redemption and abjection. In short, bodies in trans* and, we suggest, American culture occupy a field of contradictoriness, at once markers of stability and transivity, clarity and in-betweenness, rendering them, along with gender, a zone of repetition but also individualization.

From a psychoanalytic perspective, these features of trans* experience are no less integral features of the lives of all of us. Visually apprehended cisgendered bodies and selves mask gendered subjectivities far more heterogenuous and contradictory than what's publicly available. As we've argued, underneath the sharply delineated, often seamless gendered surface is a subjectivity teeming with multiple, contradictory, and situationally shifting gender identifications and ways of being and relating, always overinclusive and transgressive as they are driven by an unconscious logic of desire. Becoming a normalized self, that is, performatively cisgendered and straight pivots on an imperative to impose an order on an unruly interiority animated by phantasies of wanting it all, wanting to be all, but equally harboring powerful and deep longings for a bodily and psychic anchor, a ground to stake out a recognizable identity.

In psychoanalytical accounts, Oedipus is still at the heart of this normalizing imperative (Gilligan and Snider 2017). However much we relate this drama as one of consolidation and triumph, the sturm and drang of this transitional dynamic is ongoing. Loss and dis-ease and transivity form the shadowy life of identity coherence. And, for some, perhaps many, consolidation feels like imposition, engendering anguished drama's pivoting around authenticity and often psychic-wrenching anxieties of estrangement and dislocation. There are no psychic endpoints, no final moments, no triumphant completions to these psychic dramas, no matter how effectively one secures a hetero-gendered psychic integrity and manages a normalizing performative competence.

Indeed, we've argued that the recent emergence of liminal, transitional psychic and social spaces, along with gender questioning representations and discourses, have made possible a counter-culture of bodily/gender transsituatedness for many Americans. As the link between the sexed body and gender expression has loosened, we can speak of a generalized social condition making possible highly individualized gender trajectories.

At the same time, cisgendered normativity remains compelling and many trans* and non-trans* people continue to find in notions of maleness and femaleness and man and woman a space of psychic and social integrity and belonging.

Alongside a diamorphic sex/gender normativity are the contours of a multipolar gender culture. The variance between sexed status and gender expression, between gender expression and identity, and the growing recognition of variance among sexed bodies, including bodies situated outside of the male/female binary, are today the cultural horizons against which many Americans stake out projects of self-making and social reformation. Notwithstanding the power of cisgendered normativity, gender is increasingly recognized as an arena whose very meaning presents a multiplicity—as identity, as psychic home, as lifestyle, as an aesthetic of existence, as a site of play or eroticism, and so on. Paralleling this cultural shift is arguably an ongoing social transformation. Gender, or at least a rigid hetero-gender, is seemingly less essential for the well-enough functioning of key social roles and institutions, for example, marriage and parenting or the distribution of positions of authority and technical expertise. One result: as a focus of historically thick state and institutional administration gender is becoming a site of contestation (Davis 2017). This is perhaps the broader social context for the resonance of a transsituated standpoint, but has also made it possible.

Notes

1 Writes Jack Halberstam (2018):

> The asterisk modifies the meaning of transitivity by refusing to situate transition in relation to a destination, final form, a specific shape, or an established configuration of desire and identity. The asterisk holds off the certainty of diagnosis; it keeps at bay any sense of knowing in advance what the meaning of this or that gender variant form may be, and perhaps most importantly, it makes trans* people the authors of their own categorizations.
>
> (p. 4)

Or, alluding to the generalizability of the term:

> My use of the asterisk . . . embraces the nonspecificity of the term "trans" and uses it to open the term up to a shifting set of conditions and possibilities rather than to attach it only to the life narratives of a specific group of people.
>
> (p. 52)

2 Historically, whiteness has been the bearer of rights and authority; non-white bodies, especially black bodies, have been and still are marked by otherness, a combination of inferiority and danger. For example, driven by instinct and animal impulse, black bodies are imagined as rule violating, a threat to the very white bodies that ensure civic order and national progress (Harper 1996, Hill-Collins 2005, Jackson 2006). A history of state-enforced modes of surveillance and regulation such as disenfranchisement, incarceration, and ghettoization, aimed at containing black bodies (cf. state driven administration of trans* bodies: Currah and Spade 2003, Davis 2017, Latham 2017, Serano 2016, Spade 2008, Stone 2006).

Arguably, this changed after World War II—with the dismantling of state enforced racial apartheid, the rise of a civil rights movement and the mainstreaming, however uneven, of black Americans, which included race mixing, the rise of a black middle class and elite, and the delegitimation of flagrant forms of public racism. However precarious and contested, black bodies were now imagined as part of America.

One unforeseen consequence: white men could no longer take for granted appeals to authority based exclusively on their white bodies. Indeed, a curious reversal has been in play: the stereotypical phallic representation of the black body—uber-heterosexual, muscled, sexually potent—now functions paradoxically as a different kind of challenge: a *threat to feminize white male bodies!* Such instances of the excess and reversibility of meanings, and of the shifts in the dialectic of purity and pollution, speak to the body as a zone of transitivity.

To pursue this theme a bit further, the male body, white or otherwise, has faced a far-reaching challenge: feminism. Women's bodies were historically linked with a saturated, boundaryless sentimentality in need of male governance. But the women's movement contested men's authority; their very challenge signified their "masculinity" or the uncoupling of masculinity from male bodies, thus putting a lie to a masculinist construct that grounded authority in an exclusively male body. Feminists went further: they exposed these very bodies as sites of danger—as predatory and manifesting an out-of-control desire that assaults, rapes, and abuses women, children, and other men.

In response, especially in light of women's full-throttled participation in public life, some men have doubled down on a body-based foundationalism: invoking big, strong, hard bodies, bodies that mirror male superheroes, as if the power of an impenetrable steel framed body warrants claims to authority. But, ironically, this phallicized male body culture unintentionally authorizes a view of the body as malleable, as something that can be formed and re-formed, something accessible regardless of one's postnatal body status—hardly a secure ground of authority.

This hyperphallic masculine body is also susceptible to meaning reversibility. In ads, TV, film, and porn, the phallic man is often portrayed as receptive and seductive, as sexy figures to be looked at, desired and penetrated—by women and other men (Bordo 1999). Is the thickly muscled hard body a sign of the power of men or of women as men become objects of their gaze and desire? Do über-masculine male bodies paradoxically serve as a sign of their feminization—as representations of women's fantasies?

Furthermore, in threads of gay culture the phallicized male body not only projects masculinity but functions as an erotic object, a sexy pinup for other men.

As an object of power but also desire, as a projection of authority but also the erotic fantasy of others, the sexual and gender meanings of phallicized male bodies is suffused with an excess of ambiguous and contradictory meanings—precisely a mark of a transsituated standpoint.

References

Abelin, E. (1980). Triangulation, the role of the father and the origins of core gender identity during the rapprochement subphase. In R. Lax, S. Bach, and J. Burland (Eds.), *Rapprochment*. New York: Jason Aronson.

Adams, J. A. (2009). Psychotherapy in poor African American men: Challenges the construction of masculinity. In B. Reis and R. Grossmark (Eds.), *Heterosexual masculinities*. New York: Routledge.

Ahlm, J. (2015). Transgender biopolitics in the US: Regulating gender through a heteronormative lens. In N. Fischer and S. Seidman (Eds.), *Introducing the new sexuality studies*. New York: Routledge.

Alexander, J. (2007). *The civil sphere*. Oxford: Oxford University Press.

Altman, D. (1971). *Homosexual oppression and liberation*. New York: Avon.

——. (1983). *The homosexualization of America*. Boston, MA: Beacon Press.

Altman, N. (2011). *The analyst in the inner city*. (2nd ed.). New York: Routledge.

Anderson, E. (2005). Orthodox and inclusive masculinity: Competing masculinities among heterosexual men in a feminized terrain. *Sociological Perspectives*, 48, 337–355.

——. (2007). "Being masculine is not about who you sleep with . . ." Heterosexual athletes contexting masculinity and the one one-time rule of homosexuality. *Sex Roles*, 58, 104–115.

——. (2009). *Inclusive masculinity*. New York: Routledge.

Anderson, E. & McCormack, M. (2015). Cuddling and spooning: Hetero-masculinity and homosocial tactility among student-athletes. *Men and Masculinities*, 18, 214–230.

Anderson, E. & Robinson, S. (2016). Men's sexual flexibility. In N. Fischer and S. Seidman (Eds.), *Introducing the new sexuality studies*. New York: Routledge.

Anzieu, D. (2016). *The skin-ego*. New York: Routledge.

Anzuldua, G. (1987). *Borderlands/La frontera*. San Francisco, CA: Ann Lute Foundation Books.

Aron, L. (1995). The internalized primal scream. *Psychoanalytic Dialogues*, 5, 195–238.

Arxer, S. (2011). Hybrid masculine power. *Humanity and Society*, 35, 390–422.

Auster, C. & Collins, S. (2000). Masculinity and femininity in American society. *Sex Roles*, 43, 499–528.

Bach, S. (2006). Psychoanalysis and love. In S. Bach (Ed.), *Getting from here to there: Analytic love, analytic process*. New York: Routledge.

Balint, M. (1968) [1992]. *The basic fault*. Evanston, IL: Northwestern University Press.

Ball, C. (2011). *From the closet to the courtroom*. Boston, MA: Beacon Press.

Barber, K. (2008). The well-coifed man. *Gender and Society*, 22, 455–476.

Barker-Benfield, G. (1976). *The horrors of the half-known life: Male attitudes toward women and sexuality in nineteenth-century America*. New York: Harper & Row.

Barry, K. (1984). *Female sexual slavery*. New York: New York University Press.

Bassin, D. (1996). Beyond the he and the she: Toward the reconciliation of masculinity and femininity in the postoedipal female mind. *Journal of the American Psychoanalytic Association*, 44, 157–190.

Bataille, G. (1986) [1957]. *Eroticism: Death and sensuality*. San Francisco, CA: City Lights Books.

Beck, U. & Beck, E. (1995). *The normal chaos of love*. Cambridge: Polity.

Becker, R. (2006). *Gay TV and straight America*. New Brunswick, NJ: Rutgers University Press.

Beebe, B. & Lachmann, M. (2014). *The origins of attachment*. Nork York: Routledge.

Benjamin, J. (1988). *The bonds of love*. New York: Pantheon.

——. (1991). Father and daughter: Identification with difference—a contribution to gender heterodoxy. *Psychoanalytic Dialogues*, 1, 277–300.

——. (1995). *Like subjects, love objects: Essays on recognition and sexual difference*. New Haven, CT: Yale University Press.

——. (1996). In defense of gender ambiguity. *Gender and Psychoanalysis*, 1, 27–43.

——. (1997). Response to Ronnie C. Lesser. *Gender and Psychoanalysis*, 2, 389–398.

——. (1999). Recognition and destruction: An outline of intersubjectivity. In L. Aron and A. Harris (Eds.), *Relational psychoanalysis*. Hillsdale, NJ: Analytic Press.

——. (2004). Beyond the doer and done to: An intersubjective view of thirdness. *Psychoanalytic Quarterly*, 73, 5–46.

Bergler, E. (1956). *Homosexuality*. New York: Hill & Wang.

Bersani, L. (1986). *The Freudian body*. New York: Columbia University Press.

——. (1995). *Homos*. Cambridge, MA: Harvard University Press.

——. (1987). Is the rectum a grave? In D. Crimp (Ed.), *AIDS: Cultural analysis/Cultural activism* (pp. 197–222). Cambridge, MA: MIT Press.

Best, A. (2000). *Prom night: Youth, schools, and popular culture*. New York: Routledge.

Bianchi, S, Sayer, L., Milkie, M., & Robinson, J. (2012). Housework: Who did, does or will do it, and how much does it matter? *Social Forces*, 91, 55–63.

Bieber, I. et al. (1962). *Homosexuality: A psychoanalytic study of male homosexuals*. New York: Basic Books.

Bilbarz, T. & Stacey, J. (2010). How does the gender of parents matter? *Journal of Marriage and Family*, 7, 3–22.

Birkby, P., Harris, B., Newton, E., Johnston, J., & O'Wyatt, J. (Eds.). (1973). *Amazon expedition: A lesbian feminist anthology*. Washington, NJ: Times Change Press.

Blau, F. & Brummund, P. (2013). Trends in occupational segregation by gender 1970–2009. *Demography*, 50, 471–492.

Blechner, M. (1998). Maleness and masculinity. *Contemporary Psychoanalysis*, 34, 597–614.

——. (2005). Disgust, desire, and fascination—psychoanalytic, cultural, historical, and neurobiological perspectives: Commentary on Muriel Dimen's paper. *Studies in Gender and Sexuality*, 6, 33–45.

——. (2006). Love, sex, romance, and psychoanalytic goals. *Psychoanalytic Dialogues*, 16, 779–798.

Bloch, R. (1978). American feminine ideals in transition: The rise of the moral mother, 1785–1815. *Feminist Studies*, 4, 101–126.

Blos, P. (1984). Son and father. *Journal of the American Psychoanalytic Association*, 32, 301–324.

Blum, A., Danson, M., & Schneider, S. (1997). Problems of sexual expression in adult gay men: A psychoanalytic reconsideration. *Psychoanalytic Psychology*, 14, 1–11.

Blum, A. & Pfetzing, V. (1998). Assaults to the self: The trauma of growing up gay. *Gender and Psychoanalysis*, 2, 227–242.

Bollas, C. (1987). *The shadow of the object*. New York: Columbia University Press.

——. (1989). *Forces of destiny*. New York: Free Association Books.

Bolzendahl, C. & Myers, D. (2004). Feminist and support for gender equality: Opinion change in women and men, 1974–1998. *Social Forces*, 83, 759–789.

Bonovitz, C. (2009). Mixed race and the negotiation of racialized selves: Developing the capacity for internal conflict. *Psychoanalytic Dialogues*, 19, 426–441.

Bornstein, K. (1994). *Gender outlaw*. New York: Routledge.

Bordo, S. (1999). *The male body*. New York: Farrar, Straus & Giroux.

Botticelli, S. (2010). Thinking the unthinkable: Anal sex in theory and practice. *Studies in Gender and Sexuality*, 11, 112–123.

Brady, M. (2011). Sometimes we are prejudiced against ourselves: Internalized and external homophobia in the treatment of an adolescent boy. *Contemporary Psychoanalysis*, 47, 458–479.

Brandchaft, B. (2007). Systems of pathological accommodation and change in analysis. *Psychoanalytic Psychology*, 24(4), 667–687.

Bridges, T. (2014). A very "gay" straight? Hybrid masculinities, sexual aesthetics, and the changing relationship between masculinity and homophobia. *Gender and Society*, 28(1), 58–82.

Bridges, T. & C. J. Poscoe. (2014). Hybrid masculinities: new directions in the sociology of men and masculinities. *Sociology Compass*, 8, 245–258.

Bromberg, P. (1994). Speak! that I may see you: Some reflections on dissociation, reality, and psychoanalytic listening. *Psychoanalytic Dialogues*, 4, 517–547.

——. (1996). Standing in the spaces: The multiplicity of self and the psychoanalytic relationship. *Contemporary Psychoanalysis*, 32, 509–536.

——. (2000). Reply to reviews by Cavell, Sorenson, and Smith. *Psychoanalytic Dialogues*, 10(3), 556.

Brooks, D. (2015, September 30). The new romantics in the computer age. *The New York Times*.

Brownmiller, S. (1975). *Against our will: Men, women and rape*. New York: Simon and Schuster.

Brubaker, R. (2016). *Trans: Gender and race in an age of unsettled identities*. Princeton, NJ: Princeton University Press.

Butler, J. (1990). *Gender trouble*. New York: Routledge.

——. (1995). Melancholy gender, refused identification. *Psychoanalytic Dialogues*, 5, 165–184.

——. 1998. Analysis to the Core: Commentary on papers by James H. Hansell and Dianne Elise. *Psychoanalytic Dialogues*, 8, 373–378.

——. (2000). Longing for recognition. *Studies in Gender and Sexuality*, 1, 271–290.

——. (2004). *Undoing gender*. New York: Routledge.

Califia, P. (2000) [1994]. *Public sex*. San Francisco, CA: Cleis Press.

Campbell, L. & Carroll, M. (2007). The incomplete revolution: Theorizing gender when studying men who provide care to aging parents. *Men and Masculinities*, 9, 491–508.

Canaday, M. (2009). *The straight state*. Princeton, NJ: Princeton University Press.

Canarelli, J., Cole, G., & Rizzuto, C. (1998). Attention vs. acceptance: Some dynamic issues in gay male development. *Gender and Psychoanalysis*, Winter 4, 47–70.

Cancian, F. (1980). *Love in America*. Cambridge: Cambridge University Press.

Chodorow, N. (1976). Oedipal asymmetries and heterosexual knots. In *Feminism and psychoanalytic theory*. New Haven, CT: Yale University Press.

——. (1978). *Reproduction of mothering*. Berkeley, CA: University of California Press.

——. (1994). *Femininities, masculinities, sexualities: Freud and beyond*. Lexington, KY: University Press of Kentucky.

——. (2015). From the glory of Hera to the wrath of Achilles: Narratives of second-wave masculinity and beyond. *Studies in Gender and Sexuality*, 16, 261–270.

Cherlin. A. (2009). *The marriage-go-round*. New York: Alfred Knopf.

Clum, J. (2001). *Something for the boys: Musical theatre and gay culture.* New York: St. Martin's Press.

Cohen, J. (2002). *Regulating intimacy.* Princeton, NJ: Princeton Cohler.

Cohen, P. (2013, November 23). How can we jump-start the struggle for gender equality? *The New York Times.*

——. (2014a). *The family, inequality, and social change.* New York: Norton.

——. (2014, September 4). Family diversity is the new normal for America's children. *(Briefing paper) The council on contemporary families.*

Cohler, B. & Galatzer-Levy, R. (2013). The historical moment in the analysis of gay men. *Journal of the American Psychoanalytic Association,* 61, 1139–1173.

Cohler, B. J. & Hammack, P. L. (2007). The psychological world of the gay teenager: Social change, narrative, and "normality." *Journal of Youth and Adolescence,* 36, 47–59.

Coltrane, S. (2001). Marketing the marriage "solution:" Misplaced simplicity in the politics of fatherhood. *Sociological Perspectives,* 44, 387–402.

Coltrane, S., Parke, R., & Adams, M. (2004). Complexity of father involvement in low-income Mexican American families. *Family Relations,* 53, 179–189.

Copen, C. E., Daniels, K., & Mosher, W. D. (2013). First premarital cohabitation in the United States: 2006–2010 national survey of family growth. *National Health Statistics Report, No. 64. April.*

Corber, R. (1993). *In the name of national security: Hitchcock, homophobia, and the political construction of gender in postwar America.* Durham, NC: Duke University Press.

Corbett, K. (1993). The mystery of homosexuality. *Psychoanalytic Psychology,* 10, 345–357.

——. (1996). Homosexual boyhood: Notes on girlyboys. *Gender and Psychoanalysis,* 1, 429–461.

——. (2009a). *Boyhoods.* New Haven, CT: Yale University Press.

——. (2009b). Boyhood femininity, gender identity disorder, masculine presuppositions, and the anxiety of regulation. *Psychoanalytic Dialogues,* 19, 353–370.

Corpt, E. (2013). Peasant in the analyst's chair: Reflections, personal and otherwise, on class and the forming of an analytic identity. *International Journal of Psychoanalytic Self Psychology,* 8, 52–69.

Corrigan, E. & Gordon, P.-E. (1995). The mind as an object. In *The mind object.* Northvale, NJ: Jason Aronson.

Cott, N. F. (1977). *The bonds of womanhood: "Woman's sphere" in New England, 1780–1835.* New Haven, CT: Yale University Press.

——. (2000). *Public vows.* Cambridge, MA: Harvard University Press.

Cromwell, J. (1999). *Transmen and FTMS.* Champaign, IL: University of Illinois Press.

Cross, S. & Bagilhole, B. (2002). Girls' jobs for the boys? Men, masculinity and non-traditional occupations. *Gender, Work and Organization,* 9(2), 204–226.

Currah, P. & Spade, D. (2003). The state we're in: Locations of coercion and resistance in trans policy, part 2. *Sexuality Research and Social Policy*, 5, 1–4.

Curtin, S. et al. (2014). National Center for Health Statistics. Data Brief. No. 18, August.

Davids, M. F. (2002). Fathers in the internal world: From boy to man to father. In J. Trowell and E. Etchegoyen (Eds.), *The importance of fathers: A psychoanalytic re-evaluation*. New York: Routledge.

Davidson, C. (1998). No more separate spheres! Special Issue *American Literature (Special issue)*, 70, 443–463.

Davies, J. M. (1996). Linking the "pre-analytic" with the postclassical: Integration, dissociation, and the multiplicity of unconscious process. *Contemporary Psychoanalysis*, 32, 553–576.

——. (1998). Between the disclosure and foreclosure of erotic transference-countertransference: Can psychoanalysis find a place for adult sexuality? *Psychoanalytic Dialogues*, 8, 747–766.

——. (2003). Falling in love with love: Oedipal and postoedipal manifestations of idealization, mourning, and erotic masochism. *Psychoanalytic Dialogues*, 13, 1–27.

——. (2004). Roundtable: Dialogues of sexuality in development and treatment. *Studies in Gender and Sexuality*, 5, 371–418.

——. (2015). From Oedipus complex to oedipal complexity: Reconfiguring (pardon the expression) the negative oedipal complex and the disowned erotics of disowned sexualities. *Psychoanalytic Dialogues*, 25, 265–283.

Davies, N. & Eagle, G. (2013). Conceptualizing the paternal function: Maleness, masculinity, or thirdness? *Contemporary Psychoanalysis*, 49, 559–585.

Davis, E. C. (2008). Situating "fluidity" (trans)gender identification and the regulation of gender diversity. *GLQ: A Journal of Lesbian and Gay Studies*, 15, 97–130.

Davis, H. (2017). *Beyond trans does gender matter?* New York: NYU Press.

Dean, J. (2014). *Straights: Heterosexuality in post-closeted culture*. New York: NYU Press.

Dean, T. (2014). Uses of perversity: Commentary on Saketopoulou's "To suffer pleasure." *Studies in Gender and Sexuality*, 15, 269–277.

Degler, C. (1981). *At odds: Women and the family in America from the revolution to the present*. Oxford: Oxford University Press.

D'Emilio, J. (1983). *Sexual politics, sexual communities*. Chicago, IL: University of Chicago Press.

D'Emilio, J. & Freedman, E. (2012). *Intimate matters* (3rd ed.). Chicago, IL: University of Chicago Press.

Deutsch, F. (2007). Undoing gender. *Gender and Society*, 21, 106–27.

——. (1999). *Having it All: How Equally shared parenting works*. Cambridge, MA: Harvard University Press.

Diamond, M. (1997). Boys to men: The maturing of masculine gender identity through parental watchful protectiveness. *Gender and Psychoanalysis*, 2, 443–468.

——. (1998). Fathers and sons: Psychoanalytic perspectives on "good enough" fathering throughout the life cycle. *Gender and Psychoanalysis*, 3, 243–299.

——. (2004). Accessing the multitude within: A psychoanalytic perspective on the transformation of masculinity at mid-life. *International Journal of Psychoanalysis*, 85, 45–64.

——. (2007). *My father before me: How fathers and sons influence each other.* New York: Norton.

——. (2009). Masculinity and its discontents: Making room for the "mother" inside the male—an essential achievement for healthy, male gender identity. In B. Reis and R. Grossmark (Eds.), *Heterosexual masculinities*. New York: Routledge.

——. (2015). The elusiveness of masculinity: Primordial vulnerability, lack, and the challenges of male development. *Psychoanalytic Quarterly*, LXXXIV, 47–101.

——. (2017). Recovering the father in mind and flesh: History, triadic functioning, and developmental implications. *Psychoanalytic Quarterly*, LXXXVI, 297–331.

Dietz, T. (1998). An examination of violence and gender role portrayls in video games. *Sex Roles*, 38, 425–442.

Dimen, M. (1991). Deconstructing difference: Gender, splitting and transitional space. *Psychoanalytic Dialogues*, 1, 335–352.

——. (2003). *Sexuality, intimacy, power*. New York: The Analytic Press.

——. (2005). Sexuality and suffering, or the eew! factor. *Studies in Gender and Sexuality*, 6, 1–18.

——. (2011). *With culture in mind*. New York: Routledge.

Dinnerstein, D. (1976). *The mermaid and the minotaur*. New York: Other Press.

Domenici, T. & Lesser, R. (Eds.). (1995). *Disorienting sexuality: Psychoanalytic reappraisals of sexual identities*. New York: Routledge.

Doucet, A. (2006). *Do men mother? Fathering, care, and domestic responsibility*. Toronto, ONT: University of Toronto Press.

Drescher, J. (1998). *Psychoanalytic therapy and the gay man*. Hillsdale, NJ: The Analytic Press.

——. (2002). Causes and becauses: On etiological theories of homosexuality. In J. W. Anderson and J. A. Winer (Eds.), *Rethinking psychoanalysis and the homosexualities*. Hillsdale, NJ: The Analytic Press.

Drozek. R. (2015). The dignity in multiplicity: Human value as a foundational concept in relational thought. *Psychoanalytic Dialogues*, 25, 431–451.

Duberman, M. (1991). *Cures*. New York: Dutton.

Duggan, L. (2002). The new homonormativity: The sexual patterns of neo-liberalism. In R. Castronovo and D. Nelson, (Eds.). *Materializing democracy*. Durham, NC: Duke University Press.

——. (2003). *The twilight of equality*. Boston, MA: Beacon Press.

Dworkin, A. (1976). *Our blood: Prophecies and discourses on sexual politics.* New York: Harper & Row.

——. (1981). *Pornography: Men possessing women.* London: Women's Press.

Echols, A. (1990). *Daring to be bad.* Minneapolis, MN: University of Minnesota Press.

Eden, K. & Nelson, T. (2013). *Doing the best I can: Fatherhood in the inner city.* Berkeley, CA: University of California Press.

Ehrenberg, D. (1975). The quest for intimate relatedness. *Contemporary Psychoanalysis*, 1, 320–331.

Ehrensaft, D. (2007). Raising girlyboys: A parent's perspective. *Studies in Gender and Sexuality*, 8, 269–302.

——. (2011). Boys will be girls, girls will be boys: Children affect parents as parents affect children in gender nonconformity. *Psychoanalytic Psychology*, 28, 528–548.

——. (2014). Found in transition: Our littlest transgender people. *Contemporary Psychoanalysis*, 50, 571–592.

Elise, D. (2001). Male fears of psychic penetration. *Psychoanalytic Dialogues*, 11, 499–532.

Elliot, P. (2001). A psychoanalytic reading of transsexual embodiment. *Studies in Gender and Sexuality*, 2, 295–326.

Erickson-Schroth, L. (Ed.). (2014). *Trans bodies, trans selves.* Oxford: Oxford University Press.

Eskridge, W. (1999). *Gaylaw.* Cambridge, MA: Harvard University Press.

Ezzell, M. (2016). Healthy for whom? Males, men, and masculinity: A reflection on the doing (and study) of dominance. In C. J. Pascoe and T. Bridges (Eds.), *Exploring masculinities.* Oxford: Oxford University Press.

Faderman, L. (1991). *Odd Girls and twilight lovers.* New York: Columbia University Press.

Fairbairn, R. (1952). *Psychoanalytic studies of the personality.* London: Routledge.

Faludi, S. (1999). *Stiffed: The betrayal of the American man.* New York: William Morrow Co.

Farrell, W. (1974). *The liberated man: Beyond masculinity: Freeing men and their relationships with women.* New York: Random House.

Fast, I. (1984). *Gender identity: A differentiation model.* Hillsdale, NJ: The Analytic Press.

——. (1990). Aspects of early gender development: Toward a reformulation. *Psychoanalytic Psychology*, 7S, 105–117.

——. (1999). Aspects of core gender identity. *Psychoanalytic Dialogues*, 9, 633–662.

Feinberg, L. (1993). *Stone butch blues.* Ithaca, NY: Firebrand.

Flax, J. (1990). *Thinking fragments: Psychoanalysis, feminism, and postmodernism in the contemporary west.* Berkeley, CA: University of California Press.

——. (1996). Taking multiplicity seriously: Some consequences for psychoanalytic theorizing and practice. *Contemporary Psychoanalysis*, 32, 577–594.

Fogel, G. (2009). Interiority and inner genital space in men: What else can be lost in castration? In B. Reis and R. Grossmark (Eds.), *Heterosexual Masculinities*. New York: Routledge.

Foucault, M. (1980). *History of sexuality* (Vol. 1). New York: Vintage Press.

——. (1986). *History of sexuality: The care of the self* (Vol. 3). New York: Vintage.

——. (1990a). An aesthetics of existence." In L. Kritzman (Ed.), *Michel Foucault: Politics, philosophy, culture, interviews and other writings 1977–1984*. New York: Routledge.

——. (1990b). On the genealogy of ethics: An overview of work in progress. In P. Rabinow (Ed.), *Michel Foucault: Ethics, subjectivity and truth*. New York: The New Press.

——. (1990c). Sexual choice, sexual act: Foucault and homosexuality. In L. Kritzman (Ed.), *Michel Foucault: Politics, philosophy, culture, interviews and other writings 1977–1984*. New York: Routledge.

——. (1997). The ethics of the concern for self as a practice of freedom. In P. Rabinow (Ed.), *Michel Foucault: Ethics, subjectivity and truth*. New York: The New Press.

Frank, A. (2013). Unexpected Intimacies: Moments of connection, moments of shame. In A. Frank, P. T. Clough, and S. Seidman (Eds.), *Intimacies: A new world of relational life*. New York: Routledge.

Frank, A., Clough, P. T., & S. Seidman (Eds). (2013). *Intimacies: A new world of relational life*. New York: Routledge.

Frank, W. (2014). *Law and the gay rights story*. New Brunswick, NJ: Rutgers University Press.

Frankel. J. (1998). The play's the thing: How the essential processes of therapy are seen most clearly in child therapy. *Psychoanalytic Dialogues*, 8, 149–182.

——. (2002). Exploring Ferenczi's concept of identification with the aggressor: Its role in trauma, everyday life, and the therapeutic relationship. *Psychoanalytic Dialogues*, 12, 101–139.

Franklin, K. (2018). Queering Sexual Development Frameworks: A Dynamic Systems Approach to Conceptualizing Other-Sex Sexuality Among Lesbians. Dissertation in progress. University at Albany.

Fraser, N. (1997). *Justice interruptus*. New York: Routledge.

Fraser, N. & Honneth, A. (2004). *Redistribution or recognition? A political-philosophical exchange*. New York: Verso.

Freeman, T. (2008). Psychoanalytic concepts of fatherhood: Patriarchal paradoxes and the presence of an absent authority. *Studies in Gender and Sexuality*, 9, 113–139.

Freud, S. 1921 [1955]. Group psychology and the analysis of the ego. *Standard Edition*, 18. London: Hogarth Press.

——. (1923). The ego and the id. *Standard Edition*, 19L, 12–66.

———. (1925) [1961]. Some psychological consequences of the anatomical differences between the sexes, *Standard Edition*. V. 19, 248–258. London: Hogarth Press.

———. (1939). Moses and monotheism, *Standard Edition*. V. 22. London: Hogarth Press.

Frey, J. & Passel, S. (2014, July 17). In post-recession era, young adults drive continuing rise in multigenerational living. *Pew Research Center*.

Friedman, R. (1988). *Male Homosexuality*. New Haven, CT: Yale University Press.

Frommer, M. S. (1994). Homosexuality and psychoanalysis: Technical considerations revisited. *Psychoanalytical Dialogues*, 4(2), 215–233.

———. (2000). Offending gender: Being and wanting in male same-sex desire. *Studies in Gender and Sexuality*, 1, 191–206.

Fuss, D. (1989). *Essentially speaking*. New York: Routledge.

Gabbard, G. & Lester, E. (1995). *Boundaries and boundary violations in psychoanalysis*. New York: Basic Books.

Gadamer, H. (1975). *Truth and method*. New York: Continuum.

Gamson, J. (2002). Sweating the spotlight: lesbian, gay and queer encounters with media and popular culture. In D. Richardson and S. Seidman (Eds.), *Handbook of lesbian and gay studies*. London: Sage.

———. (2015). *Modern Families: Stories of extraordinary journeys to kinship*. New York: NYU Press.

Geist, R. (2008). Connectedness, permeable boundaries, and the development of the self: Therapeutic implications. *International Journal of Psychoanalytic Self Psychology*, 3, 129–152.

———. (2009). Empathy, connectedness, and the evolution of boundaries in self-psychological treatment. *International Journal of Psychoanalytic Self Psychology*, 4, 165–180.

Gerson, K. (2010). *The unfinished revolution: Coming of age in a new era of gender, work, and family*. New York: Oxford University Press.

Ghaziani, A. (2011). Post gay collective identity construction. *Social Problems*, 58, 99–125.

———. (2014). *There goes the gayborhood?* Princetown, NJ: Princeton University Press.

Ghent, E. (1990). Masochism, submission, surrender. *Contemporary Psychoanalysis*, 26, 108–136.

Giddens, A. (1992). *Transformation of Intimacy*. Stanford, CA: Stanford University Press.

———. (1993). *The transformation of intimate life*. Stanford, CA: Stanford University Press.

Gilligan, C. (1982). *In a different voice*. Cambridge, MA: Harvard University Press.

Gilligan, C. & Snider, N. (2017). The loss of pleasure, or why we are still talking about Oedipus. *Contemporary Psychoanalysis*, 53, 173–195.

Glassman, N. & Botticelli, S. (2014). Perspectives on gay fatherhood: emotional legacies and clinical reverberations. In S. Kuchuck (Ed.), *Clinical implications of the psychoanalyst's life experience*. New York: Routledge.

Goldberg, A. (2012). *Gay dads*. New York: New York University Press.

Goldberg, H. (1976). *The hazards of being male: Surviving the myth of masculine privilege*. Mechanicsville, MD: Nash.

Goldman, D. (2007). Faking it. *Contemporary Psychoanalysis*, 43, 17–36.

Goldner, V. (1991). Toward a critical relational theory of gender. *Psychoanalytic Dialogues*, 1, 249–272.

——. (2007). Let's do it again: Further reflections on Eros and attachment. *Psychoanalytic Dialogues*, 16, 619–637.

——. (2011). Transgender subjectivities: Introduction to papers by Goldner, Suchet, Saketopoulou, Hansbury, Salamon & Corbett, and Harris. *Psychoanalytic Dialogues*, 21, 153–158.

——. (2014). Talking sex, talking gender, a roundtable. *Studies in Gender and Sexuality*, 15, 295–317.

Goldsmith, S. (1995). Oedipus or Orestes? Aspects of gender identity development in homosexual men. *Psychoanalytic Inquiry*, 15, 112–24.

Gonzalez, F. J. (2013). Another Eden: Proto-gay desire and social precocity. *Studies in Gender and Sexuality*, 14, 112–121.

Gozlan, O. (2016). The transsexual's turn: Uncanniness at Wellesley College. *Studies in Gender and Sexuality*, 17, 297–304.

Grand, S. (2016). Unsexed and ungendered bodies: The violated self. *Studies in Gender and Sexuality*, 4, 343–341.

Green, A. (2009). The construction of the lost father. In L. Kulinish and S. Taylor (Eds.), *The dead father*. New York: Routledge.

Green, J. (2003). Growing up hidden: Notes on understanding male homosexuality. *American Journal of Psychoanalysis*, 63, 177–191.

——. (2004). *Becoming a visible man*. Nashville, TN: Vanderbuilt University Press.

Green, R. (1987). *The sissy boy syndrome and the development of homosexuality*. New Haven, CT: Yale University Press.

Greenson. R. (1968). Disidentifying from mother: Its special importance for the boy. *International Journal of Psychoanalysis*, 49, 370–74.

Greenspan, S. (1982). "The second other:" The role of the father in early personality formation and the dyadic-phallic phase of development. In S. Cath and A. Gurwitt (Eds), *Father and child: developmental and clinical perspectives*. Boston: Little, Brown, and Co.

Golombok, S. (2015). *Modern families: Parents and children in new family forms*. New York: Cambridge University Press.

Griffin, S. (1978). *Woman and nature*. New York: Harper & Row.

Guignon, C. (2004). *On being authentic*. New York: Routledge.

Gump, J. (2000). A white therapist, an African-American patient—shame in the therapeutic dyad. *Psychoanalytic Dialogues*, 10, 619–632.

Guntrip, H. (1969a). *Schizoid phenonena, object relations and the self.* New York: International Universities Press.

———. (1969b). The regressed ego, the lost heart of the self, and the inability to love. In *Schizoid phenonena, object relations and the self.* New York: International Universities Press.

Guss, J. (2010). The danger of desire: Anal sex and the homo/masculine subject. *Studies in Gender and Sexuality,* 11, 124–40.

Halberstam, J. (1998a). *Female masculinity.* Durham, NC: Duke University Press.

———. (1998b). Transgender butch: Butch/FTM border wars and the masculine continuum. *GLQ,* 4, 287–310.

———. (2018). *Trans*.* Berkeley, CA: University of California Press.

Hale, J. (1997). Leatherdyke boys and their daddies: How to have sex without women or men. *Social Text,* 15, 225–238.

———. (1998). Consuming the living, dis(re)membering the dead in the butch/FTM borderlands. *GLQ,* 4, 311–348.

Halperin, D. (2012). *How to be gay.* Cambridge, MA: Harvard University Press.

Halperin, D. & Traub, V. (Eds.). (2009). *Gay shame.* Chicago, IL: University of Chicago Press.

Hammack, P. L., Thompson, E. M. & Pilecki, A. (2009). Configurations of identity among sexual minority youth: Context, desire, and narrative. *Journal of Youth and Adolescence,* 38, 867–883.

Hansbury, G. (2005). The middle men: An introduction to the transmasculine identities. *Studies in Gender and Sexuality,* 6, 241–264.

Hansell, J. (1998). Gender anxiety, gender melancholia, gender perversion. *Psychoanalytic Dialogues,* 8, 337–352.

Harris, A. (1991). Gender as contradiction. *Psychoanalytic Dialogues,* 1, 197–224.

———. (2009a). *Gender as soft assembly.* New York: Routledge.

———. (2009b). Fathers and daughters. In B. Reis and R. Grossmark (Eds.), *Heterosexual Masculinities.* New York: Routledge.

Harris, A. & Botticelli, S. (Eds.). (2010). *First do no harm: The paradoxical encounters of psychoanalysis, warmaking, and resistance.* New York: Routledge.

Hartman, S. (2010). Ruined by pleasure: Commentary on Steven Botticelli and Jeffrey R. Guss. *Studies in Gender and Sexuality,* 11, 141–145.

———. (2011). Reality 2.0: When loss is lost. *Psychoanalytic Dialogues,* 21, 1466–1482.

Harper, P. B. (1996). *Are we not men? Masculine anxiety and the problem of African-American identity.* New York: Oxford University Press.

Heasley, R. (2004). Crossing the borders of gendered sexuality: Queer masculinities of straight men. In C. Ingraham (Ed.), *Straight thinking.* New York: Routledge.

———. (2005). Queer masculinities of straight men: A typology. *Men and Masculinities,* 7, 310–320.

Heineman, T. V. (2004). A boy and two mothers: New variations on an old theme or a new story of triangulation: Beginning thoughts on the psychosexual development of children in nontraditional families. *Psychoanalytic Psychology*, 21, 99–115.

Hennen, P. (2008). *Faeries, bears, and leathermen: Men in community queering the masculine*. Chicago, IL: University of Chicago Press.

Herzog, J. (2001). *Father hunger*. Hillsdale, NJ: Analytic Press.

——. (2005a). What fathers do and how they do it. In S. Brown (Ed.), *What do Fathers Want?*

——. (2005b). Triadic reality and the capacity to love. *Psychoanalytic Quarterly*, LXXIV, 1029–1051.

——. (2009). Constructing and deconstructing the conglomerate: Thoughts about the father in life, in death and in theory. In L. Kulinish and S. Taylor (Eds.), *The dead father*. New York: Routledge.

Hernandez, D. & Rehman, B. (2010). *Colonize this: Young women of color on today's feminism*. Berkeley, CA: Seal Press.

Hill-Collins, P. (1990). *Black feminist thought*. New York: Routledge.

——. (2005). *Black sexual politics*. New York: Routledge.

Hirsch, I. (2009). Imperfect love, imperfect lives: Making love, making sex, making moral judgments. In B. Reis and R. Grossmark (Eds.), *Heterosexual Masculinities*. New York: Routledge.

Honneth, A. (1992). *The struggle for recognition: The moral grammar of social conflicts*. Cambridge, MA: The MIT Press.

——. (2004). Redistribution as recognition. In N. Fraser and A. Honneth, (Eds.), *Redistribution or recognition? A political-philosophical exchange*. New York: Verso.

Hooks, B. (1991). *Yearning: Race, gender, and cultural politics*. New York: Routledge.

——. (2004). *The will to change: Men, masculinity, and love*. New York: Washington Square Press.

Hocquenghem, G. (1972) [1993]. *Homosexual desire*. Durham, NC: Duke University Press.

Howell, E. (2008). *The dissociative mind*. New York: Routledge.

Impert, L. (1999). The body held hostage: The paradox of self-sufficiency. *Contemporary Psychoanalysis*, 35, 647–671.

Ingraham, C. (2008). *White weddings: Romanticizing heterosexuality in popular culture* (2nd ed.). New York: Routledge.

Irigaray, L. (2002). *The way of love*. London: Continuum.

Isay, R. (1989). *Being homosexual: Gay men and their development*. New York: Avon Books.

——. (1987). Fathers and their homosexually inclined sons in childhood. *The Psychoanalytic Study of the Child*, 42, 275–292.

Jacobson, L. (1997). The soul of psychoanalysis in the modern world: Reflections on the work of Christopher Bollas. *Psychoanalytic Dialogues*, 7, 81–115.

Jackson, R. (2006). *Scripting the black masculine body: Identity, discourse, and racial politics in popular media*. Albany, NY: SUNY Press.

Jay, K. & Young, A. (Eds.). (1972). *Out of the closets: Voices of gay liberationism*. New York: Pyramid Books.

Jay, M. (2007). Melancholy, femininity, and obsessive-compulsive masculinity. *Studies in Gender and Sexuality*, 8, 115–135.

Johns, M. (2002). Identification and dis-identification in the development of sexual identity. In J. Trowell and A. Etchegoyen (Eds.), *The importance of fathers: A psychoanalytic re-evaluation*. New York: Routledge.

Kaftal, E. (2001). Outside in: Commentary on paper by Diane Elise. *Psychoanalytic Dialogues*, 11, 541–548.

——. (2009). On intimacy between men. In B. Reis and R. Grossmark (Eds.), *Heterosexual Masculinities*. New York: Routledge.

Kainer, R. (2014). *The collapse of the self and its therapeutic restoration*. New York: Routledge.

Kalinish, L. & Taylor, S. (Eds.). (2009). *The dead father: A psychoanalytic inquiry*. New York: Routledge.

Kaufman, G. (2013). *Superdads: How fathers balance work and family in the 21st century*. New York: NYU Press.

Kelan, E. (2009). Gender logic and (un)doing gender at work. *Gender, Work, and Organization*, 17, 174–194.

Kearney, M., Herhbein, B., & Jácome, E. (2015). Profiles of change: Employment, earnings, and occupations from 1990–2013. *Economic Analysis*. Washington, DC: The Hamilton Project.

Kerber, L. (1988). Separate spheres, female worlds, woman's place: The rhetoric of women's history. *The Journal of American History*, 75, 9–39.

Kimmel, M. (1994). Masculinity as homophobia. In H. Brod and M. Kaufman (Eds.), *Theorizing masculinities*. Thousand Oaks, CA: Sage.

——. (2005). *The gender of desire*. New York: State University of New York Press.

——. (2012). *Manhood: A cultural history* (3rd ed.). New York, NY: Oxford University Press.

——. (2015). *Angry white men*. New York: Nation Books.

Kinsey, A., Pomeroy, W., & Martin, C. (1948). *Sexual behavior in the human male*. New York: Random House.

Kinsey, A., Pomeroy, W., Martin, C., & Gebhard, P. (1953). *Sexual behavior in the human female*. Philadelphia, PA: Saunders.

Klein, M. (1946). Notes on some schizoid mechanisms. In *Envy and Gratitude*, (Vol. 3). New York: Basic Books.

——. (1957). *Envy and gratitude*. New York: Basic Books.

Klinenberg, E. (2012). *Going solo*. New York: Penguin.

Knoblauch, S. (1996). The play and interplay of passionate experience: Multiple organizations of desire. *Gender and Psychoanalysis*, 1, 323–344.

Koedt, A., Levine, E., & Rapone, A. (Eds.). (1973). *Radical feminism*. New York: Quadrangle.

Koestenbaum, W. (1993). *The queen's throat*. New York: Poseidon Press.

Kohut, H. (1971). *The analysis of the self*. Madison, CT: International Universities Press.

——. (1977). *The restoration of the self*. Chicago, IL: University of Chicago Press.

Kramer, K. & Kramer, A. (2014). The rise of stay at home father families in the US: The role of gendered expectations, human capital, and economic downturns. University of Illinois, School of Labor and Employment Relations (Working Paper).

Kramer, K. Z., & Kramer, A. (2016). At-home father families in the United States: Gender ideology, human capital, and unemployment. *Journal of Marriage and Family*, 78, 1315–1331.

Kuklin, S. (Ed). (2014). *Beyond magenta: transgender teens speak out*. Somerville, MA: Candlewick Press.

Lachmann, F. (1996). How many selves make a person? *Contemporary Psychoanalysis*, 32, 595–614.

Laing, R. D. (1960) [1990]. *The divided self*. New York: Penguin.

LaMarre, N. (2016). Sexual narratives of "straight" women. In N. Fischer and S. Seidman (Eds.), *Introducing the new sexuality studies*. New York: Routledge.

Lampere, L. & Rosaldo, M. Z. (Eds.). (1974). *Women, culture, and society*. Stanford, CA: Stanford University Press.

Langer, S. J. (2006). Trans bodies and the failure of mirrors. *Studies in Gender and Sexuality*, 17, 306–316.

Laplanche, J. (1997). The theory of seduction and the problem of the other. *International Journal of Psychoanalysis*, 78, 653–666.

Latham, J. R. (2017). Making and treating trans problems: The ontological politics of clinical practices. *Studies in Gender and Sexuality*, 18, 40–61.

Lawrence-Clark, T. (2016). Mid-life transition. In M. Brown (Ed.), *A herstory of transmasculine identities*. Miami, FL: Boundless Endeavors.

Layton, L. (1998). *Who's that girl? Who's that boy? Clinical practice meets postmodern gender theory*. Northvale, NJ: Jason Aronson.

——. (2006a). Racial identities, racial enactments, and normative unconscious processes. *Psychoanalytic Quarterly*, 75, 237–270.

——. (2006b). Attacks on linking: The unconscious pull to dissociate individuals from their social context. In L. Layton, et al. (Eds.), *Psychoanalysis, class and politics: Encounters in the clinical setting*. London: Routledge.

Lee, J. (1979). The gay connection. *Urban Issues*, 8.

Lemma, A. (2013). The body one has and the body one is: Understanding the transsexual's need to be seen. *International Journal of Psychoanalysis*, 94, 277–292.

Levine, M. (1998). *Gay macho: The life and death of the homosexual clone*. New York: NYU Press.

Lewes, K. (1988). *The psychoanalytic theory of male homosexuality*. New York: Meridan Books.

Liebman, S. M. A. & Abell, S. (2000). The forgotten parent no more: A psychoanalytic reconsideration of fatherhood. *Psychoanalytic Psychology*, 17, 88–105.

Livingston, G. (2014). Growing number of dads home with the kids. *Pew Research*, June 5.

Lorber, J. (2005). *Breaking the bowls: Degendering and feminist change*. New York: Norton.

Lorde, A. (1984). *Sister outsider: Freedom*. Berkeley, CA: The Crossing Press.

Love, H. (2007). *Feeling backward: Loss and the politics of queer history*. Cambridge, MA: Harvard University Press.

Luhmann, N. (1986). *Love as passion*. Cambridge: Cambridge University Press.

Lystra, K. (1989). *Searching the heart: Women, men and romantic love in nineteenth-century America*. New York: Oxford University Press.

Magee, M. & Miller, D. (1998). *Lesbian lives: Psychoanalytic narratives old and new*. New York: Routledge.

Marks, M. (2002). Letting fathers in. In J. Trowell and A. Etchegoyen (Eds.), *The importance of fathers: A psychoanalytic re-evaluation*. New York: Routledge.

Marmor, J. (1980). *Homosexual behavior*. New York: Basic Books.

McCormack, M. (2012). *The declining significance of homophobia*. Oxford: Oxford University Press.

McDermott, M. (2016). *Masculinity, femininity, and American political behavior*. New York: Oxford University Press.

McDonald, J. (2013). Conforming to and resisting dominant gender norms: How male and female nursing students do and undo gender. *Gender, Work, and Organizations*, 20, 561–578.

McGraw, P. C. (2001). *Self matters: Creating your life from the inside out*. New York: Simon & Schuster.

Meissner, W. W. (2005). Gender identity and the self: I. Gender formation in general and in masculinity. *The Psychoanalytic Review*, 92, 1–27.

Messner, M. (2007). The masculinity of the governator. *Gender and Society*, 21, 461–480.

Messner, M, Greenberg, M. A., and Peretz, T. (2016). *Some men: Feminist allies and the movement to end violence against women*. Oxford: Oxford University Press.

Miles, C. (2012). Racial differences in therapy. *Psychoanalytic Inquiry*, 32, 205–220.

Miller, C. (2014, November 7). Paternity leave: The rewards and the remaining stigma. *The New York Times*.

———. (2015, May 8). Out of wedlock births are falling, except for older women. *The New York Times*.

Miller, D. A. (1998). *Place for us: Essay on the Broadway musical*. Cambridge, MA: Harvard University Press.

Miller, J. (1993). *The passion of Michel Foucault*. New York: Anchor.

Miller, L. (2013, Aug. 29). The roar of young male rage. *New York Magazine*.

Mitchell, J. (2003). *Siblings*. London: Polity Press.

Mitchell, S. (1978). Psychodynamics, homosexuality and the question of pathology. *Psychiatry*, 41, 254–263.

——. (1981). The psychoanalytic treatment of homosexuality: Some technical considerations. *International Review of Psychoanalysis*, 8, 63–80.

——. (1991). Contemporary perspectives on self: Towards an integration. *Psychoanalytic Dialogues*, 1, 121–148.

——. (1993). *Hope and dread in psychoanalysis*. New York: Basic Books.

——. (1997). Psychoanalysis and the degradation of romance. *Psychoanalytic Dialogues*, 7, 23–42.

Molofsky, M. (2013). The language of yes in a world of no: A gay man rediscovers his voice. *American Journal of Psychoanalysis*, 73, 43–61.

Moraga, C. (1983). *Loving in the war years*. Boston, MA: South End Press.

Moss, D. (2012). *Thirteen ways of looking at a man*. New York: Routledge.

Murphy, M. (2017). *Queer youth activism: Generational change in the US LGBTQ movement*. PhD Dissertation. Dept. of Sociology. SUNY-Albany.

Myron, N. & Bunch, C. (Eds.). (1975). *Lesbianism and the women's movement*. Baltimore, MD: Diana Press.

Namaste, V. (2000). *Invisible lives: The erasure of transsexual and transgendered people*. Chicago, IL: University of Chicago Press.

——. 2006. *Sex change, social change: Reflections on identity, institutions, and imperialism*. Toronto, ONT: Women's Press of Canada.

Nardi, P., Sanders, D., & Marmor, J. (Eds.). (1994). *Before stonewall: Life stories of some gay men*. New York: Routledge.

Nestle, J., Howell, C., & Wilchins, R. (2002). *Genderqueer: Voices from beyond the binary*. Los Angeles, CA: Alyson Press.

Nicholson, L. (1986). *Gender and history: The limits of social theory in the age of the family*. New York: Columbia University Press.

——. (1994). Interpreting Gender. *Signs* (Autumn), 1, 79–105.

O'Connor, N. & Ryan, J. (2004). *Wild desires and mistaken identities: Lesbianism and psychoanalysis*. New York: Routledge.

Ogden, T. (1989a). The threshold of the male oedipal complex. *Journal of the American Psychoanalytic Association*, 53, 394–419.

——. (1989b). *The primitive edge of experience*. Lanham, MD: Jason Aronson.

——. (2004). The analytic third. *Psychoanalytic Quarterly*, 73, 167–195.

Orbach, S. (2004). Beyond the fear of intimacy. *Psychoanalytic Dialogues*, 8, 561–572.

Padawer, R. (2012, August 8). What's so bad about a boy who wants to wear a dress? *The New York Times Magazine*.

Parker, K. & Wang, W. (2013). Modern parenthood: Roles of moms and dads converge as they balance work and family. *Pew Research Center*, March 14.

Pecora, N. (1992). Superman/superboys/supermen: The comic book hero as socializing agent. In S. Craig (Ed.), *Men, masculinity, and the media*. Newbury Park, CA: Sage.

Perelberg, R. J. (2015). *Murdered father, dead father: Revisiting the Oedipus complex*. New York: Routledge.

Pew Research Center. (2010, November 18). The decline of marriage and the rise of new families.

———. (2013, June 14). The new American father.

———. (2013, December 11). On pay gap, millennial women hear parity—for now.

Phillips, S. (2001). The overstimulation of everyday life: New aspects of male homosexuality. *Journal of American Psychoanalytic Association*, 49, 1235–1267.

———. (2003). Homosexuality: Coming out of the confusion. *International Journal of Psychoanalysis*, 64, 1431–1450.

Pollack, W. (1998). *Real boys*. New York: Henry Holt and Co.

Powell, A., Bagilhole, B., & Dainty, A. (2008). How women engineers do and undo gender: Consequences for gender equality. *Gender, Work, and Organization*, 16, 411–428.

Prager, J. (2013). Intimacy undone: Stories of sex and abuse in the psychoanalytic consulting room. In A. Frank, P. T. Clough, and S. Seidman (Eds.), *Intimacies: A new world of relational life*. New York, NY: Routledge.

Prosser, J. (1998). *Second skins: The body narratives of transsexuality*. New York: Columbia University Press.

Pullen, A. & Simpson, R. (2009). Managing differences in feminized work: Men, otherness, and social practice. *Human Relations*, 62, 561–87.

Putnam, E. (1988). The switch process in multiple personality disorder and other state-change disorders. *Dissociation*, 1, 24–32.

Raeburn, N. (2004). *Changing corporate America from inside out: Lesbian and gay workplace rights*. Minneapolis, MN: University of Minnesota Press.

Rehel, E. (2014). When dad stays home too: Paternity leave, gender and parenting. *Gender and Society*, 28, 110–132.

Reinhart, R. (1986). *A history of shadows: A novel*. Boston, MA: Alyson.

Reis, B. (2009). Names of the father. In B. Reis and R. Grossmark (Eds.), *Heterosexual masculinities*. New York, NY: Routledge.

Reis, B. & Grossmark, R. (Eds.). (2009). *Heterosexual masculinities*. New York, NY: Routledge.

Reiff, P. (1979) [1959]. *Freud: The mind of the moralist* (3rd ed.). Chicago, IL: University of Chicago Press.

———. (1966) [2006]. *The triumph of the therapeutic*. Chicago, IL: University of Chicago Press.

Rich, A. (1977). *Of woman born*. New York: Bantam.

———. (1980). Compulsory heterosexuality and lesbian existence. *Signs* (Summer), 5, 631–660.

Richards, A. (2009). Introduction to Part III. In L. Kalinish and S. Taylor (Eds.), *The dead father: A Psychoanalytic inquiry.* New York: Routledge.

Risman, B. (2009). From doing to undoing: Gender as we know it. *Gender and Society*, 23, 81–84.

Rosenfeld, M. (2007). *The age of independence: Interracial unions, same-sex unions and the changing American family.* Cambridge, MA: Harvard University Press.

Ross. J. (1979). Fathering: A review of some psychoanalytical contributions on paternity. *International Journal of Psychoanalysis*, 60, 317–327.

Roughton, R. (2001). Four men in treatment: An evolving perspective on homosexuality and bisexuality, 1965 to 2000. *Journal of American Psychoanalytic Association*, 49, 1187–1217.

———. (2002). Rethinking homosexuality: What it teaches us about psychoanalysis. *Journal of the American Psychoanalytic Association*, 50, 733–763.

Rousseau, J.-J. (1782a). France, P. (Trans.). (1980). *Reveries of a solitary walker.* London: Penguin Books.

———. (1782b). Scholar, A. (Trans.). (2000). *The confessions.* Oxford: Oxford University Press.

Rosin, H. (2012). *The end of man.* New York: Riverside Books.

Rotundo, A. (1993). *American manhood.* New York: Basic Books.

Rozmarin, E. (2007). The other in psychoanalysis. *Contemporary Psychoanalysis*, 43, 327–360.

———. (2009). I am yourself: Subjectivity and the collective. *Psychoanalytic Dialogues*, 19, 604–616.

———. (2010). Better identity politics. *Psychoanalytic Dialogues*, 20, 181–190.

———. (2017). The social is the unconscious of the unconscious of psychoanalysis. *Contemporary Psychoanalysis*, 53, 459–469.

Rubin, G. (1984). Thinking sex. In C. Vance (Ed.), *Pleasure and danger.* New York: Routledge.

Rubin, H. (2003). *Self-made men: Identity and embodiment among transsexual men.* Nashville, TN: Vanderbilt University Press.

Rundel, M. (2015). The fire of Eros: Sexuality and the movement toward union. *Psychoanalytic Dialogues*, 25, 614–630.

Rupp, L. & Taylor, V. (2013). Queer girls on campus: New intimacies and sexual identities. In A. Frank, P. T. Clough, and S. Seidman (Eds.), *Intimacies.* New York, NY: Routledge.

Russo, V. (1987). *The celluloid closet.* New York: Harper & Row.

Ryan, J. (2015). From transgender to trans*: The ongoing struggle for the inclusion, acceptance, and celebration of identities beyond the binary. In N. Fischer and S. Seidman (Eds.), *Introducing the new sexuality studies.* New York: Routledge.

Safran, J. (2016). The unbearable lightness of being: Authenticity and the search for the real. *Psychoanalytic Psychology*, 34, 69–77.

Saketopoulou, A. (2014). To suffer pleasure: The shattering of the ego as the psychic labor of perverse sexuality. *Studies in Gender and Sexuality*, 15, 254–298.

Salamon, G. (2010). *Assuming a body: Transgender and rhetorics of materiality.* New York: Columbia University Press.

Samois (Ed.). (1982). *Coming to Power.* Boston, MA: Alyson Press.

Samuels, A. (1996). The good-enough father of whatever sex. In C. Clulow (Ed.), *Partners becoming parents: Talks from the Tavistock marital studies* (pp. 101–118). London: Sheldon Press.

——. (2006). Working directly with political, social and cultural materials in the therapy session. In L. Layton, N. C. Hollander, and S. Gutwill (Eds.), *Psychoanalysis, class, and politics: Encounters in the clinical setting.* London: Routledge.

Sartre. J.-P. (1943) [1984]. *Being and nothingness.* New York, NY: Washington Square Press.

——. (1962). *Existential psychoanalysis.* Washington, DC: Regnery Publishing.

Savin-Williams, R. (2006). *The new gay teenager.* Cambridge, MA: Harvard University Press.

——. (2016). *Becoming who I am: Young men on being gay.* Cambridge, MA: Harvard University Press.

——. (2017). *Mostly straight: Sexual fluidity among men.* Cambridge, MA: Harvard University Press.

Sayer, L. (2005). Gender, time and inequality: Trends in women's and men's paid work, unpaid work and free time. *Social Forces*, 84, 285–303.

Scarfone, D. (2017). On "that is not psychoanalysis:" Ethics as the main tool for psychoanalytic knowledge and discussion. *Psychoanalytic Dialogues*, 27, 392–400.

Schiller, B.-M. (2010a). Permeable masculinities: Gender reveries in Richard Serra's torqued sculptures. *Studies in Gender and Sexuality*, 11, 35–46.

——. (2010b). Incompleting masculinity: Engendering a masculine of sexual difference. In *Thinking with Irigiray.* Albany, NY: SUNY Press.

Schrock, D. & Schwalbe, M. (2009). Men, masculinity, and manhood acts. *Annual Review of Sociology*, 35, 277–295.

Schwartz, A. (1997). *Lesbians, gender and psychoanalysis.* New York: Routledge.

Schwartz, D. (1995). Current psychoanalytic discourses on sexuality: Tripping over the body. In T. Domenici and R. Lesser (Eds.), *Disorienting sexuality.* New York: Routledge.

Scott, A. O. (2014, September 11). The death of adulthood in American culture. *The New York Times Magazine.*

Searcey, D., Porter, E., & Gebeloff, R. (2015, February 22). Health care opens stable career path, taken mainly by women. *The New York Times.*

Sedgwick, E. (1990). *Epistemology of the closet.* Berkeley, CA: University of California Press.

Segal, L. (1994). *Straight sex.* Berkeley, CA: University of California Press.

Seidman, S. (1991). *Romantic longings: Love in America, 1800–1980*. New York: Routledge.

——. (1992). *Embattled Eros*. New York: Routledge.

——. (1997). The politics of sexual difference in late twentieth-century America. In *Difference troubles: Queering social theory and sexual politics*. New York: Cambridge University Press.

——. (2004). *Beyond the closet*. New York: Routledge.

——. (2009). Critique of compulsory heterosexuality. *Sexuality Research and Social Policy*, 6, 18–28.

——. (2013). State and class politics in the making of a culture of intimacy. In A. Frank, P. T. Clough, and S. Seidman (Eds.), *Intimacies: A new world of relational life*. New York, NY: Routledge.

Seligman, S. (2017). *Relationships in development*. New York: Routledge.

Serano, J. (2016). *Whipping girl: A transsexual woman on sexism and the scapegoating of femininity*. Berkeley, CA: Seal Press.

Shamir, M. (2002). The manliest relations to men: Thoreau on privacy, intimacy, and writing. In M. Shamir and J. Travis (Eds.), *Boys don't cry: Rethinking narratives of masculinity and emotion in the U.S.* New York, NY: Columbia University Press.

Shamir, M. & Travis, J. (2002). Introduction. In M. Shamir and J. Travis, (Eds.), *Boys don't cry: Rethinking narratives of masculinity and emotion in the U.S.* New York, NY: Columbia University Press.

Shaw, D. (2014). *Traumatic narcissism*. New York: Routledge.

Shenkman, G. (2016). Classic psychoanalysis and male same-sex parents. *Psychoanalytic Psychology*, 33, 585–598.

Sherman, E. (2005). *Notes from the margins: The gay analyst's subjectivity in the treatment setting*. Hillsdale, NJ: Analytic Press.

Shifman, P. and Tillet, S. (2015, February 3). To stop violence, start at home. *The New York Times*.

Shows, C. & Gerstel, N. (2009). Father, class and gender: A comparison of physicians and emergency medical technicians. *Gender and Society*, 23, 161–187.

——. (2004). Masculinity at work: The experiences of men in female dominated occupations. *Work, Employment and Society*, 18, 349–368.

Singer, J. (1992). The privatization of family law. *Wisconsin Law Review*, 1442–1562.

Slochower, J. (1999). Interior experience within analytic practice. *Psychoanalytic Dialogues*, 9, 789–809.

——. (2011). Analytic idealizations and the disavowed: Winnicott, his patients, and us. *Psychoanalytic Dialogues*, 21, 3–21.

Smith-Rosenberg, C. (1986). *Disorderly conduct: Visions of gender in Victorian America*. New York: Oxford University Press.

Sorcarides, C. W. (1968). *The overt homosexual*. New York: Jason Aronson.

Sojka, C. J. (2016). Identities, inequalities, and the partners of trans folks. In N. Fischer and S. Seidman (Eds.), *Introducing the new sexuality studies*. New York: Routledge.

Spade, D. (2008). Documenting gender. *Hastings Law Journal*, 59, 731–841.

Spelman, E. (1988). *Inessential woman*. Boston, MA: Beacon.

Stacey, J. (2011). *Unhitched*. New York: New York University Press.

Stacey, J. & Biblarz, T. (2001). How does the sexual orientation of parents matter? *American Sociological Review*, 66, 159–183.

Starobinski, J. (1988). *Jean-Jacques Rousseau: Transparency and obstruction*. Chicago, IL: University of Chicago Press.

Stein, A. (2013). Who's your daddy? Intimacy, recognition and the queer family story. In A. Frank, P. T. Clough, and S. Seidman (Eds.), *Intimacies: A new world of relational life*. New York: Routledge.

Stein, R. (1998). The enigmatic dimension of sexual experience: The "otherness" of sexuality and primal seduction. *The Psychoanalytic Quarterly*, 67, 594–625.

——. (2004). Roundtable: Dialogues of sexuality in development and treatment. *Studies in Gender and Sexuality*, 5, 371–418.

——. (2008). The otherness of sexuality: Excess. *Journal of the American Psychoanalytic Association*, 56, 43–71.

Stern, D. (1985). *The interpersonal world of the infant*. New York: Basic Books.

Stern, D., Sander, L., Nahum, J., Harrison, A., Karlen R. L., Morgan, A., Bruschweilerstern, N., & Tronick, E. (1998). Non-interpretive mechanisms in psychoanalytic therapy: The "something more" than interpretation. *International Journal of Psychoanalysis*, 79, 903–921.

Stoller, R. (1968). *Sex and gender, Vol. 1: The development of masculinity and femininity*. London: Hogarth Press.

——. (1972). The bedrock of masculinity and femininity: Bisexuality. *Archives of Genderal Psychiatry*, 26, 207–212.

——. (1985). *Observing the erotic imagination*. New Haven, CT: Yale University Press.

Stolorow, R. D. (2011). *World affectivity, trauma: Heidegger and Post-Cartesian psychoanalysis*. New York: Routledge.

Stolorow, R. & Atwood, G. (1992). *Contexts of being: The intersubjective foundations of psychological life*. Hillsdale, NJ: Analytic Press.

Stone, S. (2006). The empire strikes back: A poststranssexual manifesto. In S. Stryker and S. Whittle (Eds.), *The Transgender Studies Reader*. New York: Routledge.

Strenger, C. 2014. *The designed self*. New York: Routledge.

Stryker, S. (2008). *Transgender history*. Berkeley, CA: Seal Press.

Suchet, M. (2004). A relational encounter with race. *Psychoanalytic Dialogues*, 14, 405–422.

——. (2007). Unraveling whiteness. *Psychoanalytic Dialogues*, 17, 867–886.

——. (2010). Searching for the ethical: A reply to commentaries. *Psychoanalytic Dialogues*, 20, 158–171.

Sweetnam, A. (1996). The changing contexts of gender: Between fixed and fluid experience. *Psychoanalytic Dialogues*, 6, 437–460.

Sycamore, M. B. (Ed.). (2012). *Why are faggots so afraid of faggots?* Oakland, CA: AK Press.

Target, M. & Fonagy, P. (2002). Fathers in modern psychoanalysis and in society: The role of the father and child development. In J. Trowell and A. Etchegoyen (Eds.), *The importance of fathers: A psychoanalytic re-evaluation.* New York: Routledge.

Taylor, C. (1992a). The politics of recognition. In A. Gutmann (Ed.), *Multiculturalism: Examining the politics of recognition.* Princeton, NJ: Princeton University Press.

——. (1992b). *The ethics of authenticity.* Cambridge: Harvard University Press.

Thomson-Salo, F. & Campbell, P. (2017). Understanding the sexuality of infants within caregiving in the first year. *Psychoanalytic Dialogues*, 27, 320–337.

Townsend, N. (2002). *The package deal: Marriage, work and fatherhood in men's lives.* Philadelphia, PA: Temple University Press.

Trilling, L. (1972). *Sincerity and authenticity.* Cambridge, MA: Harvard University Press.

Trowell, J. & Etchegoyen, A. (Eds.). (2002). *The importance of fathers: A psychoanalytic re-evaluation.* New York: Routledge.

Twenge, J. (1997). Changes in masculine and feminine traits over time: A meta-analysis. *Psychology of Women Quarterly*, 21, 35–51.

US Census Bureau of Household and Family Statistics. (2000). www.census.gov/main/www/cen2000.html (Accessed August 12, 2018).

Valerio, M. W. (2006). *The testosterone files.* Emeryville, CA: Seal Press.

Valentine. D. (2006). I went to bed with my own kind once: The erasure of desire in the name of identity. In S. Stryker and S. Whittle (Eds.), *The transgender studies reader.* New York: Routledge.

Vance, C. (Ed.). (1984). *Pleasure and danger.* New York: Routledge.

Vavrus, M. (2002). Domesticity patriarchy: Hegemonic masculinity and television's "Mr. Mom." *Critical Studies in Media Communication*, 19, 352–375.

Wachtel, P. L. (2014). *Cyclical psychodynamics and the contextual self: The inner world, the intimate world, and the world of culture and society.* New York: Routledge.

Walker, D. (2016). Waiting for the third line. In M. Brown (Ed.), *A herstory of transmasculine identities.* Miami, FL: Boundless Endeavors.

Walters, S. (2001). *All the rage: The story of gay visibility in America.* Chicago, IL: University of Chicago Press.

Wang, W. (2013a, May 29). Single mothers. *Pew Research: Social and Demographic Trends.*

——. (2013b, May 29). Married mothers who out-earn their husbands. *Pew Research: Social and Demographic Trends.*

Ward, J. (2015). *Not gay: Sex between straight white men.* New York: New York University Press.

——. (2008). Dude-sex: White masculinities and "authentic" heterosexuality among dudes who have sex with dudes. *Sexualities*, 11, 414–434.

Warner, M. (2002). *Publics and counterpublics*. Cambridge: Zone Books.

Waterman, B. (2003). Winnicott meets daddy & papa—how gay men father and mother. *Fort Da*, 9, 59–76.

Weber, M. (1993) [1920]. *The sociology of religion*. Boston, MA: Beacon.

Weeks, J. (2007). *The world we have won*. New York: Routledge.

——. (1995). *Invented moralities*. New York: Columbia University Press.

Welter, B. (1968). The cult of true womanhood: 1820–1860. *American Quarterly*, 18, 151–174.

West, L. (2017). *Shrill: Notes from a loud woman*. New York: Hachette Books.

Weston, K. (1991). *Families we choose*. New York: Columbia University Press.

White, E. (1980). *States of desire*. New York: Dutton.

White, E. & Silverman, C. (1977). *The joy of gay sex*. New York: Simon & Schuster.

Wilchins, R. (1997). *Read my lips*. Ann Arbor, MI: Firebrand Books.

Williams, B. (1985). *Ethics and the limits of philosophy*. Cambridge, MA: Harvard University Press.

Williams, C. (1995). *Still a man's world*. Berkeley, CA: University of California Press.

Williamsinstitute.law.ucla.edu/research/census-lgbt-demographics-studies/same-sex-couples-census-2010-race-ethnicity/#sthash.7wpXr9f7.UAZP7A8B.dpu (Accessed August 12, 2018).

Winer, J. & Anderson, J. W. (Eds.) (2002). *Rethinking psychoanalysis and the homosexualities*. Hillsdale, NJ: The Analytic Press.

Winnicott D. W. (1965a) [1949]. Reparation in respect of a mother's organized defense against depression. In *Through pediatrics to psychoanalysis*. New York: Brunner/Mazel.

——. (1965b). Ego distortion in terms of true and false self. In *The maturational processes and the facilitating environment*. London: Routledge.

——. (1965c) [1960]. The theory of parent-child relationship. In *The Maturational Processes and the Facilitating Environment*. London: Routledge.

——. (1986). *Home is where we start from*. New York: Norton.

——. (1988). *Human nature*. London: Free Association Books.

——. (1989) [1968]. *On the split-off male and female elements in psychoanalytic explorations*. Cambridge, MA: Harvard University Press.

——. (1992) [1949]. Mind and its relation to the psyche-soma. In *Through pediatrics to psychoanalysis*. New York: Bruner/Mazel.

Wittman, C. (1972). A gay manifesto. In K. Jay and A. Young (Eds.), *Out of the closets*. New York: NYU Press.

Wolf, E. (1991). Contemporary perspectives on self: Towards an integration (Discussion). *Psychoanalytic Dialogues*, 1, 158–172.

Wurtzel, E. (1999). *Bitch: In praise of difficult women*. New York: Anchor.

Wyrem, H. K. (2001). Breakthroughs and phallacies: Commentary on paper by Diane Elise. *Psychoanalytic Dialogues*, 11, 533–540.

Index